LOVE
AROUND THE
WORLD

Also by Lailan Young
SECRETS OF THE FACE

LOVE
AROUND THE
WORLD

LAILAN YOUNG

HODDER AND STOUGHTON
LONDON SYDNEY AUCKLAND TORONTO

British Library Cataloguing in Publication Data

Young, Lailan
  Love around the world.
  1. Love
  I. Title
  152.4   BF575.L8

  ISBN 0-340-35684-7

To Robin,
with
love around the world

ACKNOWLEDGMENTS

These men, women and organisations have variously given me inspiration, knowledge, experience or assistance in the research and preparation of this book. I thank each for a special contribution: Tony Benn, Clare Bristow, British Airways, Simon Cardew, Pat Conway, Ken Cook, Monica Cunningham, Dabber and Paddy Davis, Marcel Delannoy, Nigel Dempster, Placido Domingo, Hans Eysenck, The Garden in Guangzhou, Corinne Hall, Anthony Howard, Morven Knowles, Mary Loring, Andrew Lownie, Penny Mansergh, Stan Marks, Bogunia Masseron, André Maurois, Christine Medcalf, the Museum of Mankind, Luciano Pavarotti, Pema Lhundup Lama, Lady Ponsonby, the Peninsula Group, the Royal Anthropological Institute, Celia Sanders Hornung, Andrés Segovia, Sheraton Corporation, Jane Sinclair, David Snelling, Sammy Suzuki, Paul Tortelier, my editor Ion Trewin, Louise Tulip, Arnold Tunbridge, Kay Whalley, Ken White, B. B. Young, K. G. Young.

My gratitude also goes to these writers and my precursors in the field: Lynn Bennett, Joseph Braddock, E. E. Evans-Pritchard, Edward S. Gifford, Edgar Gregersen, Barbara E. Harrell-Bond, Ruth Webb Lee, Kenneth Lo and Wang Wu, Maung Maung, Reay Tannahill, Lawrence Wright, and the authors of the love manuals the *Kama Sutra*, *The Perfumed Garden*, and the *Koka Shastra*.

CREDITS

Cover drawing: Prafulla Mohanti
Book design: Ian Hughes with Lawrence Back
Drawings: Martin Lubikowski
Photographs: Boy George (Rex Features); Sri Lankan painting (Camerapix Hutchison); coco-de-mer (Photo Eden, Seychelles); Chinese wedding (Sally and Richard Greenhill); Toothless is beautiful (Philippe de Roy, Vision International); Korean wedding (C. K. Kim, Camera Press); Mehinacu girl (Carlos Pasini, Camerapix Hutchison); Falklands war (Camera Press); Mursi women (Leslie Woodhead, Camerapix Hutchison); Mangbetu woman (Camerapix Hutchison); Valentine card (courtesy of Phillips, auctioneers); Dinka and cattle (Sarah Errington, Camerapix Hutchison); Jean Harlow (Kobal Collection); Solomon Islander (Michael MacIntyre, Camerapix Hutchison)

CONTENTS

CHAPTER ONE
LOVE AROUND THE WORLD

At this moment 1,680,466,201 people around the world think they are in love. Of these, 7,666,667 are actually making love – 57,000 of them with more than one person. If you think this is a lot of people you still have to add on the 424 million who are recuperating from the effects of love.

Different races see themselves as the world authority on love. The French have more ways of saying 'to make love' than anyone, though the ancient Peruvians had hundreds more. Italians believe they are the experts in the different ways of kissing, but I know that the Khyoungthas, who live in the foothills of the Himalayas, have more ways. Portuguese sing the saddest love songs, Arabs are craziest about virgins, the Japanese and Chinese spend most money on love potions, and Americans are best at grand weddings and big divorces.

The English are wittiest in love but are jealous of the French, so the French commiserate by referring to 'melancholy' as *le mal anglais*. The Ambriz of Angola adore anyone with four front teeth missing, while the Trarsa men of the western Sahara are uncontrollably attracted to very fat women. Fulani men in Nigeria welcome gays, but you are no one in the United Arab Emirates unless you are married to your first cousin.

Spare a thought for the Burusho bride spending her wedding night in the Himalayas; she has to share the bridal bed with her mother-in-law until the marriage is consummated.

The Greeks have written scholarly books about the art of loving, and three Indians and one Tunisian have created fascinating guide books to love-making. But top place for the most imaginative manual on love goes to the Chinese.

Huang-ti, also known as the Yellow Emperor, is to some the father of Chinese civilisation for the compass, silk, and the lunar calendar date from his time. To others he is simply an old roué, who lived to the great age of 120. No one knows how many wives he had, but so numerous were his children that his descendants were able to rule the country for over 1,000 years.

Such was the Emperor's preoccupation with the pleasures of the body that he spent many years preparing the world's first manual on love and sex. Some of the practical details are so explicit that his translators retreated into Latin, which means that some of us will miss out on the best bits:

'The Yellow Emperor said: "Cum coitum perpetrate desideranti Caulis mihi jaspius surgere nolet, utrum sollicitare eum debeo an non?"

'The Dark Girl said: "Certainly not!"'

There are no international rules that govern the way we love, nor should we be shocked about the love habits of other races, though admittedly some are very strange. There is always the chance that our own love practices are reviled – or worse, laughed at – by people in other lands.

I have been wandering around the world for twenty years gathering material for first a lecture and then a book called *Love Around the World*. The lecture has been given to more than 2,000 organisations in many countries. In Australia a columnist for the *Sun* newspaper asked: 'If I give you a scale of zero to ten how would you rate the British man as a lover?' I rated British men 8, the French 6, Indians 7. Then came the crunch. 'What about us?'

Next day the rating of 2.5 for Australian men became newspaper headlines and thirty press, radio and television reporters began the pursuit of the woman who dared insult Australian manhood. The Channel 9 television network referred to me on their main evening news as 'the world famous sexologist', which sounded immensely gratifying till I was reminded that almost anyone can be some type of -ologist in Australia, including garbologists who have been known to send 'Seasonal Greetings from your friendly garbologist' at Christmas. In my Australian childhood they were simply 'dustmen' or 'garbage collectors'.

A week after I left Australia the following letter was published in the Melbourne *Age* newspaper:

No wonder Australian men are lousy lovers. Look what
they have to practise on.
(signed) A. DRIVE of Hampton

So what is love? Since the beginning of life on earth, what passes for love has been as varied as life itself. Some love practices are grimly unjust, others are tragic, many are hilarious, and most are fascinating.

I believe that someone somewhere in the world likes what you have got, and if you could meet that person you could have fun making a life of love together.

———————————————♡———————————————

The sexual behaviour of the inhabitants of Siwa oasis has raised Egyptian eyebrows for generations. Though Moslems, many women and boys work as prostitutes and are especially busy at festivals in honour of local saints.

The British writer Robin Maugham was told about an elaborate Siwa wedding at which an English guest was accompanied by a high-ranking Egyptian official. Both were scandalised to find that the wedding was between a man and a boy.

An *imaam* – a Moslem holy man – was immediately despatched from Cairo to improve the morals of the Siwas. Two years later he, too, 'married' a boy.

———————————————♡———————————————

Towards the end of the last century, a bishop from England, accompanied by a young English clergyman, visited a Maori village in New Zealand. After the welcome banquet speeches were made and the Maori chief thanked his visitors for taking the time to visit his country. At bedtime, the chief called for 'A woman for the bishop!'; but the young clergyman said that this was unacceptable. Momentarily baffled, the chief then shouted more loudly: 'Two women for the bishop!'

One hundred years later, news of 500 broken marriages among the Church of England's 9,000 vicars and curates in Britain was made public by some of the wives of the unfaithful clergy. The jilted wives said their husbands were the prey of sex-hungry single women who, in the true spirit of predators, set out to catch a curate off-guard.

———————————————♡———————————————

THE J SPOT

Japanese men do not particularly enjoy kissing a woman's mouth and few are attracted to her bosom. The reason is quite simple: they prefer her Secret Spot, which enlightened foreign visitors (male), returning from Japan, call the J or Japanese Spot. Men also have a J Spot, but it is usually smaller.

Everyone should know about the J Spot because it gives an entirely new outlook on love. I shall try to help you discover the Spot, but would advise you to follow the directions in privacy. If you are reading this in a tube, bus or train it would be advisable to turn the page and come back to the J Spot after everyone has gone to bed tonight.

The problem about locating the J Spot is that its exact position varies according to the growth of hair in the target area. The apparent hairline is apt

3

to vary according to posture, and whether the object of your attentions is lying down or bending backwards.

The first step is to raise the index finger of your right hand (left if you are left-handed) and quietly run it along the hairline, that is, along the roots of the hairs. This is not easy. Return the finger to the very centre of the hairline and lo! Exactly one inch immediately below the centre is the J Spot. In case some of you had difficulty following these instructions a drawing of the nape of the neck and the hairline, including the J Spot, can be found on page 69.

———————————————♡———————————————

The British think the French know a lot about love. The French think the British know nothing. In 1983 the runaway best-seller in France was a love encyclopedia published in ninety-six weekly parts, which claimed to help people to enjoy 'better love relationships'. The first two parts contained double-page photo-spreads of 'amorous positions', and sold 1,300,000 copies. What few people in France realised was that the encyclopedia was translated from a British work.

———————————————♡———————————————

Woman is a calamity, but no house ought to be without this evil.
Iranian

———————————

A woman's advice is often fatal.
Icelandic

———————————

When the hen clucks, the cock is doomed.
Spanish   French   Japanese
Polish   Fulfulde (Niger)
Pashto (Afghan)

———————————

Three kinds of men fail to understand women – young men, old men, and middle-aged men.
Irish

═══════════════♡═══════════════

BELLY BUTTONS

The Ilas, who live along the banks of the Zambesi River, love big, protruding navels. If Mr. Dearing had known this all his problems might have been solved.

Mr. Dearing is an American plastic surgeon, who suggested to a patient that she might like a change of site for her navel to suit a re-positioning of her breasts, which the surgeon had already done successfully. The patient was disappointed with the result.

'In the first place it is eight inches above the site of my old navel,' she said. 'Mr. Dearing assured me that the navel he intended to create would resemble a small walnut. I have finished up with something more like a coconut.'

Defending himself, the surgeon said he had tried for the desirable walnut shape, but the patient's skin was not good enough. He had tried to make up for her disappointment by offering to marry her, but she had declined.

♡

The *South Wales Echo* published a page of photographs of navels. Beside each craterous hole was a text telling you how to judge a man's character. Here are some of the findings:

Protruding: Thinks he is God's gift to women
Low: Never let him out of your sight if you want to see him again
Deep: Secretive, strong, silent; unquenchable passions

———————————————♡———————————————

The Walbiri tribesmen of the central Australian desert do not only shake hands with men from another tribe. Such is their love of fellow men that they show complete trust by putting their male organ into the other man's hand, too.

———————————————♡———————————————

Once President Coolidge visited an American government farm with his wife. They were taken to separate areas, and when the First Lady reached the chicken house she asked the inspector how many times a day a healthy rooster would perform his duty. 'Dozens,' said the inspector. Impressed by this, Mrs. Coolidge asked him to 'please tell that to Mr. Coolidge'. When the President passed the chicken house and was told about the rooster's prowess, he asked whether the rooster chose the same hen each time. 'A different one each time,' was the answer. 'Tell that to Mrs. Coolidge,' said the President.

———————————————♡———————————————

The Editor
The Daily Telegraph
Fleet Street
London EC4

Dear Sir,

Does my husband hold a record in failing to remember our wedding anniversary throughout 20 years of marriage?

Strangely, he never forgot our dog's birthday, which fell three days after mine, during the dog's 11 years of life.

MAUREEN M. HOUSE

Basildon, Essex
9 April 1984

The Editor
The Daily Telegraph
Fleet Street
London EC4

Dear Sir,

Mrs Maureen House complains that her husband never remembers their wedding anniversary. I am in perfect sympathy with him.

I think the reason is that many men, like myself, do not remember ever getting married. I was, I believe, in such a state that it took months, even years for me to accept the fact and by that time the event had lost all relevance.

JAMES BLAKE

Plymouth, Devon
14 April 1984

Early this century Dr. Ludwig Jacobsohn of St. Petersburg wrote to leading professors of physiology, neurology, and psychiatry in Russia and Germany asking if they considered sexual abstinence harmless. Four replied that they 'had no personal experience'.

On the island of Bali and among the Aymaras of Bolivia and Peru twin brothers and sisters are allowed to marry because it is assumed that they have already been intimate in their mother's womb.

If you are really repulsive your best chance of finding a temporary partner is among the Trobriand Islanders in the Pacific Ocean. The Trobriands only have close physical relationships with those whom they love, but will always service those who would normally be outcasts in other societies.

Women who have been described as being repugnant and 'far beyond the toleration of a drunken sailor' have eventually found partners on these Pacific islands. Even Trobriand village idiots have 'been pleasured'.

The Trobriands are not too keen on bald men, but if such a man wears a band of fuzzy hair tied around the forehead, he will find a sweetheart. The bald man with the best chance of success is one whose hair-band comes from the shaved heads of bereaved men who have lost a close relative. Bald or not, a Trobriand man's virility is judged by the size of the yams he grows.

4 CASES OF RAVISHMENT

Kágaba women of north Colombia not only practise free love, but free rape as well, and few men are safe. In fact, many men are impotent because their sex initiation was provided by wizened, toothless widows.

♡

In the dead of night, and the darker the better, a Samoan man creeps furtively towards the house of a loved one. He is called a *moetotolo*, or sleep-crawler, and the girl he stalks has rejected him, preferring the favours of another. The sleep-crawler has taken off his *lava-lava* (loin cloth) and greased his body thoroughly with coconut oil so that he can slip through the fingers of pursuers. Stealthily he lifts the blinds and enters the house. To his astonishment he sometimes finds that the girl is pleased to see him, but there is another danger; they sleep until morning and the family finds the couple together. Catching a sleep-crawler is a great sport and an event in which everyone joins in. International 'experts' on the life of Samoans call this whole business 'surreptitious rape'.

♡

One of the regular chores of Trobriand women is to weed the gardens in their villages. It is a task that requires little skill, and it is best enlivened by gossip and chatter. Every Trobriand woman envies the weeders in the villages of Okayaulo, Bwaga, Kumilabwaga, Louya, Bwadela and Vakuta: they have the right to ravish a man whom they have never seen before. A male visitor to these villages who has not been warned about the lady weeders is in for a tough time. The women pull off his pubic leaf, and then do everything possible to awaken his passion. At the end of the encounter many men – who arrived in the village feeling happy and virile – are too weak to get up and leave for home.

♡

The Wentworth Courier, published in the Australian state of New South Wales, reported the case of a rapist who arrives and departs naked and has been terrorising women in the suburbs of Sydney for more than a year. Detective Inspector C. J. Mackie stated: 'He has not harmed anyone yet beyond raping them.'

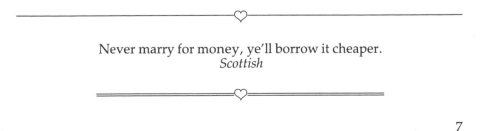

Never marry for money, ye'll borrow it cheaper.
Scottish

THE KITCHEN CURSE

In Sierra Leone menstruating women are not permitted to prepare or cook meals for fear of spreading pollution and bringing a curse on their husbands. Many Anglo-Saxon women also call their monthly period 'the curse'.

I warmly recommend Sierra Leone's important custom to any woman who would like an excuse to stay out of the kitchen. A clever one can avoid kitchen duties at least eighty-five days a year.

The *British Medical Journal* stated in 1878 that 'it is an undoubted fact that meat spoils when touched by menstruating women'. French writer Simone de Beauvoir wrote in *A History of Sex* about parts of rural France where peasants still think that a menstruating woman causes mayonnaise to separate and prevents cider from fermenting and bacon from salting.

———————————♡———————————

Many communities in the Pacific islands offer visitors a night of love with the wives and women members of their families. Others noted for such hospitable acts are the Dards in Pakistan and Kashmir, the Hunzas and Hazaras in Afghanistan, and in Africa, the Bantu and the Masai.

In eastern Siberia the Koryaks, although keen to please their visitors, will probably kill a man who turns down an offer of a wife or daughter. On the other hand, the *nomadic* Koryaks, who rarely settle for longer than a few weeks in one area, often kill their wives if they suspect them of adultery.

The Monguors of Mongolia also believe in making their guests feel part of the family, but if a daughter gets pregnant by a visitor, she is 'married' to the belt he has to leave behind for such an emergency. In other parts of Mongolia the daughter will be 'married' to a prayer mat in a special family ceremony.

═══════════════♡═══════════════

A TALE OF TWO CITIES

Stockholm: a group of women called the 'sex vigilantes' take photographs of men leaving sex shops. The photographs are published on posters around the city under the slogan: 'We can see you.'

Bangkok: a world record of 1,202 Thai men responded to a plea 'to have a vasectomy for the King' to celebrate King Bhumibol's fifty-fifth birthday. Many volunteers said that they had been influenced by the number three song in the Thai hit parade: *'I'm vasectomized.'*

———————————♡———————————

If you are an Ait Sadden Berber in Morocco, and your family want you to marry a man of their choice, there is little you can do if you do not like your husband-to-be. Your family will expect you to put on your finest clothes and sit with other female members of the household while the man's family inspects you. However, a small number of Ait Sadden girls have scared off fiancés by behaving on these occasions like women at funerals – the custom being that they scratch their faces and smear themselves un-appetisingly with cow dung.

═══════════════♡═══════════════

CHRISTINE OR BORIS?

Christine is the sexiest name for a girl, according to a poll conducted among New York students. The 'least sexy' are Ethel and Elvira, but Eurolinda does not have much in her favour either. Here are the poll results:

10 sexiest names	*3 least sexy names*	*Other 'turn-offs'*
1 Christine	Ethel	Edna
2 Candice	Elvira	Alma
3 Cheryl	Eurolinda	Florence
4 Melanie		Mildred
5 Dawn		Myrtle
6 Heather		Silvana
7 Jennifer		
8 Marilyn		
9 Michelle		
10 Susan		

The problem also exists in Russia where a lot of men are called Tractor, which was a popular name during the great farm collectivisation of the Stalinist era of the 1930s. Many women were called Electricity during the same period in homage to Lenin's ideas of progress. One acronymic name among middle-aged men is Melsor, which stands for Marx, Engels, Lenin, Stalin, and October Revolution. Luckily, the Soviet authorities have announced that those who would like to change their over-patriotic names and become ordinary Boris or Tanya may do so.

———————————♡———————————

Men of the Tchambuli tribe in New Guinea are considered a nuisance by the women, except as candidates for breeding purposes. The men live separately in special quarters where they do their own cooking. They are nervous of women, and in mixed company are constantly at the ready to disappear. That is why they customarily stand near a door or with one foot on the house-ladder.

Tchambuli women expect to be courted, so the men dance gracefully and coquettishly, but are afraid to put a foot wrong because they are outnumbered by women. The tiny community is only 500 strong, but the majority of men are conspicuous maladjusts, subject to neurasthenia, hysteria and maniacal outbursts.

In January 1984 after a law court in Delphi had sentenced him to two years for the offence, Mr. Eleftherios Saridis expressed his profound apologies for beating Mrs. Maria Kouralis. He said he had mistaken her for his wife.

---

4 WAYS TO A WOMAN'S HEART

Men of the Macusi Indians in Guiana are sewn up in a hammock full of fire ants. The men who make the best husbands are those who can stay put longest.

In the dry eastern desert region of Ethiopia between the mountains and the Red Sea, a Danakil man must endure physical pain to win a wife. Relatives of the woman he wishes to marry whip him with strands of raw hippopotamus hide, but unlike the Macusi Indians who can suffer privately inside their hammocks, the Danakil man must be seen to be enjoying himself.

Dr. Audrey Richards spent several years living among the Bembas in Zimbabwe. She told a group of them an English folk tale about a young prince who climbed glass mountains, crossed canyons, and fought dragons to win the hand of the maiden he loved. The Bemba thought about the story for a long time, then the old chief asked: 'Why not take another girl?'

Lord Chesterfield wooed Fanny Shirley by letter, begging her to spend a night with him. If she would consent, he would like to visit her early one evening:

'. . . I shall confess to you ingenuously that I have intimate relations with a married lady . . . She is an abandoned lady, who welcomes all comers, but who nevertheless behaves rather well. She is bizarre and uncertain to a supreme degree, now of a marvellous tranquillity, now wild as the devil. Our rendezvous are every morning at seven o'clock; I throw myself completely nude into her arms, even without a shirt, and as she is of appalling size, I have not the least difficulty in getting at her . . . I do not love her, and proof of that is that I shall tell you who she is: She is the Sea, the wife of Monsieur the Doge of Venice, and I hope that he and you will pardon me this affair.'

In Italy latter-day Casanovas who accept invitations to their loved ones' bedrooms risk up to three years in gaol if any other member of the family objects. In 1984, after six years of legal argument, Italy's Supreme Appeals Tribunal ruled that a married man called Luigi had 'violated a domicile' when a nineteen-year-old beauty of the city of Montesilvano invited him up to her room while her parents were out. The mother and father returned unexpectedly, and caught the couple in bed. Judge Armando Gallo upheld a four-month suspended sentence against Luigi on the principle of *Escludendi alois* – the right to shut out those you do not want in the house.

Mothers are more important in some societies than others. Among the Cubeo Indians in Colombia, a boy has no choice but his mother for his first sexual experience. Put another way, we would call this compulsory mother–son incest. However, they are not permitted to marry.

Among the Tutsi of central Africa, a bridegroom is allowed to cure any sign of impotence on his wedding night by copulating with his mother.

IF LOVE IS A BORE

Some people think making love is a bore. Manus women of the Admiralty Islands live in houses on stilts over salt lagoons, and have told visiting anthropologists: 'Copulation is revolting. The only bearable husband is one whose advances one can hardly feel.'

Madame de Maintenon was the mistress of Louis XIV, and married him when she was nearing middle age. The Abbé Gobelin, one of her close advisers, wrote how 'she had a marked disgust for the state of marriage . . . she submitted to the conjugal duties only with regret, and her spiritual director had to exhort her to conquer herself on these painful occasions'.

Sex without passion was endured by many in Victorian times in the British Isles and America. William Hammond, an American surgeon, said that decent women felt not the slightest pleasure in intercourse. Dr. William Acton wrote a text book on the reproductive system, and included the belief that anyone who thought that women had a sexual appetite was casting 'a vile aspersion'. In Switzerland, an eminent gynaecologist named Fehling said that sexual desire in women was 'pathological'.

All these distressed people would have been suited to life in the tenth century, when some rigid English theologians recommended abstention on:
- Thursday in memory of Christ's arrest
- Friday in memory of his death
- Saturday in honour of the Virgin Mary
- Sunday in honour of the Resurrection
- Monday in commemoration of the departed

This leaves Tuesday and Wednesday, but these were largely accounted for by a ban on intercourse during fasts and festivals, which included forty days before Easter, Pentecost, Christmas, and before Communion.

Nearer in time, Evelyn Waugh gave his opinion. 'All this fuss about sleeping together. For physical pleasure, I'd sooner go to my dentist any day.'

When the Chicago-based columnist Mike Royko asked his nationwide American readers their opinions about sex, most of the golfers and anglers who replied were quite sure of their priorities. One Chicago correspondent wrote: 'You get to set your own pace without nagging for speed and performance. A golfer is guaranteed 18 opportunities for success in one round. While playing, your partners give you encouragement and praise – even when you aren't doing well. I don't remember that ever happening in my bedroom.'

Another correspondent replied from St. Louis about his wife: 'I mentioned to her I had to compare the pleasure of sex with her to sinking a forty-foot birdie. She told me the odds of either happening in the near future were about the same.'

———————————————————— ♡ ————————————————————

The Celibacy Club of New York exists so that its members can go out in groups to avoid sexual entanglements. One member explained: 'It is hard enough for a woman to get ahead in business without waking up in a different bed every morning.'

The United Nations has published details of where men and women wishing to marry should go. Greenland is best for women, for here nearly six out of every ten males are available to marry. The best prospects for men are in the French island of Réunion in the Indian Ocean, which not only has a better climate than Greenland, but here fifty-eight per cent of the women are eligible.

If you are interested in outliving your partner, for whatever reason, then it is worth noting from the UN report that women in Ireland live longest, while Japan has the longest expectation of life in the world for men.

───────────────────────────── ♡ ─────────────────────────────

There are more ways of making love than meet the eye if you are a Zulu or a member of the Ganda race. If a Ganda woman jumps over her husband she has committed a sex act. The Zulu just has to step over someone of the opposite sex to qualify.

Elsewhere in Africa, the Edo and Ibo of Nigeria and the Mossi along the Volta River must not cough during their love-making, for it means a serious illness will follow.

A good Moslem will not make love facing Mecca, out of respect. But the Rif of Morocco do, because a child conceived in this way will be blessed and have a face 'shining like the sun and moon'.

That irrepressible gossip the Seigneur de Brantôme recorded how a French lady of his acquaintance insisted on taking the woman-superior position with her lovers, so that she could always protest her innocence if anyone accused her of 'allowing a man to mount her'.

═════════════════════════════ ♡ ═════════════════════════════

CHECKMATE

Infidelity is encouraged by the Múria who belong to the Gond group of people in central India. At an early age boys and girls are expected to sleep in the *ghotuls*, which are communal houses for young people. They sleep together, but if a boy spends more than three nights in a row with the same girl he is punished. The Múrias believe that storing up sexual energy is unnatural and therefore harmful.

Strict taboos are put on making love *al fresco* by many African people: the Dogon, Mossi, Edo, Edda, Ibibio, and the Twi. The Tallensi and the Mongo-Nkundus are especially incensed if they discover anyone copulating in the open, and purify the place where the forbidden act took place by throwing grass or branches on it.

Pygmies have no such regulations, much preferring forest trysts to love indoors. A few Africans are against love-making in the daylight: these are Zulus (who think sunlight is only suitable for dogs), the Bambara (who fear that the daylight produces albinos), the Fang, Ganda and the Masai.

Paintings dating from the last century of Chinese lovers show them lying outdoors on hot summer nights. Some of the couples are seen making love at the same time as sipping tea or exchanging greetings with friends passing by the garden wall.

---♡---

> Some Sudanese brides receive a *hugg* as a wedding present. A *hugg* is a large red cylindrical box about a foot high, with a mushroom-shaped lid. It contains pieces of scented sandalwood. When a woman wants her husband to make love to her she puts the box where he cannot miss it with the lid open so that the scent of sandalwood escapes.

---♡---

Impotence makes any man feel dejected, and it can occur among all races. In 1981 an Indian urologist, Dr. D. D. Gaur of Bombay, invented a technique for implanting two rigid silicon tubes fitted with hinges into the male member so that it was permanently extended, but capable of being hinged up or down.

Dr. Gaur claimed that his invention cost a fraction of the price of more sophisticated devices used in America, and whereas American pumps would sometimes let users down, he said his special silicon tubes would never fail.

Indian hinges sometimes do. One of Dr. Gaur's patients had his total satisfaction marred by a hinge malfunction. The doctor told a group of journalists the man now tucks his organ up against his abdomen for most of the time and 'is still quite happy'.

---♡---

The Soviet newspaper *Pravda* gave as the most common causes of marital breakup in the Soviet Union adultery, incompatibility, wife-beating and mental cruelty. But the great hazard of the late twentieth century is having to stand in queues every day. *Pravda* calculated that the Russian population spends thirty-seven billion hours a year standing in queues. Not only do Russian wives get varicose veins from so much standing, but many find that their husbands have given up waiting for dinner and have run off with another woman.

Ghoonj is the art of muscle manipulation that a woman can apply during the love act. By squeezing then relaxing her internal muscles a woman can provide the most fantastic thrills a man can ever hope to experience. Young girls in China are sometimes instructed in the art of *ghoonj* by older, experienced women, so *ghoonj* can obviously be learnt! Egyptians, Hindus and Ethiopians are also *ghoonj* experts.

---♡---   ---♡---

In the southern Indian state of Kerala, Pulaya women return to the fields to tend the crops soon after the birth of their babies, while the husband goes to bed. The rest of the family ministers to his needs until he recovers. The Andamans of the islands that bear their name also follow this custom, and an especially anxious husband will stay in bed for up to six months.

$\heartsuit$

WHAT IS LOVE?

BBC television cameras went to Harbin, a city of two million people in north-east China. Viewers saw a girl of nineteen in a hospital ward, and doctors described her symptoms: the patient is excitable, fidgety, and vain because she likes to use cosmetics. She thinks of her boyfriend all the time and dreams of becoming a queen. Diagnosis: schizophrenia.

I thought she was simply in love.

A Chinese sex manual gives the following advice to men: avoid wearing tight clothes, especially trousers; renounce alcohol, cigarettes, and anything which – like tight trousers – might excite passions; think about politics.

$\heartsuit$

Radio Moscow frequently broadcasts interviews with farmers and factory workers. In the 1960s love was inspired by achievements in the production of pig-iron, in the seventies it was iron and steel, and in the eighties the farmer who lifts his, or her, grain output is especially lovable. Here is a conversation between a collective farmer (man) and a tractor driver (girl) broadcast on October 20 in 1952:

Girl (sighing): How wonderful it is to work on such a beautiful night under the full moon and do one's utmost to save petrol.
Boy: The night inspires me to over-fulfil my quota by a higher and still higher percentage. I fell in love with your working achievement from the very first moment.

$\heartsuit$

A school in Buckinghamshire for the children of American Forces personnel in England has a rule that 'loving will be strictly according to the rulebook of PDA'. PDA stands for Public Displays of Affection. Under PDA the pupils are allowed to hold hands and give, or receive, a peck on the cheek. 'But any long term embraces and we are in with a crowbar,' says the headmaster. 'I'm not a party pooper,' he added, 'but I have to intervene. I'm running an academic institution.'

The editor of the school magazine drew the attention of everyone to the problem when she revealed that 'the amount of cuddling going on has exceeded PDA'. The commander of the American base to which the school is attached clarified the situation: 'PDA is a commonly accepted term to us. It could be tough for healthy youngsters, as any adult appreciates, but just because you're in love the whole world doesn't have to know about it.'

The Roman Catholic public school Downside, in Somerset, briefly admitted girls in 1981 and the monks introduced a rule that boy and girl pupils must keep a minimum of six inches apart except during sporting activities.

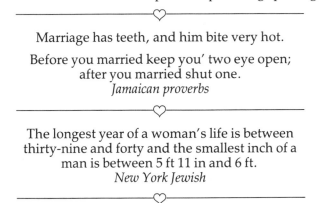

Marriage has teeth, and him bite very hot.

Before you married keep you' two eye open;
after you married shut one.
Jamaican proverbs

The longest year of a woman's life is between
thirty-nine and forty and the smallest inch of a
man is between 5 ft 11 in and 6 ft.
New York Jewish

Some people are not allowed to mention their husband's first name either to his face or behind his back. Most Hindu women refer to their husband as 'my husband' or by his family name, but among the Barea of Eritrea a wife cannot even utter a word that is in any way connected with his name. If, for example, her husband is called Lerotholi, which means 'drop', she cannot say 'a drop of water', but will say 'vomiting of rain' or 'dribble of dew'.

In 1622 England observed similar rules. William Gouge made a written plea to wives requesting them not to call their husbands by the popular terms of endearment of the time, such as sweet, heart, sweetheart, love, joy, dear, duck, chick or pigsnie. The only proper way to address one's husband, he wrote, was 'Husband'.

One October day in 1984 in New Orleans, Mrs. Cecil Jude Lions had no time or patience to address her husband by name. Mr. Lions, a former St. John the Baptist parish sheriff's deputy (who had run for sheriff in 1983), died of gunshot wounds inflicted by his wife. She was, at the time, the parish rabies control officer.

NAKED APES

A popular time in France to seduce a woman is at supper, but it has to be like one of those special *petits soupers* that the French arrange with the skill needed for the marriage of love and gastronomy to flourish.

The Duc de Richelieu's small, intimate suppers were famous in the eighteenth century. His guests, accompanied by their mistresses or lovers, dined in the nude – except for their wigs.

A hundred years ago the English were still fretting about the effects that nudity might have. Some old maids were reluctant to go to bed in rooms containing men's portraits, and many families covered the legs of tables and pianos for decency's sake. Trousers were referred to as 'unmentionables', pregnant members of the family were 'visiting in the country', and in many libraries books by male and female authors were segregated. Two books popular at the time had such engaging titles as *How to Woo and How to Win* and *Courtship As It Is and As It Ought To Be*.

♡

Shanghai, 1984. A French tourist emerged naked from her bath in a Shanghai hotel and was seen by a room-boy in the bedroom. He rushed out and the woman was later admonished by a Communist Party official for the incident. When she protested the man explained: 'It is not permitted to be naked in hotel rooms, only in the bathroom. You have made the boy upset and he will have to go home and rest.'

CHAPTER TWO
BODY LOVE

♡Some people love particular parts of the human body rather than the whole thing. But not everyone has the same priorities, and in some countries the most fancied parts are quite different. The belly button, the teeth, the liver, and the nostrils all have their followers.

Before taking a look at the human body let me first draw your attention to the following chart. This special guide is recommended to those who have not yet found the 'right' man or woman, those who would like a change or a brief encounter, or those who feel they could do better.

If you are satisfied that you have already found *absolute perfection* in love you may proceed to page 21 where an examination of the body and its parts begins.

SOMEBODY LOVES YOU SOMEWHERE

YOU	WHO LOVES YOU
Up to six front teeth missing	Nilotes, Sudan (See p. 48) Ovaherero, Namibia and Batoka of Mozambique Mussurongo of the Congo River; Ambriz, Angola (See p. 125)
Teeth missing from any part of mouth	Nilotes, Sudan; Aborigines, central Australia (See p. 125) Wagogo of Tanzania; Nandi of Kenya; Bageshu of Uganda
Black teeth	Trobriand Islanders; Masai of Kenya; Yapese

YOU	WHO LOVES YOU
Black gums	Masai
Gap between two top, centre teeth (female)	Kuwaiti
Lips as red as a bloody scimitar	Iranians
Gigantic, thick, fat lips	Sara near Lake Chad
Small mouth and short fingers (female)	Chinese men (See p. 47)
Can be ugly, but private parts must function properly (male)	Japanese women; Swahili-speaking women of Zanzibar
Big, drooping labia (female) Note: This is sometimes called the Hottentot apron.	Ganda, Gisu, Nama, Dahomey, Thonga, Venda, Marquesan, Kusaian
Enormous mons pubis	Bushmen of the Kalahari
Large clitoris	Easter Islanders
Abundant pubic hair	Chukchi of eastern Siberia
Fat calves	Tiv of Nigeria
Thick ankles	Ila, especially those near the Zaire–Botswana border
Tiny feet (female)	Old Chinese men
Very long neck (male)	Women of Padaung, Burma
Broad shoulders (female)	Marquesans
Virgins	Lots, but especially Arabs (See Chapter Six)
Young virgins under thirteen, full breasts, full lips, round buttocks	Lots, but especially Somali
Pale, tactful, quiet, compliant, polite, gracious, virgin	Baluchi men of Oman
Young, pale-skinned, strong, wealthy & willing to buy jewels; lets his wives visit their parents	Baluchi women of Oman
Hairless body	Trobriand Islanders
So repugnant as to be 'far beyond the toleration of a drunken sailor' (female)	Trobriand Islanders

YOU	WHO LOVES YOU
Flat head	Kwakiútl of British Columbia
Single, widowed or divorced with lots of children (female)	Antandroy of Madagascar (See p. 198)
Nymphomaniac	Yapese bachelors (See p. 192)
Over-sexed man	The Korongo and Mesakin women of Sudan; Babua of Zaire; Dahomey (Nigeria) women (See p. 23)
Lazy, but well-built man	Sotho of Namibia (See p. 23)
Gay (female)	Zande, central Africa; Woleaians in the Pacific; Tupinamba of Brazil; Chukchi of eastern Siberia; some Kuwaiti; Mongo along the Congo River (See p. 201)
Drooping, pendulous breasts (female)	Hottentots; Zande; Ganda of Uganda; Kaffir of South Africa; Mpongwe of west Africa (See p. 29)
Plump breasts protruding like pomegranates or hand-grenades (female)	Palestinians
Small, flat breasts (female)	Lepcha of the Himalayas
Red nipples (female)	Chinese (See p. 27)
Old man	Some Indonesians (See p. 134)
Willing to work hard without getting tired & retaining youthful looks (female)	Mexicans; Vietnamese
Tattooed body	Sudanese; Mongo; Tupi of Brazil; Mangbetu (central Africa); Basonge of Zaire; most Polynesians (See p. 51)
Protruding buttocks	Chinese
Immensely protruding buttocks that resemble a shelf or ledge	Hottentots, Somali, Bushmen of the Kalahari (See p. 32)
Extremely big hips	Mangaians and Hawaiian men
Very broad hips (female)	Cypriots, Yemeni, Shi'ites, Mangaians of the Cook Islands (See p. 188)

YOU	WHO LOVES YOU
Heavy buttocks	Marquesans
Narrow hips	Yakut of Siberia
Scars or big blemishes on buttocks (female)	Lala of Nigeria (See p. 34)
Social outcasts because of physical or mental defects	Trobriand Islanders (See p. 6)
Large, deep belly button	Masai of Kenya
Protruding belly button	Ila of the Zambesi River
Protruding abdomen (female)	Sudanese
Facial scars	Kipsigi of Kenya & Nandi of Ethiopia (See p. 45)
Flat, broad nose	Cantonese; Australian Aborigines; Trobriand Islanders
Short-sighted	Chinese (See p. 47)
Cross-eyed	Mayan
Small eyes	Trobriand Islanders
No eyebrows or eyelashes	Mongo of the Congo River regions
Joining eyebrows	Syrians
Extremely thin body	Dobuans in the Pacific
Short woman	Arabs (See p. 50)
Fat body and narrow forehead	Men & women of Guiana
Fat (female)	Punjabis (See p. 52)
Very fat (male or female)	Makololo of the Zambesi River; Trarsa of western Sahara
Very fat (female)	Men of Calabar in Nigeria (See p. 52)

NAKED TRUTH

Some people never give nudity a second thought. For others the problem is always there: shall I or shall I not take off my clothes?

In France during the Middle Ages the problem about naughty nakedness was solved by the *chemise cagoule*, which was a type of heavy nightgown with a hole suitably placed through which a wife could be impregnated without any further physical contact. One husband, a Monsieur Jean de Brasseuse, was such a prude that his wife was never permitted to see his naked body 'except for his neck, his face, his hands and sometimes, but only rarely, his feet'.

Not many people can resist giving their opinion about nudity:

The trouble with nude dancing is that not everything stops when the music stops.
Australian dancer and actor, Sir Robert Helpmann

When the candle is taken away, every woman is alike.
Greek

All women look the same with a sack over their heads.
Australian

A woman may be naked and yet behave like a lady.
Mrs. Bishop, the traveller in Japan

The nude is nearer to virtue than the *décolleté*.
French

He seduced many ladies, particularly American heiresses; but these seductions usually entailed stripping them naked in his apartment, frying a couple of eggs, putting them on the women's shoulders and, without a word showing them to the door.
Luis Buñuel speaking about Salvador Dali

In Congo-Brazzaville, young Nkundo girls are strictly forbidden to see their parents naked. If they do they cry out: 'Heavens! I have seen where I come from.'

———————————————— ♡ ————————————————

The favourite holiday beaches in the Soviet Union are by the Black Sea, where exposed fat and flab sizzle and quiver in the hot summer sun. In the 1960s nude bathing was popular in rivers, and from that period comes this Russian story.

An American was crossing Siberia by train when he saw a beautiful girl sunbathing naked by a river. He married her and they went to live in Dallas. Twenty years later they returned to her village. When the train was a mile away from the village, the conductor closed all the curtains. The couple asked him why. 'It's been like this for twenty years, and I don't understand why, but when a train comes here all the people come down to the railway line and take off their clothes.'

---♡---

Mixed bathing in public bath-houses is a way of life in Japan. It is not the nakedness which is immodest, but looking at someone else.

---♡---

The love life of men with a keen sex drive is good and plentiful if they belong to the Rega community in Zaire. Rega women give themselves freely to men. So do the Babua of Zaire, and Korongo and Mesakin women of Sudan, who enjoy showing their bodies and speak openly of free love. Without a hint of embarrassment they compare themselves to goats: 'Goats copulate when they want to, and so do we.'

Dahomey women of Nigeria who belong to the snake cult drop their grass skirts and expose themselves to the man they desire.

The truly lucky men are the Sothos in Namibia. Not only are Sotho women allowed to have lovers, but their husbands pay an allowance to a lover. The Sotho word for lover is *cicisbei*.

---♡---

When Cuchulainn landed in pre-Christian Ireland he was greeted by the Queen of Ulster who, like the ladies of the court accompanying her, was naked above the waist. All the women wasted no time raising their skirts to show their feelings towards Cuchulainn, and to make him feel at home.

English ladies lined the cliffs of Dover and lifted their skirts over their heads to welcome returning Crusaders from their holy wars.

Nearer in time British women took off their T-shirts and brassières at the quaysides when waving their menfolk off to the Falklands War, and several went out in yachts and stripped off completely when the victorious soldiery returned.

---♡---

Thirty-five years after the Communist Revolution swept China, art schools were allowed to use nude models for the first time. It was announced that those applying to pose must have attractive and healthy bodies, must themselves possess artistic creativity, and had to be Party Comrades in good standing.

At the same time women in Sweden's gaols had their plea to sunbathe nude turned down for fear they might excite male prisoners. No one mentioned how the prison officers might have felt.

---♡---

A HAIRY LOT

The shrewd grow bald.
Hungarian

Hairy husband, smooth happiness.
Estonian

♡

In his book *Ways of Sex* the Chinese writer Yeh Te-hui described the meanings of different types of hair that grow around the private parts:

Black like the feathers of a glossy bird	Strong-willed; obstinate
Brown with golden tints	Easy-going; generous
Fine, silky, short	Quiet and retiring
Very thick and sweeps down and under	Able to abandon himself or herself to total pleasure
Patchy or dry	Lacks warmth; chilly disposition

♡

Some people love their hair more than anything else in the world. Masuriya Din of Uttar Pradesh grew the longest moustache in the world – 8 ft 6 in (2.59 m). The British record belonged to John Roy until he sat on his 6 ft 2 in moustache in the bath and tore off 3 ft. Hans N. Langseth of Eidsroll in Norway grew a 17 ft 6 in (5.33 m) beard, while the much-admired beard of the bearded lady Janice Deveree of Kentucky, USA, reached 14 in (36 cm).

♡

The man is slim, around 5 ft 7 in tall with brown, shoulder-length hair. He also has a beard, which would make him noticeable if he was wearing a dress. Anyone who can help the police should call Hackney police station, telephone 488 7111.
Hackney Gazette

♡

The Diary of Tseng Kuo-ting was published in 1932 in Peking and contained this description of the merits of Western women:

'For us the Western woman is extremely voluptuous. She has large limbs and large breasts, her eyes are of many colours and round, and her laughter is uninhibited and free. Every time a Western female laughs, I imagine it is an invitation to the bedchamber . . . There is also the glory of her hair, the range of colours, the different textures, straight and curly, wavy and fluffy. This, too, is a most exciting characteristic.

'But there are two features of Western women that can hardly gain favour with the Chinese male. The rawness of her odours is exactly as one would expect from "raw" barbarians, and no amount of soap or scent can change this. Secondly, the pubic hair of many Western women – how coarse it seems after the Chinese female. It reminds one of riding camels and donkeys bareback, rough and wiry, and sometimes extending in a fuzz towards navel or knees.'

♡

A Batoro bride in the area between Lakes Albert and Edward in east Africa has the hair on her head shaved by the village barber and the hair on her body by a female member of the family before she can marry. Every hair is removed, then the girl is oiled from top to toenails.

Julius Caesar is another who liked to keep his body plucked clean of hair. He fussed so often with his thinning locks that Cicero once observed: 'When I see his hair so carefully arranged and observe him adjusting it with one finger, I cannot imagine that it should enter into such a man's thoughts to subvert the Roman state.'

Many Turks also spend time removing hairs from their bodies. Women shave as many as they can find, but men are more concerned with their armpits. Other removalists are the Bororos in Brazil and the Bantu Ila bride in Africa, who plucks out her husband's pubic and chin hairs on the morning after their marriage.

♡

The longer the hair,
the smaller the brain.
German

Hair long;
wisdom little.
Hindi saying

BOSOMS

In Victorian times a man could not offer a lady a chicken leg, only its breast, which he had to call the 'bosom'.

———————————♡———————————

Lepcha men of the Himalayas are not particularly attracted to women's breasts, but will tweak them in public as an invitation to love-making.

Desmond Morris told of an incident in *The Naked Ape* when a boy did this, but the woman replied by aiming her breast and squirting milk over him.

———————————♡———————————

Police in Britain often do dangerous work with little reward or praise, but Detective Constable Terry Lewitt won a public commendation from Judge Edwin Jowitt for the fortitude with which he had endured his 'suffering'. The detective constable had told Leicester Crown Court that while keeping watch at an ex-servicemen's club he had been obliged to lick the nipples of a stripper named Claudia. On another night she had fondled him while his sergeant buried his face in her breasts. Mr. Lewitt said that he and the sergeant had endured their ordeal to preserve their anonymity. The judge observed that it must have been very unpleasant for them.

———————♡———————

Phryne the courtesan had the loveliest breasts in ancient Greece. When an Athens law court condemned her to death for heresy, she exposed her beautiful bosom to the judges, and was immediately acquitted.

Agnès Sorel also had a beautiful bosom. The mistress of Charles VII of France, she displayed her mammary supremacy by wearing dresses bare to the waist. When other women copied her, she showed only one breast. The general opinion of the time was that the best breast filled one hand of an honest man.

The French Ambassador to England saw the ageing Elizabeth I in 1597, and reported that her uncovered bosom was wrinkled and that she kept pulling open her dress 'so that one saw the whole of her stomach'.

———————♡———————

Investigators at the University of Illinois have found that American men who prefer women with small breasts are either suffering from mild depression or hold fundamentalist religious views.

Mr. Hansen of Los Angeles could never suffer from mild depression, or could he? Famous for his party catering in Los Angeles (he has even made a birthday cake for Ronald Reagan), he once produced a cake of a life-sized naked woman lying on a marble slab. One chef took two days to decorate it, the longest time being spent on the lady's breasts. The cake was delivered to the client, a film company, in a rented hearse.

Marcia Seligson, writing in *The Eternal Bliss Machine*, quotes American wedding-dress designer, Frank Rizzo:

'The wedding dress has to be a little sexy, with a bit of breast showing. Girls are obsessed with bosom; they start taking birth control pills six months ahead of the wedding just to increase their bust two inches.'

A famous commander-in-chief of the Ming armies, Hung Cheng-tsou, was captured by Emperor Tai Tsung of the Chings. The great soldier refused to collaborate with his enemies, so a beautiful woman was sent to speak to him. She gave him a cup of poison and told him that if he drank it he would die for his own emperor. Naturally, Hung drank it, and as he waited to die the woman disrobed. Hypnotised by the beauty of her nipples, which were as red as ripe cherries, he felt a surge of passion. After a night of love he said he would serve the Ching emperor after all. That day he was presented to the emperor, and beside him was the empress, the lady with the red nipples with whom he had spent a passionate night of love.

P.S. The potion he drank was ginseng, believed by Chinese all round the world to be a great aphrodisiac. There is more about ginseng in the chapter on 'The Food of Love'.

MAKING A CLEAN BREAST OF IT

According to Islamic rules a woman can ask to be paid for breast-feeding her child, and her husband is obliged to pay from his earnings. But if another woman volunteers to do the job, the wife loses her right to ask for payment.

In the highlands of New Guinea no man considers a woman's breasts erotic. It is quite common to see bare breasts, usually when a woman suckles a pig. Pig meat is highly valued.

The Nyikas of Tanzania consider it disgusting if a man wants to suck or touch a woman's breasts. In fact, a wife can divorce her husband if he insists.

A Navaho Indian man is allowed to suck milk from a nursing mother, if she has too much.

In the Jumla region of Nepal a high-caste Brahmin-Chetri bridegroom sucks his mother's breast at the wedding ceremony as a symbolic end of the nursing relationship between mother and son.

In the Bwaka communities in Sudan the only women who cover their breasts are prostitutes.

TITBITS

The Government of Burma keeps a close watch over newspaper proprietors and bans all photographs of women's breasts because they are 'likely to arouse immoral passion in men'.

♡

From today it will be an offence to import and/or distribute the following undesirable publications:
1001 Erotic Dreams (Richard Sterling)
Bosom Pals (an omnibus edition) (Molly Parkin)
Western Areas Table Tennis Association Souvenir Brochure – 2nd Open Championship 1983 (Western Areas Table Tennis Association)
Johannesburg Star

———————————————♡———————————————

There is never a shortage of advice to women about the bosom and its care.

One French love guide called *La Cour d'Aimer* advised frequent baths and use of rose-water before meeting a lover. Then, 'when you are with your lover, embrace him tenderly and offer him your breast as a cushion. When he has left you, do not mention his visit to anyone and when you meet him in public, pretend that you do not know him'.

That prolific French writer on health and morals, Dr. Venette, warned against the flabbiness that gradually overtakes the flesh. It is most undesirable for a woman to have flabby breasts, he warned, because it makes people think the afflicted woman is lascivious and that she likes the bottle. To help overcome the embarrassment of women whose breasts are as large as cushions, Dr. Venette suggested a decoction of red wine boiled with ivy, myrrh, parsley and hemlock. 'One can also wear lead moulds smeared with henbane oil to reduce the size of the breasts,' he told his women followers.

Culpeper, the most famous British herbalist, believed that the wild flower called lady's mantle helps 'women who have over-flagging breasts, causing them to grow less and hard'.

Burmese women advocate a much tougher treatment: to improve size and texture, massage each breast with stinging nettles. Just feel the pain, but watch the benefits.

———————————————♡———————————————

Most people know or suspect that the Chinese invented gunpowder, the compass, silk and chopsticks, but few realise that they claim the credit for the brassière too.

At the beginning of the eighth century a favourite concubine of Emperor Tang Hsuan-tsung had an affair with one of his generals. One night the general bit and scratched her bosom too passionately, so she camouflaged the marks with a decorative red silk binding. The emperor simply adored her like that, and asked her to wear it often. Soon the cloth binding became fashionable, and many women embroidered theirs with pornographic scenes.

'Brassière' is a French word, but the French themselves call it a *soutiengorge*, meaning a 'throat support'. The early Christian Church did not mind what it was called, but it considered the lace openings to all types of feminine bodices and intimate apparel to be 'the gates of hell'.

In fourteenth-century France fashionable ladies laced their breasts so high that 'a candlestick could be placed on them'. Four hundred years later the medical officer for the West Riding in England agreed with doctors that tight lacing was a bad thing, and he wrote an epitaph for the tomb of a young lady:

> Mary had a little waist
> She laced it smaller still;
> A stone o'er Mary has been placed
> Out on the silent hill.
>
> And on that stone these words are writ:
> 'Oh let us hope she's gone
> Where angels never care a bit
> 'Bout what they have got on.'

———————————♡———————————

The English novelist Mrs. Frances Trollope confessed that she was baffled by what she saw in America. Readers of her *Domestic Manners of the Americans* were told about the woman who breast-fed her baby in a New York theatre and yet how some people were offended if you said 'corset' in front of the ladies. She also noted 'a universal defect in the formation of the bust, which is rarely full or gracefully formed.'

———————————♡———————————

Not many men – or women – prefer sagging, pendulous breasts to the high-rise species. But the Hottentots do, and so do the Zande, Ganda, Kaffir and Mpongwe – all of Africa.

Young Mpongwe girls bind tight-fitting cloths around the top of their breasts to make them sag like those of very old women. Ganda and Zande girls often tug at their breasts and sing: 'Oh, let my breasts droop.'

Kaffir and Hottentot men are charmed by their women's low-slung bosoms, some of which assume such enormous dimensions that the normal way to suckle is to carry the baby on the back and throw the breast over the shoulder.

———————————♡———————————

BOTTOMS

In the steep mountain ranges of New Guinea live the Arapesh. Those who live near the sea are plumper than the Arapesh who live inland. Coastal-dwelling or not, Arapesh men and women know two important signals: if a man wishes to copulate with a particular woman he takes hold of her breasts. A woman need not be shy either; if she desires a man she just grabs his buttocks.

$\diamondsuit$

FEELING THE PINCH

Dangerous though it is to generalise about the love habits of a whole nation, it does appear to be true that Italian men have a penchant for pinching women's bottoms, particularly in department stores, in crowded market streets, and on buses.

Indian men also enjoy bottom-pinching and nipple-tweaking, and a law has been passed by the Government of India forbidding this. The illegal sport is still avidly pursued, particularly on board the country's crowded buses and in markets, as this report in the Calcutta *Statesman* shows:

> Puja's new Market inspectors have launched a campaign
> against men who molest female shoppers. Chief Inspector
> Amwar Singh has declared: 'Our market must not become
> a hunting ground for eve-teasers. We have been receiving
> up to thirty complaints a day, and I am sorry to report that
> of those caught red-handed many are married men with
> impeccable reputations and large bank accounts. One was
> an executive engineer of the State Government; another
> was a Colonel; and the third I shall mention – a doctor
> who worked for the Geological Survey of India. However,
> considering the social status of these molesters, the
> Inspectorate decided to let them off – with the exception of
> the Colonel, a third offender. He was made to do twenty
> press-ups in front of a large crowd.'

In France, though, bottom-pinching is sanctioned by law. In December 1984 an appeal court held that it was 'a normal gesture in the framework of a certain familiarity that arises out of the closeness of daily work' and acquitted M. Jean-Luc Sage, proprietor of Le Relais de la Diligence at Arnod in eastern France, of tormenting an eighteen-year-old waitress by constantly pinching her bottom during the two years she worked for him.

Outraged by the court's decision and M. Sage's unrepentant declaration that he felt entitled to go on pinching his employees' bottoms, a commando of women led by Miss Marinette Volpini ambushed M. Sage and in Miss Volpini's words 'were as familiar with him as possible. We pinched him as hard as we could for forty-five minutes. If we hear that he is still pinching his waitresses' bottoms we are coming back again armed with our ultimate weapon – clothes pegs'.

♡

The Chinese are fascinated by the thought of a pair of attractive buttocks. The Yellow Emperor, Huang-ti, not only spent a good part of every day researching all aspects of bodily love, but also committed to posterity one of the most famous couplets in Chinese literature:

To understand the head
Investigate well the tail.

Almost 4,900 years later in 1927, Yeh Te-hui wrote a best-seller in China called *Ways of Sex*. Like the Yellow Emperor, Yeh was also fascinated by what the tailpiece was worth. Here are his findings:

TYPE OF BUTTOCKS	DIAGNOSIS
High & protruding	'Comfortable cushion for the sex battle.' Their owner is demanding and hard to satisfy.
Flat as a featureless plain	This person is not destined to be a great lover. If a woman, she will be suited to working tirelessly in the kitchen or about the house.
Narrow	Seldom enjoys love-making, but pretends to
Droop over the back of the thighs	Lazy, passive

―――――――――――――♡―――――――――――――

As early man made love in the old primate mating posture, he had a back view of his partner, and was therefore attracted to nicely rounded buttocks. One problem was that the woman had no view at all.

Now, 'civilised' races generally prefer what is labelled the 'missionary position' by anthropologists, which got its name from the position advocated by missionaries who were shocked to see 'uncivilised' races mating like animals.

When Tahitian girls experienced the ordinary mating habits of Captain Cook's men, they thought the face-to-face position resembled the copulating manner of beetles. The Trobriand Islanders also despise the European position, calling it impractical and improper.

One islander described it like this: 'the man overlies heavily the woman; he presses her heavily downwards, and she cannot breathe or respond'.

The most wonderful Lady-of-the-Buttocks is one who has a 'dainty, slim body, sweet voice, medium passion, a rapid walk, and no taste for love-battles'.

This extract is taken from the *Koka Shastra*, one of the great Indian books on love. Such a lady can be found in Gauda and Vanga in West Bengal. But the truly great woman 'famous for love and world-famous for her wantonness' comes from the western state of Gujarat.

Hugely curved buttocks, which protrude so much that you could almost balance a glass on their shelf-like form, are highly rated by Hottentots and men in Somalia.

Charles Darwin mentioned an Englishman who saw 'a beauty' whose buttocks were so big that if she sat on the ground she could not stand up without first pushing herself along until she came to a slope.

Rich young Somali men say that enormously protruding buttocks belong to an exciting 'bedfellow'. These men will invite girls to stand in a line, and they will choose the one whose posterior sticks out furthest behind as a wife.

THE PANTY & THE OBI

Panties were invented when Catherine de Medici, wife of Henri II, announced she would ride side-saddle at the next hunt. She was a spoilsport because until then the gentlemen of the court had been able to enjoy some unusual sights when ladies' skirts flew high on windy days. Many people protested, but some, like writer Henri Estienne, approved. He thought the new garment would be 'useful for women – they help to keep them tidy, prevent the onslaught of dust and cold and stop them showing too much of their body whenever they happen to fall from a horse. It also affords them a certain measure of protection against dissolute young men who, when they stealthily slide their hand under a lady's skirt, will no longer come into direct contact with her flesh'.

Meanwhile, French shepherdesses continued to wear nothing under their skirts.

When girl jockey Lee Custance romped home a two lengths' winner on an outsider called Regal Segment at Australia's Port Lincoln racecourse in November 1984, she was given a dressing down by the stewards. It was because her red panties showed through her flimsy jodhpurs, and the course officials feared her male competitors might have stayed behind for a better view.

The *obi* is part of the Japanese woman's national costume. Resembling a belt, it is generally made from bright or elaborate fabric. When knotted in front, it has the effect of drawing the kimono tightly over the buttocks, showing off the wearer's form to any roving eye. Many wives and virgins wear the *obi* at the back, which most men would take as a message to stay away.

---♡---

The organisers of the 1982 Commonwealth Games arranged a big cover-up operation in Brisbane, Australia before the Queen arrived. In the athletes' village the graffiti, which included 'Streakers repent – your end is in sight', was covered with posters showing the beauties of the Australian countryside.

---♡---

A group called the Social Democratic Union of Swedish Women – the SSKF – has launched a campaign to 'liberate love'. SSKF ladies are against 'on-the-job bottom-pinching and other such sexual impertinences'. Their plan is to set up 'erotic-free zones'. If they are successful maps of Sweden will have to be re-drawn to show the lie of the land.

---♡---

FOUR BRITISH TALES

In a national poll conducted by the *Sunday Times*, British women rated 'small and sexy buttocks' as the physical attributes they most desired in men. 'Muscular chest and shoulders' came tenth in a list of eleven features.

♡

British television has turned snooker players into sex symbols, and their female admirers are unanimous about what makes them stay up late to watch: 'It's his sexy bottom!' reported the *Daily Mirror*.

One fan, Janette Austin, writes poetry about player Kirk Stevens.

> His performance was a dream come true
> He's shown us how to pot 'em.
> But my only dream would be
> To pinch his sexy bottom.

According to a psychologist quoted in the *Daily Mirror*, Janette's reactions are quite normal: 'There is nothing surprising about the poem or the lady's liking for Kirk Stevens' bottom. Snooker is exciting, and the way men play, constantly leaning over the table, adds to the excitement for many women – especially as the younger players wear tight trousers . . . I think that while men usually watch the snooker carefully, women look at the players' bodies more. It will be interesting to see how men react if women's snooker becomes more popular.'

♡

Catching on to the British preoccupation with a fine pair of buttocks, *The Sun* featured 'girls who chase their men and always catch them'. Debra Smith, a 21-year-old girl from Bristol, apparently goes on the prowl with another girl. She told *The Sun* reporter: 'Our technique is to walk past a bloke we fancy and pinch his bum. That usually gets their attention.'

♡

Another tabloid, the *Daily Star*, organised what it called Britain's cheekiest contest, Top of the Bottoms. Readers sent in photographs of the buttocks of thousands of men and women, some clad, others naked. I thought the most curious of all was the photograph of a girl called Sally whose 'admiring uncle' submitted a shot of her in tights. Sally did not win the contest, which had been nicknamed The Rump Stakes.

---♡---

A Lala man of Nigeria appreciates a woman whose buttocks and thighs are scarred. A girl wearing clothes will excite him if she opens her skirt and shows him her scars.

Sir Winston Churchill once made a speech in Paris in which he looked back over his past: 'Quand je regarde mon derrière, je vois qu'il est divisé en deux parties.'

---♡---   ---♡---

34

HEARTS

Hearts will never be practical until they can be
made unbreakable.
The Wizard of Oz to the Tin Man

What they called heart is located far lower than
the fourth waistcoat button.
Georg Lichtenberg

Man combs his hair every morning, why not his
heart?

Chinese saying

♡

Sir John Suckling was the greatest gambler and
card-player of his time (1609–42), and invented
the game of cribbage. His life was largely one
of extravagance and dangerous adventures. He
wrote:

> Love is the fart
> Of every heart
> It pains a man when 'tis kept close
> And others doth offend when 'tis let loose.

———————♡———————

Some people think better of their liver than their heart. Some of the Berber
women in northern Morocco say 'You have captured my liver' to a man they
would like to marry. The liver is considered the centre of love because a
healthy one promotes good digestion and therefore happiness.

In a seventeenth-century erotic Chinese novel, the hero, who is called the
Night-time Scholar, addresses Delicate Scent as 'Dearest heart and liver'.

At the same time in France, the venerable Dr. Venette wrote that the liver
is full of fire and sulphur and that lascivious men have such fiery kidneys
that they inflame adjoining organs, dry up the brain, and make them
prematurely bald.

———————♡———————

In medieval France the Dame de Fayel kept her
deceased lover's heart in a casket. When her
husband discovered it he had it served up in a
casserole. Historical accounts disagree as to who
ate it.

———————♡———————

IN 1984:

British scientists disclosed that if a man cannot openly show affection he is more likely to develop heart problems than an extrovert lover. In fact, lack of affection was found to be more of a killer than lack of exercise, bad diet or smoking.

American doctors in Illinois examined the effects of sexual intercourse on the hearts of male volunteers. During the tests the men wore masks to measure oxygen intake, but these also prevented them from kissing or talking. Neither could they move freely, being restricted by wires and other pieces of equipment. The most difficult task for the volunteers was signalling to the doctors the precise orgasmic moment. For this they had to press a button.

Professor Jean-Paul Broustet of Bordeaux University in France warned that making love to a mistress was more likely to give a fatal heart attack than making love to a wife. 'At around fifty, having sex with your wife is like climbing three floors or taking a three-and-a-half-mile walk in the country. But with a girlfriend it is like racing up the stairs of a skyscraper or sprinting five miles.' The professor fired a final word of warning: 'Men should also avoid lying under their partner because this position speeds up the return of blood through the veins and overloads the left ventricle of the heart.'

---♡---

'My true love hath my heart and I have his.'

Wrong. The lady and gentleman in Philip Sidney's poem have each other's pituitary glands, which does not sound romantic at all.

Some American psychologists, including John Money, have discovered that the pituitary gland regulates a large number of hormones, and if it is in poor working order, 'falling in love' may be impossible.

Money says that people whose pituitaries are below par may 'date and even marry, but their marriages are typically based on companionship, not sex or love'. Put another way, their hearts are not in it.

LEGS

Life is good if you happen to be a Bulungo nymphomaniac living on the Congo River banks. Among the Bulungos the woman is boss, and if she lies on the ground and commands a man to 'get on my knee!', no man can refuse her. Men are also required to carry a woman on their shoulders if she needs transport.

When love grows cold
The legs grow old.
Czech-Bohemian proverb
———

One joins married people by their hands, and
with their feet they run asunder.
Austrian saying

———♡———

The Amazons broke their captives' arms and legs
in the belief that by weakening one part of the
body the erotic powers of another would increase. One Amazon queen, Antiara, thought
the lame were the best performers.

———♡———

That Chinese gown with the high 'mandarin' collar and thigh-high side
slits – the *cheongsam* – was designed like that because while it was permissible to show her leg no proper Chinese lady would dare uncover her neck and
bosom. Under Chairman Mao the *cheongsam* was banned, and the campaign
against 'spiritual pollution' still continues, though every now and then some
brave Chinese woman tries to change the fashion by revealing an inch of
thigh or baring a bit of throat.

Another country which thinks a lot about legs is Japan. If a man rolls up a
trouser leg, for whatever reason, the public stops goggle-eyed to look at the
bare flesh. Uncovered legs excite considerable interest on stage in cabarets,
too. A popular calendar in Japan shows the legs of golfers (female). A
company spokesman whose organisation has promoted one of the leggy
calendars, said that his clients liked 'a cute blonde with nice legs and a warm
atmosphere' for all year round.

In Britain Gallup conducted a survey about the female body. Twice as
many men chose legs as their favourite part, especially when they were
encased in black stockings with a tantalising glimpse of suspender. Gallup
found that only two in five women owned a suspender belt, although the
figure rose with age. But that is the time when men shift their interest from
thighs to ankles, said Gallup.

———♡———

A Mongo-Nkundu wife in Congo-Brazzaville
can tell if her husband has committed adultery:
he will refuse to take their child on his knees,
believing that by doing so he will harm the child.
Hence, 'father's bad knee' is another way of
saying 'adultery'.

———♡———

> If you could see my legs when I take
> my boots off, you'd form some idea
> of what unrequited affection is.
> Mr. Toots in *Dombey and Son*

———————————♡———————————

> For the love of his religion, Swami
> Maujgiri Maharij stood for more
> than seventeen years, performing
> the Tapasya. He leant against a
> plank when he slept in case he fell
> over and broke his penance. He
> died, aged eighty-five, in 1980.

———————————♡———————————

It is easier to tell whether a man has enjoyed
himself in a love session than a woman. But the
Japanese offer guidelines, based on paintings
done by the artists Koryusai and Shuncho. They
painted scenes of lovers at the end of the eighteenth century, and the three clues to a woman's
satisfaction are: she closes her eyes, she leans
back, and she curls up her toes.

Catherine the Great of Russia liked to have her
feet tickled. She had an *éprouveuse* called Miss
Protas, whose job it was to sample prospective
lovers and report on their skills.
Actress Sophia Loren reveals in her book on
health and beauty that one of her favourite erotic
sensations is to run her feet back and forth over a
rolling pin while she watches television. She told
members of the world's press that she gets an
almost orgasmic kick out of buying a pair of
shoes. She compares this to a brief, sad love
affair, complete with desire, satisfaction, disillu-
sionment and pain, all condensed into one afternoon in a shoe shop.

═══════════════♡═══════════════

PRIVATE PARTS

Is that a pistol in your pocket or are you happy
to see me?
Mae West

———————————————— ♡ ————————————————

Once in a while the message of Mohammed requires explanation by Ibn Abbas, who on one occasion wrote:
'If the male organ rises up, it is an overwhelming catastrophe for once provoked it cannot be resisted by either reason or religion. For this organ is more powerful than all the instruments used by Satan against man.' Ibn Abbas continues: 'The Prophet warned men: "Do not enter the house of those who have absent ones (meaning women whose husbands are away) for Satan will run out from one of you, like hot blood."'
You have been warned.

———————————————— ♡ ————————————————

Between the two World Wars Dr. John R. Brinkley made twelve million dollars from transplanting goat testicles into 16,000 men. His clients were influenced by the advertisements of the time: 'Your glands wear out'; 'Are you giving your wife the companionship she craves?'; 'Are you suffering from tired love?'; 'He didn't even kiss me goodnight'.
Brinkley's practice was so successful that he was able to raise his own flock of Toggenberg goats, whose social advantage was that they, and their costly parts, were colourless. His patients were allowed to choose their own goat.

———————————————— ♡ ————————————————

In many Moslem societies a professional man or woman is employed to deflower virgins. Sometimes the defloration ceremony is done publicly.
One famous expert of this profession was killed in Khartoum when the city came under siege by the rebel Mahdi Mohammed Ahmed. His fame derived from the power and beauty of his organ. Many Sudanese women committed suicide when they learnt of the destruction of so magnificent an organ. The story is still told that it survived the city siege and was bought for an undisclosed sum by a local rich woman, and still exists somewhere in Sudan today.
There is nothing new in preserving parts of the body for posterity. A number of Americans have had the body of a loved one frozen in the hope that one day it can be revived. Parts of the body of Napoleon Bonaparte were also distributed among some of his admirers: a wisdom tooth, his heart, stomach and his hair. But strangest of all is his penis, which was offered for

sale at Christie's in 1972 and listed as 'a small dried-up object'. It failed to reach the reserve price.

———————————————————♡———————————————————

Most people feel sorry for eunuchs, but many have wielded considerable power in the harems and courts of Asia. The Chinese referred to what the castrated men had lost as their 'precious', and these were kept in a special jar as a child would keep the first tooth that fell out. Any eunuch seeking promotion would present his pickled precious to the chief eunuch for inspection, although sometimes he might borrow or hire a superior set from a friend.

Sir Richard Burton, the scholar who translated the *Arabian Nights* and the *Kama Sutra*, was the top expert in oriental attitudes to love and physical pleasures. In the following passage he explains a curious matter:
'The *erectio et distensio* penis which comes on before dawn in tropical lands does not denote any desire for women. Some Anglo-Indians call this a urine-proud pizzle.'

————————♡————————   ————————♡————————

Such was the fear in Victorian times that boys might be tempted to explore their bodies that cages were sometimes put over their private parts at night and carefully locked. For extra security some had spikes sticking out.

It was not a new phenomenon that the English should feel shame about their bodies. In 1786 the British Minister in Naples wrote to the president of the Royal Society about how he had seen peasants in Isernia worshipping 'the great toe of St. Cosimo'. 'Toe' was his euphemism for 'phallus', but did the president realise this when he read that the women kissed 'the toe' and said: 'Blessed St. Cosimo, that's how I want it to be'?

———————————————————♡———————————————————

Never at a loss for words, the Renaissance French had about 400 erotic names alluding to the private parts. Ancient Sumerians referred to their hot fish, and the late Victorians to their live rabbits, goose necks, sausages and hot puddings.

The Tunisian author of the sixteenth-century classic *The Perfumed Garden* devoted two chapters to this subject, using a variety of names for women's parts: the voluptuous, the one with the little nose, the hedgehog, the crusher, the yearning one, the vast one, the glutton, the two lipped, the biter, the sucker, the hot one, the delicious one.

For the male member the author of *The Perfumed Garden* suggested: the liberator, the tinkler, the extinguisher of passion, the bald, the one with an eye, the pusher, the hairy one, the rummager, the crowbar, the rubber, the flabby one, the ransacker, and many more.

A Burmese man talks about his beautiful flower, and his friend says she will steal it if he will not give it to her.

With one eye on the ancient pillow books (many of which were lavishly illustrated) a Chinese man may refer to his little monk, or wonderful thing, his jade stem, turtle head or positive peak, while thinking about her precious estate, jade gate, cinnabar cleft, jewel terrace or the fire inside her jade pavilion.

Although *The Perfumed Garden* was written more than 400 years ago, the advice its author gives to men who feel that their manly vigour is beginning to wane or may have already left them still holds true today. Here are some of the causes given for loss of strength:

* too much sleep
* silk cloth worn against the skin (it impairs energy)
* greasy liquid
* snuff
* bashfulness
* smelling something disagreeable
* jealousy because the object of your love is not a virgin

The book's author suggests ten cures:

* absence of all care and worry
* unembarrassed mind
* bodily health
* natural gaiety
* good nourishment
* wealth
* a variety of women's faces
* a variety of women's complexions
* a nightcap of thick honey mixed with twenty almonds and a hundred grains of pine kernels
* rub your private parts with asses' milk

The art of reading character and personality from the shape of faces was popular among the ancient Greeks and Romans. The poet Ovid remarked that a man with a big nose would be well endowed sexually, an opinion shared by the Frenchman Dr. Venette, who wrote a book about the human body in 1696. The Chinese disagree. According to their system of face-reading, which is called *Siang Mien*, a big nose means that its owner is more interested in money than love.

In Vanuatu (the New Hebrides) in the Pacific a Tanna man must not catch sight of another man's vital organ because it is considered unlucky. That is why men wrap them up in yards of calico to form preposterous bundles sometimes two feet long.

Men in other countries are not as coy. The Suk and Nandi tribes of Kenya cover their bodies in elaborate clothes, but leave their sexual organs exposed. In Zaire, where a Rega father of twins is thought to have supernatural powers, he lies down outside the hut where the twins were born and displays his instrument for all to see.

The love life of the royals in some Lunda kingdoms in Zaire brightens when a new king is enthroned. During the ceremony he goes through a ritual in which he lifts up his sister's skirt and looks at her private parts. Among the Luba of Zaire the king has to sleep with his sister.

The Cape Nguni in South Africa refer to a girl's private parts as her 'father's cattle' because she will fetch him a good bride-price if she looks fertile. Many societies buy wives for cattle in Africa (see page 198).

Twelve paintings of the amorous adventures of Pharaoh Rameses III were made on papyrus by an unknown painter in about 1100 BC, and have been preserved in Turin. They show a woman bending over a chariot, with her head turned towards Rameses. He has a lute in one hand and is using the other to effect the entry of his phallus into the lady. Beside them is a small man with his phallus in a state of excitement. He carries a small bag. Nearly 4,000 years later scholars are still arguing about what the paintings mean.

The Gisus live in Uganda. If a Gisu woman is not satisfied with her husband, she will shout loud enough for the whole neighbourhood to hear: 'My husband's penis has died!'

The ancient Romans invented some revolting 'cures' for impotence, but many are on record as being extremely successful. Pliny the Elder's ointment was one, and the ingredients and instructions are given as: rub the affected part with earth moistened by the urine of a bull who has just had a cow; bind or attach to the same part the liver of a frog enclosed in the skin of a crane; hang the eyetooth of a crocodile on your arm, then lean your body against the right side of an elephant's trunk.

Apparently it was very important to know right from left in these matters.

Hindu preparations usually contain honey, while lion's fat was included in many Italian medieval recipes. The Chinese listed horrible items such as chili powder, baked earthworms and turtle's blood, and recipes for Moslems mentioned the gall bladder of a jackal, the fat from a camel's hump, and the blood of numerous animals, all of which were to be massaged in while the man read the *Koran*.

The ancient Greeks were keen on ointments containing nettles, and more recently Dr. William J. Robinson, formerly a leading physician at a New York hospital in the Bronx, recommended this simple home-made ointment: crush and strain cloves of garlic then mix with lard. Rub on the male part and on the patient's back.

There is more about love foods and aphrodisiacs in the chapter on 'The Food of Love'.

ORGAN WORSHIP

To many races and tribes the phallus is more worthy of worship than anything else on earth or in the skies. Images of the phallus have something in common: they are usually larger than life.

Ancient cave paintings of the human reproductive organs – some dating back tens of thousands of years – have been found in countries as far apart as Senegal and Niger, Australia, France, China, Japan and India, and are proof of man's fascination with the generative power of the human body.

The Romans used phallic charms to ward off evil spirits and bad fortune. The god Priapus was a firm favourite, and he was usually depicted as a huge phallus with a human face whose eyes could see and solve his devotees' sex problems. Phallic figures graced the triumphant chariot of a victorious general, and shop signs often included sketches of a phallus; some are still on show over doorways in Pompeii. In the Roman town of Lanuvium, festivals in honour of phallic gods lasted an entire month, and public sexual acts took place to propitiate the gods.

In Mexico feathered serpents representing the vital sex organs were painted by the Aztecs and Toltecs, while over in the Pacific the Polynesians chose as their phallic symbol the eel.

In Hindu temples stone carvings of the lingam and yoni are often placed side by side. The lingam represents Shiva, god of creation and destruction, and the yoni stands for Shakti, goddess of energy. There are countless numbers of unclothed holy men in India who have given up life in a consumer world in order to wander in search of 'the truth'. Some of the lucky ones have their genitals stroked, even kissed, by strangers as an act of reverence to fertility gods.

In parts of Africa statues in the shape of the phallus are put up to protect the crops; in Upper Egypt they are made of clay, while the Mbole in the rain forests of the Congo River shape theirs in wood. In Zimbabwe and north Transvaal sacred huts are constructed in the shape of a phallus.

The favourite god in many Chinese homes is Shou-lao, the god of longevity. Some statues show him with an enormous bald head that resembles a lingam.

At the annual Hadaka festival in Okayama in Japan, hundreds of completely nude young men jostle against each other for several hours on a small platform at the Saidaiji temple. Their purpose is to arouse the passions of the men and women crowded around the platform.

———————————————♡———————————————

A Venice art-school teacher named Giorgio Spiller was charged with offending public decency for dressing up as a male sexual organ at the Carnival of Venice in 1982. At his trial the defendant said that, as a behavioural artist specialising in matters of life and love, he had never been in trouble before. In fact, no one had been upset at the previous year's festival when he had paraded as a female sexual organ.

———————————————♡———————————————

There are islands in the Caribbean, Mediterranean, and Pacific and Indian oceans which claim to be 'the island of love'. My vote goes to the Seychelles, a group of ninety-odd islands scattered over 400,000 square miles of the Indian Ocean.

Here, most people are born on the wrong side of the banana leaf, but it is no insult to be called a bastard. At one time the Catholic Church baptised illegitimate children on Fridays and the legitimate on Sundays.

In the Seychelles is a double-breasted island called The Boobs. Unfortunately, the magnificent fifty-rupee bank note is now a collector's item: its group of palm fronds spell out 'Sex'. The unanswered question is, did the note's designer or the bank governors know what they were doing or was it an accidental artistic coup?

General Gordon fell in love with Praslin Island, identifying it as the original Garden of Eden. Today it is the second most populous island in the Seychelles. Here can be found the unique coco-de-mer palm tree, whose huge female seed resembles a smooth, well-rounded, life-size pair of buttocks. The male part of the coco-de-mer is even more explicit – long, shapely and erect but, like most phallic symbols, it is much larger than life. This male organ, or catkin, is strikingly decorated with yellow flowers and is a happy hunting ground for chameleons and green geckoes. (See page 67.)

———————————————♡———————————————

Margaret Thatcher, acompañada de su marido, Penis . . .
El Dia, Tenerife
March 1983

44

FACES

A woman's mouth never takes a
holiday.
Martinique

———————————♡———————————

When she speaks to a man an Ainu
woman of Japan covers her mouth
with one hand.

———————————♡———————————

Facial scars are thought to be erotic by the Kipsigi
and Nandi communities in Ethiopia. Scars can be
made in two ways: first by burning, then cutting,
after which the scars are given 'highlights' by
rubbing in vegetable ash. The other method is to
stick moistened strips of the plant yeroyat
directly on to the cheeks with saliva, then pull
them off after they have dried.

═══════════════♡═══════════════

LOVE UNDER WRAPS

There is a saying in Afghanistan that 'a woman without a veil is like food
without salt – unattractive!' There is a saying in the West that 'beauty is in
the eye of the beholder', in which case one could ask how can you tell what
the face is like if it is hidden by a veil?

While non-Moslems think that the purpose of the veil is to prevent
Moslem women from liberating themselves from a subordinate role to men,
it is worth quoting Muhammed Naccache, who said of the Lebanese forty
years ago: 'Just as it is inhuman to force a young girl to wear the veil today, so
it is also to make an old woman, who has been accustomed to wear the veil
all her life, unveil in the name of progress.' Many will say that those words
could have been written today.

Choosing a new *burqa*, which is the opaque 'mask' that covers the middle
of the face, is for some women as exciting as buying a new hat or dress is for
others. *Burqas* can be made to order, and there are fashion trends: shall I hide
my cheekbones or make them look higher? Will I go for the broad face or the
narrower one, and . . . what colour? A lot of thought goes into the curve of
the *burqa*, for a curve in the right place can make the difference between a
sneer, a leer, or a seductive come-with-me-to-the-bedroom look.

Some Moslem ladies would rather die than be seen without their veils. In
some cases anyway a glimpse underneath would probably be a worse shock
than meeting a man whose beard has just been shaved off.

A popular social event in Moslem societies is a *tafrita*, which is an afternoon tea party at which women meet for a gossip. In the Yemen it is customary to chat, chew *qat*, and hire a singer to entertain one's guests. In Oman the favourite topics of conversation are infidelity, virginity, illnesses, prices, and how to lose weight (one way is to chew *qat*, because it kills the appetite).

If a man enters a house when a *tafrita* is in progress, it is safest if he says 'Allah! Allah!' several times so that the women can cover their faces quickly.

And finally, some lightly veiled relief from Chad and Sudan: in Chad some women wear veils, but go bare-breasted. Among the Tuaregs of Sudan it is the men, and not the women, who are veiled. I have it on good authority that this is necessary because of the disruptive sexuality of the men.

———————————————————♡———————————————————

READING FACES

More than 2,000 years ago the Chinese devised a system of physiognomy whereby they could look at the faces of total strangers and tell whether they were mean or generous, healthy, honest, jealous, reliable or sensuous.

Last century physiognomy became fashionable in Europe. The most famous exponent of this fascinating art was John Caspar Lavater, the twelfth child of a Member of the Government of Zurich. Lavater's *Essays on Physiognomy* became a classic, but the author's observations are limited mostly to Swiss and German faces. The Chinese system of *Siang Mien* is universal, the result of minute analyses of faces from every country with which the Chinese have had contact, and it is still practised today.**

In Victorian England and America there developed a passion for face-reading, and many books were published on the subject. One particularly well illustrated one was John Spon's *Faces: How to Read Them*.

Each of these three systems of physiognomy permits a face-reader to learn something about the sexuality of others. Here are examples from each system.

Swiss System

Very thin lips	Emotionally cold
Very fleshy lips	Sensual
Droopy eyelids	Very amorous
Large, sparkling, rapidly blinking eyes (male)	A violent love of women
Projecting canine teeth (female)	More voluptuous than a beautiful woman
Brown, hairy or bristly warts on chin (female)	Frenzied in love

** See *Secrets of the Face: the do-it-yourself guide to the Chinese art of reading faces* by Lailan Young (Hodder & Stoughton/Coronet Books)

Chinese System of Siang Mien

Small mouth	Imaginative lover
Eyebrows like new moons	Loses control in love-making (female) Sexually demanding (male)
An almost three-dimensional, fleshy circle in mid-chin	Rocky love life; powerful sex drive
Clusters of red *dots* in whites of eyes	Incipient sex maniac
Small ear lobes	Many sex hang-ups
Short-sighted	Sincere, but likely to be an eccentric lover
Thick lips and big mouth (female)	Large, thick labia
Small mouth and short fingers (female)	Easily satisfied in love-making
Bald	Good sex drive

Victorian English and American System

Red, moist upper lip	Magnetic lover, but over-demanding
Red, wrinkled upper lip	Brutish, carnal
Wrinkles under the eyes (before age 25)	Dissipated; sexually greedy
Large, wide, clear eyes with a strong, direct gaze	Loves once in a lifetime; if remarries after a bereavement, will be faithful
Large, dark, very powerful and luminous eyes	Mysterious in love; fascinated by the occult
Short, thick, muscular neck (male)	Amorous
Thick, wrinkled, red neck (male)	A sensualist
Soft, slender, moderately long neck (female)	Amorous
Large, fat neck with tucks or folds (female)	Prefers eating to making love
Hair on upper lip and/or chin (female)	Lusty and lustful

Free of her lips, free of her hips.
Romany

♡

In the eyes of a lover pockmarks are
dimples.
Japanese

———————

There are eyes that fall in love with
bleared ones.
Spanish

════════════♡════════════

The Nilotes of Sudan dislike a toothy face and a
grin that reminds them of the muzzle of a wild
animal. When their aversion is overpowering
they will take teeth out for beauty's sake. This
destructive orthodontistry is commonly practised on children with big white smiles. One
explanation of the custom is that it stems from
the Nilotes' admiration for the toothless look
often apparent in their cattle.

————————————————————

ODD SPOTS

Egyptians say of a woman whose body is losing
its beauty that she has reached *Sin El Ya'as*, the
age of despair and of no hope.

The French are kinder: they refer to her as *une
femme d'un certain âge*, which is more gallant than
'middle-aged', the phrase used by English-
speaking people.

The problem does not arise in Botswana. Here,
regardless of sex or age, 'Love paralyses the
joints'.

————————————♡————————————

The Germans, Indians, Irish and Swedes share a
problem:

Lust, fire, cough, these three things are not
concealed.
Hindi saying
Love, fire, the itch, a cough, and gout are not to
be concealed.
German
The love disease and thirst know no shame, but
the itch beats them hollow.
Irish
Love or the fire in your trousers is not easy to
conceal.
Swedish

───────────────♡───────────────

Henry VII of England sent envoys to Valencia in 1505 to report on the
physical charms, if any, of the widowed Queen of Naples. The envoys were
to pay particular attention to the queen's mouth and bosom.

They had to note 'her breasts and paps, whether they be big or small'.
They were able to report that 'the said Queen's breasts were somewhat great
and full' because they were 'trussed somewhat high, after the manner of the
country'.

They were gratified to find that her lips were 'somewhat round and thick',
but best of all was that she had no hair on her upper lip. Then they had 'to
approach as near to her mouth as they honestly may, to the intent that they
may feel the condition of her breath, whether it be sweet or not, and to mark
at every time when they speak with her if they feel any savour of spices,
rosewater, or musk by the breath of her mouth or not'. The envoys described
her as 'well aired'.

═══════════════♡═══════════════

LOVE RIDDLES

'If my body were divided into two which half would you prefer – the top or
the bottom?'

This was the question a high noblewoman asked a slightly lower noble-
man in an imaginary discussion written in a book on love by André le
Chapelain in the twelfth century.

He said the top, fearing her scorn if he chose the bottom half. She replied
that the top was useless without the part containing the entrance to Venus,
and the man who chose the half which granted fruition was a better man
than one who preferred preliminary acts. And, she added, the foundations

of a building are more important than the top storeys.

The suitor countered this by pointing out that trees are more valued for their tops than their bottoms.

A lot of people speak in riddles, when the subject is love, lust or anything to do with the body. Here is a Mongolian riddle:

'If the body holds itself erect, what matter if the shadow be crooked?'

Over to Thyra Samter Winslow for the last word:

'Platonic love is from the neck up.'

───────────────♡───────────────

Chinese, Indian and Arab men hold hands, if they are feeling friendly. American football players wear such heavy protective gear that no form of physical contact is possible. Heterosexual American and Australian men avoid close physical contact with other men at all costs, except for mouth-to-mouth resuscitation, certain sports such as wrestling, and when shaking hands.

───────────────♡───────────────

HANDS OFF!

Around the world certain things cannot be touched because they are taboo. Here are four.

The nape of a Japanese woman's neck should only be touched by a man during the love act because it is an erotic zone. Hairdressers have a difficult time in Japan.

The top of a Thai woman's head is taboo because of religious beliefs. (The Chinese say that if a man or woman has a mole right in the centre of the top of the head you ought to touch it for luck. The big problem is knowing if someone has a mole there.)

In Victorian Britain a lady used to describe her pain to a doctor by pointing its position on a doll so as to avoid making an indelicate gesture. Advertisements for women's underclothes showed a pair of briefs folded so as to hide the crotch.

The Mangias of central Africa do not eat fish because they associate it with the scent of human private parts.

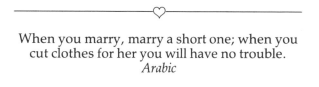

When you marry, marry a short one; when you
cut clothes for her you will have no trouble.
Arabic

───────────────♡───────────────

50

Large eyes are usually associated with beauty, but Trobriand Islanders dislike them, comparing them to puddles of water. They prefer small eyes. Trobriands also hate the Western-type nose which is 'sharp like an axe blade'. They like them broad and flat.

Love is not blind. It merely doesn't
see.
German

Love enters a man through his eyes; woman through her ears.
Polish

Choose a wife by your ear rather than by your eye.
Canadian

Love takes away the sight and matrimony restores it.
Greek

Only four per cent of the body of Wilfred Hardy of Huthwaite, England, is free from tattoo marks. Even his eyebrows and the insides of his cheeks, tongue and gums have fallen under the needle. Mrs. Rusty Skuse, also English, has come to within fifteen per cent of total body coverage under the expert hand and needle of her tattooist husband. She says that he always had designs on her.

Tattooing of the reproductive organs is favoured by Sudanese women in the Kordofan, and Mongo women in Congo-Brazzaville, whilst the same areas of the body are deemed desirable (for themselves) by Mangaian men in the Cook Islands in the Pacific. Others who enjoy pictures drawn on their private parts are Tupi Indians in Brazil and the Mangbetus and Basonges of central Africa.

'Tattoo' is a Maori word, and the art of tattooing was accepted in most parts of Polynesia until twenty years ago as a form of beauty treatment. Many Polynesians liked every part of the body to be done except the eyeball, but certain parts of the body were considered more desirable if they were tattooed. Easter Islanders liked arched lines on the forehead, edges of ears, and the thickest parts of the lips. On Samoa and Tonga the favoured areas were legs and arms. The inhabitants of the Marquesas liked the tongue best.

Every November the Miss World contest is beamed by satellite from London to television viewers on six continents. Since the Women's Liberation Movement objected to this 'cattle market' the organisers have dropped the announcement of the contestants' body measurements. Soon a whole generation of people will not know what 35-24-36 means.

Desmond Morris, author of *The Naked Ape* and *Manwatching*, compiled these ideal vital statistics of past civilisations (all in inches, believe it or not):

Miss Old Stone Age: 20,000 BC   96-89-96

Miss Indus Valley: 2,000 BC   45-34-63

Miss Cyprus of Late Bronze Age: 1,500 BC   43-42-44

Miss Amlash: 1,000 BC   38-44-78

and her neighbour, *Miss Syria: 1,000 BC*   31-26-36

———————————————♡———————————————

FAT IS BEAUTIFUL

A fat woman is a quilt for the
winter.
Punjabi saying

In the Calabar region of Nigeria, brides-to-be spend weeks in 'fattening huts' so as to be ready for their wedding day. Some need several months of fattening before they reach the desired plumpness.

By the banks of the Zambesi River Dr. Livingstone met Makololo women, who made themselves fat by drinking a brew called *boyáloa*.

Among the Trarsa, a Moorish tribe in the western Sahara, the women consume immense quantities of milk and butter to make themselves attractive to men.

——————————♡——————————

TOILET BEAUTY

All her teeth were made in Blackfriars, both her eyebrows in the Strand, and her hair in Silver Street . . . She takes herself when she goes to bed in some twenty boxes.

A husband's description of his wife
in *The Silent Woman* by Ben Jonson

♡

Americans like clean bodies. One brand of deodorant reminded all clean-living people:

Whether it's May or December
REMEMBER that it's August under your arm.

Further evidence of American love of cleanliness is shown in a suggestion made by an employee of the New York City Department of Health in response to an appeal to reduce water consumption during a particularly bad drought. The employee proposed a revision of the standard sign that is required by law in all restaurant washrooms. The suggested wording was:

BY ORDER OF THE BOARD OF HEALTH
All Employees Must Wash
One Hand
Before Leaving This Room

Frenchmen consider not washing to be a sign of virility, revealed a survey by the French Beauty Products Confederation in 1985. The results showed that nine out of ten Frenchmen and women wash all over before going to the doctor, but only half bother before an intimate soirée. Indeed, two-fifths of the French think that a body can be sexually attractive without being clean.

CHAPTER THREE
LOVE AND KISSES

How many ways of kissing do you know? Two, three . . . Some of you are up to eight already, but others are stuck on one and are thinking: Is there another way?

Kisses can be very exciting, but not all are erotic. Some are merely introductions to love. For instance, when a Frenchman meets a woman for the first time he takes her hand and lifts it to his lips, looks her straight in the eyes, and as he gently kisses her fingers he murmurs *'Enchanté'*, by which he means 'I am enchanted to meet you'.

What do Americans, Canadians, Australians, Irish, Britons and other non-Latins do? When a man meets a woman, in all probability they will shake hands and say: 'How do you do?' Some shake so hard that your hand will feel dismembered for some time.

'How do you do?' Think about that a minute. I consider this little question of four words to be one of the dirtiest you could possibly ask a person you have just met. No matter how you choose to ask it or where you put the emphasis:

How do you do?

How *do* you do?

How do *you* do? (which is probably the filthiest way of all)

How do you *do*?

It all boils down to asking someone you have never set eyes on before for details of a highly personal nature. If you are attracted to each other why do you need to ask him or her how she or he does it? But worse, if you are *not* attracted to this stranger why bother to ask? If a young Frenchman thinks the hand-kiss requires altogether too much gallantry, he will pop a question instead: 'Comment allez-vous?', which literally means 'How are you going?' Despite this bizarre interest in the lady's travel plans, I think the French win this round of the kissing game.

No one knows who exchanged the first loving kiss, though it was unlikely to be Adam and Eve because the Bible mostly refers to kisses planted on cheeks, foreheads, hands, feet, the neck, and occasionally on beards. The Chinese and Japanese of early times did not think much of kissing, and still do not, nor is it known exactly what the ancient Celts, Egyptians and prehistoric men and women of Africa did in passionate moments.

In medieval Europe a vassal used to kiss his lord's feet and, for a special treat, his thigh. It is said that the first Duke of Normandy, when receiving the province from King Charles the Simple, kissed the monarch's feet by lifting them to his mouth as he stood upright.

Holy kisses have always been plentiful, and today the toe of St. Peter's statue in Rome is kissed by Roman Catholics, Jews kiss the Western Wall in Jerusalem, and Moslems kiss the black stone of Ka'ba in Mecca, believing that it comes from paradise.

Moslems and Indians have brought to the world a number of love manuals, each of which contains advice about kissing. The author of *The Perfumed Garden* describes one type of kiss, which he claims is 'more intoxicating than wine drunk to excess'. I quote his 'prescription'.

'The best kiss is the one impressed on humid lips combined with the suction of the lips and tongue, which latter particularly provokes the flow of sweet and fresh saliva. It is for the man to bring this about by slightly and softly nibbling his partner's tongue, when her saliva will flow sweet and exquisite, more pleasant than refined honey, and which will not mix with the saliva of her mouth . . . The kiss should be sonorous . . . and is full of voluptuousness.'

'A person who cannot kiss properly cannot make love well,' say the French. There now follow accounts of how the French, and others, kiss.

---♡---

Mistaking his friend's farewell peck on his
fiancée's cheek as a gesture of amorous intent,
Mr. Harry Arthur flew at Mr. Kevin Allen (75)
and bit off his ear. 'I did not intend to bite
Kevin's ear off,' said Mr. Arthur, 'but in our
struggle it came away in my mouth. Sandra and
I kept the ear for a while, but later on I threw it
in the dustbin.' Interviewed at his home, Mr.
Allen said: 'We have been friends for 20 years,
so this came as a surprise. I was too
embarrassed to tell my wife or the police about
it. But my attitude changed when I heard that
Harry had thrown it away.'
South London Press

---♡---

TASTE-BUDS

Dr. Bubba Nicholson, a highly respected skin expert from Tampa, Florida, revealed in the *British Journal of Dermatology* that a glue-like substance named sebum is the clue to why we kiss. Sebum is secreted on to the skin from the sebaceous gland, and kissers enjoy licking and sucking sebum. Although it is found all over the body, the best places to drink up large quantities are the face, neck, scalp, and the female nipples. Pregnant women produce plentiful sebum, and so do young people at puberty. It is the flush of sebum in pubescent youth that is the most common cause of acne.

♡

There are wine-tasters some of whom are Masters of Wine. There are tea-tasters and tasters of cheese, coffee, and (newspaper) copy. Some connoisseurs of love can identify the flavour of their loved-one's kisses. For those in the know, the kisses of Poppaea, Nero's second wife, were identified as tasting of wild berries.

♡

> After 1,315 days of self-imposed silence, the guru Bhagwan Shree Rajneesh spoke again in 1984 at his followers' retreat in the desert of Oregon. His message could hardly have pleased many: 'No kissing, sterilisation of eating and drinking utensils, and particular awareness of personal habits.'

═══════════════════♡═══════════════════

KISS-TALK

Give me a kiss = Give me an osculation, peck, smack, smacker, smooch, mash, buss

Kiss = impact between balls both of which are in motion (billiards)
    = a sugar-plum
    = a drop of sealing-wax accidentally dropped beside the seal

Kisser = the mouth

Kiss of life
Kiss of death
Goodnight kiss
Butterfly kiss = blinking your eyelashes against someone's cheeks
Kiss-curl = a tight hair-curl on forehead or cheek

Kiss your money goodbye
Kiss my foot! = Australian for 'Rubbish!'
Give someone the kiss-off
Kiss and make up (after a quarrel)
Kiss the canvas = get knocked flat (in boxing)

Kiss my arse = Kiss me where I sit on Sunday (old English proverb)
Kiss the dust = die

Sweet sixteen and never been kissed
Never been kissed = Number sixteen in bingo
Kiss-me-quick
Kiss-behind-the-garden-gate = a pansy (horticultural)
Kiss and tell
Kiss me, Hardy = attributed to Nelson as his last words
Kissing-gate = a gate that allows only one person to pass at a time
S.W.A.L.K. = Sealed with a loving kiss (a letter)

═══════════════════════════════○═══════════════════════════════

EXTRA SHARP KISSES

A kiss is not a kiss for some people without a bit of biting and scratching.
Here are some cases from around the world.

Because a lot of Sudanese men bite and suck the woman's lower lip many
women have their lips tattooed to hide the bruising effects of kissing. They
call their bruises 'blushing of the lips'. Fewer young women consent to
having tattoos done, but still the 'blushing' goes on.

♡

Bite at her arms, and neglect no part of her body.

Clasp her to you, suck her breath, bite her.
Two quotes from *The Perfumed Garden*

♡

The only people on the Japanese islands who like kissing are the Ainus; an
Ainu kiss is a big bite on the cheek. Nor do most Japanese believe in shaking
or touching hands (they prefer to bow to each other). Touching is for babies,
lovers, adolescent best friends, and drunks.

♡

Solomon Islanders scratch and bite each other at the key moment of passion,
and proudly display their scars to anyone interested.

♡

At the festival of Kimali (which means 'scratching') girls and young women
on Melanesian islands scratch the shy men with their fingernails as an
invitation to 'come with me'.

♡

The *Kama Sutra* has advice to give about love bites: nail marks should be
made on the thighs or breast of a loved-one about to make a journey; these
marks are called 'tokens of remembrance'. The writer of the Indian classic
states that 'all the places that can be kissed, are also the places that can be

bitten, except the upper lip, the interior of the mouth, and the eyes'. Some teeth, though, are superior than others for biting, the best being those that are equal in length, bright, unbroken, and with sharp ends. The most unsatisfactory are blunt teeth, protruding teeth, and those which are large and loosely set.

♡

One Swiss couple applied the advice of the *Kama Sutra* in a passionate session of love. Their case made newspaper headlines around the world, for Yolanda Fluck almost bit off Fredi Fluck's manhood early one morning in October 1984 in the tiny Swiss village of Lavpersdorf. Mr. Fluck recovered after hospital treatment.

♡

Police in Thailand in February 1983 had little difficulty finding two men after each had attacked women. One had his tongue bitten off at the scene of the crime. The second man was a policeman, who also lost part of his tongue to a bite while trying to steal a kiss.

♡

Such is the passion of the Trobriand Islanders that they will bite a lover's lips till they bleed. Some also bite off each other's eyelashes – taking it in turns, one supposes – at the moment of orgasm. Less passionate Trobriands will settle for biting each other's cheeks, or snapping at the nose and chin. Those least fascinated by the love game are content simply to pull out the hair of their partner.

♡

Among Europeans, Americans, Australians and other Western peoples the most popular places to receive a love bite are:
On the man – his left shoulder
– the flesh just below his collarbone

On the woman – the left side of her neck
– the flanks of her abdomen

♡

Written about 1,600 years ago, the *Koka Shastra* still has a huge number of followers seeking guidance in the techniques of love. The book has a chapter on love marks. Passionate lovers should have, says the author, nails with large, strong tips. They should never be dirty, nor have ridges or cracks. A light touch on the cheek or between the breasts, given with all five nails, is enough to set the hairs on end.

♡

A black widow spider can devour twenty 'husbands' in a single day.
A male praying mantis can continue copulating with the female even after she has begun to eat him.

♡

Lots and lots of love,
Kiss the baby.
*How Harry Truman signed his letters to
his wife Bess*

I kissed my first woman and
smoked my first cigarette on the
same day. I have never had time for
tobacco since.
Arturo Toscanini

♡

THE FRENCH WAY

A clever Frenchwoman could, 200 years ago, 'speak' with her fan without having to utter a word. For instance, lifting her fan to her lips meant 'Kiss me'. Closing it with a loud snap was a sign of displeasure. Waving it one way meant 'pay attention to my bosom', but waving it the other way indicated to a bosom pal that all was not right for love. This is another example of how important it is to know one's right from one's left, if only to receive the right love message. A lady who wished to encourage a man's passion might allow him to kiss her fan. Fans are coming back into fashion in France.

♡

A woman should put perfume on the places where she wants to be kissed.
*Coco Chanel, creator of the
world's most famous perfume*

♡

The nineteenth-century French idea of an intuitive lover was one who never kissed an arm too high above the elbow, never squeezed a hand too long, and never seized a foot too eagerly.

♡

A kiss is nought when the heart is silent.
French proverb

A kiss can be a comma, a question mark, or an exclamation mark. That's basic spelling everyone ought to know.
The French actress, Mistinguette

♡

Frenchwomen have a habit of calling a man by his pet name in the middle of a kiss. Particularly popular are the names of animals, cakes and vegetables. 'My little cabbage', 'my great, big, adorable rabbit', 'my little mouse', and 'my tasty tartelette' are whispered to big, strong men in Nancy in the north east of France and down the country to Nice in the south.

♡

Prosper Mérimée, who edited the letters of Napoleon, commented that some of the French emperor's letters to Josephine consisted only of kisses. 'He can talk of nothing but kisses – kisses everywhere – and upon portions of the anatomy not to be found in any Dictionary of the Académie Française.'

♡

In Deerfield, Illinois, kissing in vehicles is restricted within the drop-off zone at its commuter railway station, but permitted in another part of the station. Signs tell you which zone you are approaching: one has a couple kissing, the other shows the same couple with a line through them.

Meanwhile in London, a couple was charged with 'committing an act of a lewd, obscene and disgusting nature and an outrage to public decency'. Police Constable Donald MacLennan said he had become suspicious when he noticed the 'sideways movement of the car on its springs', but Mr. Gerald Selby and Miss Anne Rosa said in their defence that they had only been kissing. Mr. Selby produced expert evidence that there was insufficient room for him to have been in the kneeling position described by the police, and that the fogged up windows would have prevented the police from seeing in. In court a similar car was produced, but the jury was unable to agree on a verdict.

A footnote to the London case: P.C. MacLennan had already arrested ninety couples for the same offence in the eighteen months preceding the Selby case, but only the Selby incident became famous and was dubbed the 'Kiss in the Car' case.

A kiss is a contraction of the mouth due to an enlargement of the heart.
Anonymous

KISS RECIPES

To one piece of dark piazza add a little moonlight; take for granted two people. Press in two strong ones a small, soft hand. Sift lightly two ounces of attraction, one of romance; add a large measure of folly; stir in a floating ruffle and one or two whispers. Dissolve half a dozen glances in a well of silence; dust in a small quantity of hesitation, one ounce of resistance, two of yielding; place the kisses on a flushed cheek or two lips; flavour with a slight scream, and set aside to cool. This will succeed in any climate, if directions are carefully followed.

A *Receipt for Kisses* by Charles Dana Gibson, creator of the Gibson Girls

♡

Ingredients: 1 telephone; 1 G-string; ½ bikini (bottom part); 2 'resting' actors, musicians, or very extrovert amateurs – one male, one female; a sense of the bizarre.

Wait by the telephone for a call from Goole, Hamburg, Bognor Regis or Abu Dhabi for a Kissogram, and despatch man in G-string or lady in ½ bikini.

♡

The Kissogram is an American invention, probably originating on the East Coast, but California and more recently Britain have perfected what some might say has become an art form.

After the Kissogram came the

Rolypolygram, in which sixteen and a half stone Bertha of England rips off her dress, wags her charms, kisses the 'lucky' recipient of the Rolypolygram, then heads back to base for orders for her next victim. A Gross-a-gram features a delivery of kisses conveyed by a woman larger than Bertha. A Bellygram consists of a writhing naked lady emerging from a box and a Flan-a-gram involves getting the recipient into the right place to receive a lady descending from a ceiling with a custard pie ready to slam into his face.

Since the Kissogram was launched, there is no end to the type of greetings available. Pregnant women have appeared at weddings to embarrass the bridegroom, Big Bertha lookalikes smother their victims in kisses and tickle them while taking off their trousers, and a G-string clad Mr. Dale Roberts turns up as a caveman or mad vicar, depending on the job booked. Mr. Roberts, a former mechanic, said that some women try to pull off his G-string, but he loves the job *and* gets paid for going to parties and kissing people.

STAR KISSES

Hollywood actor Robert Mitchum recalled his passionate screen love scenes with the gloriously formed Jane Russell: 'She's a really pleasant lady. In the kissing scenes she'd pop her chewing gum up your nose.'

The first Hollywood kiss happened in 1896. American audiences were shocked not by what they saw, but the thought of what would follow. Next, actress Theda Bara, who started life as a Miss Goodman of Cincinnati, was promoted as 'the wickedest woman in the world' in vamp roles. Her method of kissing excited the comment that 'she just glues herself on a man and drains the strength out of him'.

Favourite male kissing expert was Rudolph Valentino, nicknamed 'the international aphrodisiac'. His speciality was an incendiary look from narrowed eyes, followed quickly by throwing women on to massive silk-draped beds or on to the backs of horses, or both.

The filming of most Hollywood kisses began with the hand, travelled up and along an arm, round the back of the neck, and – circumstances permitting – down to the least defended target. The music always gets loud when a Hollywood kiss is in progress.

In 1922 the censors decided that the kissing had to stop, and began by banning open-mouth varieties. Making love was timed by stop-watch, and it was agreed that Byron's Don Juan knew best: 'for a kiss's strength/I think it must be reckoned by its length.'

Screen kisses are banned in India, where more films are made each year than anywhere else. But who needs a kiss? Indian directors create their own form of excitement: the man gazes into the half-closed eyes of the young woman and, breathless with passion, fondles her heaving, seductive diaphragm. Their lips move closer and, with one ecstatic movement, the camera rises into the leafy boughs of an old banyan tree. Birds twitter, mosquitoes buzz, the sun's rays shimmer and in all probability – but out of sight – the couple kiss.

In every Indian film the heroine, who is chosen for her ample curves, is caught in a storm or falls into a river for her wet *saree* scene. When Prince Charles visited a Bombay film set the Indian starlet Padmini pecked him on the cheek. Within hours that kiss had made headline news all over India.

A Kissing Workshop, where budding actors and actresses are taught the art of kissing, is fully attended at Bretton Hall College near Barnsley in Yorkshire. 'A kiss can mean so many different things,' said the man in charge of the course. 'It can be anything from just a friendly greeting to a strong sexual signal, and anyone who wants to be successful on stage must know how to do them all properly.' The course lasts one afternoon.

HAIRY KISSES

Being kissed by a man who didn't wax his moustache was – like eating an egg without salt.
Rudyard Kipling

♡

When kissing, the suitor must not scrape his mistress's cheek with his bristles and should never disarrange her hair. No whiskers should appear from his nostrils.
Ovid

♡

A handsome lieutenant of the French Hussars kept a splendid moustache nicknamed 'Marquise', on which he spent a great deal of time and money, using exotic perfumes and lotions. One tragic day, while he was curling it he singed one of the ends, so rather than decrease its magnificent size, he decided to shave it off. Since shaven faces were forbidden in the army he sent in his resignation. A little later he died of grief.

♡

One moustache that got in the way of kissing and eating belonged to Masuriya Din, who lived in the Partabgarh district in Uttar Pradesh, India. His had a span of 8 ft 6 in (2.59 m). Indians excel at hairy records; Karna Ram Bheel grew a moustache of 7 ft 10 in (238 cm) while he was in prison in New Delhi, but he would have had fewer opportunities of kissing.

♡

Women went into ecstasies over a man with a moustache, and Frenchwomen last century spoke about the delicious flavour of a kiss through a veil. The heroine of Guy de Maupassant's story *La Moustache* wrote about kisses in a letter to a friend:

'A man without a moustache is not a man at all. I do not like beards much, they give a man an unkempt appearance, but a moustache . . . ah, a moustache is indispensable to a virile physique . . . Never allow yourself to be kissed by a man who has no moustache; his kisses have no taste, none whatsoever! No charm, no spice . . . Have you ever felt a moustache upon your neck? It intoxicates you, quivers down your back, vibrates to the tips of your fingers, makes you wriggle, shake your shoulders, throw your head back . . . And I adore them too, my dear, because they are so French. They are a legacy from our forefathers the Gaulois, a symbol of our national character.'

[See page 24 for more hairy details.]

———————————○———————————

In a pamphlet on marriage the Church of England tells us that there are many ways of 'making love'. Keen to be helpful, the writer describes some of them: the farewell kiss when husband or wife leaves for work in the morning, holding hands while shopping; a caress while reading the newspaper together; or 'simply a smile while sitting in the bus'.

═══════════════○═══════════════

THE SNIFF KISS

Some people enjoy sniffing each other rather than a straight lip-to-lip type of kiss. The Vietnamese, Thais, Santals of India and Andamanese go in for nose-sniffing and nose-rubbing. Another way to sniff is by applying the nose to the cheek of someone then inhaling. Inhalant specialists include the Khyoungthas, who live in the foothills of the Himalayas. So intriguing are their kisses that there are times when the number of anthropologists observing Khyoungthas exceeds the population of the Khyoungthas themselves.

A Khyoungtha kiss begins when the kisser inches his (or her) nose towards the cheek of the desired one. This is followed by a deep inhalation, then a series of lip-smacking motions, which could last for twenty-five minutes or more. I suspect that after twenty years of marriage the noise of lip-smacking could become a bore, but one or two Western anthropologists have described a Khyoungtha kiss as the highlight of their anthropological careers.

There is a famous Khyoungtha saying: If a man runs after a woman he falls into marriage; if a woman runs after a man she falls into ruin.

♡

The Maoris, Sandwich Islanders, Tongans, Eskimos, Trobriand Islanders and many Malay races rather enjoy a spot of nose-rubbing. Charles Darwin described this type of kiss as 'the Malay kiss', though he never revealed whether he had tried it for himself. The Yakuts of Siberia, many Mongolians and the Lapps of Lapland also practise this type of kiss, but Lapps usually clasp each other round the neck first and then rub noses.

♡

The joy of nose-rubbing is ascribed to the silent ecstasy of smelling one another's skins, as some animals do. The ancient Egyptians used the same word for 'smell' and 'kiss', proof that the sniff kiss has been around for a long time.

———————————————♡———————————————

Every time Martyn Feanley kissed his wife he got an electric shock. He is a 999 emergency ambulance man at a station near York. To save Mrs. Feanley from more shocks the West Yorkshire ambulance chiefs ordered the carpet at the station to be watered three times a week.

Julie Brown's kisses are also electrifying. When she kisses her husband Robert a sharp tingling pain in her lips is intense enough at times to make her jump backwards. Friends suggested she wear wellington boots, but she 'did not think that the sight of me in wellies would turn Robert on'. The couple, who live in Norfolk, hope to solve the problem and save the marriage. Robert is an electrician.

———————————————♡———————————————

In love there is always one who
kisses and one who offers the
cheek.
French

═══════════════♡═══════════════

There are strict rules of etiquette to observe when you are presented to, or in the company of, members of the British royal family: when and to whom to curtsy, when to offer a helping hand (never to the Queen, unless she asks for help) and how to dress.

Jon Kimura Parker, the ebullient 24-year-old Canadian who won the Leeds Piano Competition in England in 1984, raised eyebrows of every shape and hue when, in full view of the audience and television cameras, he planted a kiss firmly on each cheek of the Duchess of Kent in complete defiance of royal protocol.

———————————————♡———————————————

64

'A person who cannot kiss properly cannot make love well,' say the French. Boy George is poised for a Three Degrees kiss, but the chapter on *Love and Kisses* tells of dozens of different ways of kissing.

This voluptuous figure, a wall painting in a hill fortress in Sigiriya, represents a Sri Lankan ideal. Similarly nipped waists, prominent breasts and buttocks were achieved in Europe and America through the efforts of the corset and girdle industry (see pages 28 and 29), but in Bangwa, Cameroon, fat is beautiful, and both men and women can let it all hang out. For a selection of ideal vital statistics turn to page 52.

These are the biggest 'his' and 'hers' in the world. The huge female seed of the coco-de-mer palm tree from the Seychelles 'islands of love' resembles a woman's pelvis, while the erect male part of the tree is decorated with yellow flowers and is a happy hunting ground for lizards. Some races make a cult of particular parts of the body: buttocks, breasts, the belly button... See the chapter on *Body Love*.

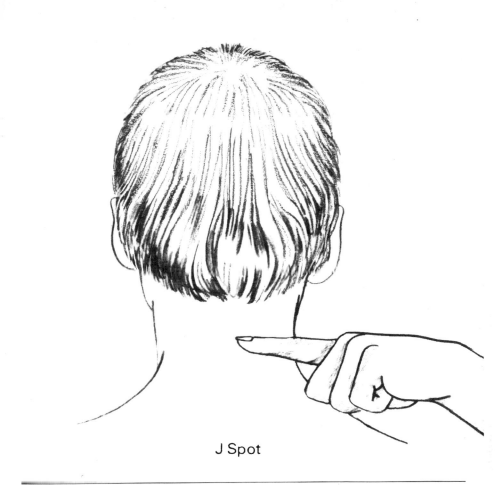

J Spot

This is the J Spot which, when kissed or stroked, gives an extraordinary sensation. Full details of how, when and where are given in Chapter One.

'Something borrowed' is an essential part of a white wedding in China. In the two photographs opposite the brides' dress, veil and the bouquet are the same, and so are the grooms' clothes. Only the bridal pairs are different. The complete outfits are hired by couple after couple trooping through the photographer's studio to record their happy day.

Toothless is beautiful in parts of Kenya, Australia, Mozambique, Uganda and Angola. There are races and tribes who particularly fancy people with black teeth, drooping labia, thick ankles, cross-eyes and flat heads. See the *Somebody Loves You Somewhere* Chart on pages 18 to 21.

These Moonstruck couples were all married by the Rev. Sun Myung Moon at a mass wedding for 5,837 couples in Seoul, South Korea – the biggest on record. He matched many of the couples himself. For more mischievous matchmakers see the chapter on *Go-Betweens*.

While deep suntans and slim legs are desirable in the West, Mehinacu girls reaching puberty are locked in dark huts on the banks of the Amazon. Tight bands are tied around their knees and ankles. After six months they emerge with their skins blanched and their calves bulging, ready for the sexual games they are to play with eligible marriage partners. To make them even more beautiful all their body hairs, including eyelashes and pubic hairs, are pulled out. More alluring ways of enticing lovers are described in the chapters on *Love Nests* and *Vows, Oaths and Curses*.

A BIRD IN THE HAND IS WORTH . . .

A favourite Turkish kiss is for men only. On seeing a beautiful woman a man kisses his own hand, and then places it on his forehead. Some men have been known to faint from the pleasure such a kiss bestows.

♡

In Yugoslavia, Serbian women like to kiss a man's hand as a sign of greeting.

♡

In parts of central Morocco people greeting those they regard as equals do so by joining their hands with a quick motion, separating them immediately. Each then kisses his own hand.

Arab men sometimes kiss their hand and wave it in the direction of a storm. In Biblical times the hand was waved towards the sun and moon; today, some Greek men kiss their hand to the sun.

♡

Kiss the hand you cannot bite.
Rumanian

The hand which you can't cut off
you kiss.
Swahili

An itchy nose means you will walk into a post,
shake hands with a fool, or be kissed.
Whichever one, it will happen before midnight.
Old English saying

Men used to rave like wild beasts about the kisses and embraces of the famous fourteenth-century courtesan, Lucretia. She liked to have three suitors with her at any one time: one would pick up her glove, kiss it and hand it to her; the second took her arm; and the third would buy whatever fruits or other edible delights she fancied. Her success was attributed to her skill at luring men on by refusing to give them what they craved. To do this she sometimes subdued them by the sheer weight of her kisses.

If you want to get into the *Guinness Book of Records* for kissing, the time to beat for 'the most prolonged osculatory marathon' for two people kissing is 17 days 9 hours, which was successfully achieved in southern California in 1983.

Another osculatory record to try for is Jonathan Hook's 4,106 women in 8 hours at a rate of one woman every 7.01 seconds; Mr. Hook accomplished his task at Newcastle University in 1983. If your skills are not suited to these categories there are three more: the Kiss of Life, with a record to beat of 240 hours with 224,029 inflations done by a team of five in ten days (their 'patient' was a dummy); the longest screen kiss (the record is 185 seconds held since 1940 by Regis Toomey and Jane Wyman, who became the first Mrs. Ronald Reagan); and 'the most protracted kiss underwater', with a time of 2 minutes 18 seconds to break. This last record is held by a Japanese couple.

SWEET AND SOUR

Among the Kabyles of Algeria a kiss on the mouth of another's wife or husband constitutes adultery. If the couple runs away and hides they can expect no help from the villagers who have given them refuge once their hideout has been discovered, for both the guilty pair and their helpers, if caught by the 'wronged' families, will be put to death. Death is not instant for all concerned: the man will probably be killed off quickly, but the woman is restored to her own family, who will not spare her. Committing adultery among some of the tribes in Burma includes holding the hand of another's wife, but punishment by death is unlikely.

♡

Near the Uganda–Sudan border, the Ganda women are renowned for the clever way they tickle their men under the armpits to arouse them. Observers say this is more potent than the average European kiss to get a man going.

♡

At Russian weddings everyone kisses everyone else, irrespective of sex. In the Yemen it is not unusual for one man to kiss another. Sheik Nefzawi, the eminent Arab erotologist and author of *The Perfumed Garden*, wrote that the gifts of God are the kiss on the mouth, on the two cheeks, upon the neck, as well as the sucking up of fresh lips.

Both the Danes and the English believe they were first to think it lucky to kiss under the mistletoe. According to the old English custom each time a couple kisses the man should pluck a berry, but the kissing has to stop when the last berry has gone. The Danes say it is bad luck to say no to someone who wants to kiss you under the mistletoe because the plant is a symbol of love.

An attractive lady offered Casanova a lift in her carriage. They kissed, and this was followed by progressively greater liberties, though this was not the first time the famous lover had worked so fast in a carriage. They parted without exchanging names. Some days later, Casanova saw the lady at another's house, but she gave no sign of recognition. When he asked if she had forgotten him already, she said: 'A frolic does not constitute an introduction.'

This reply has been translated into many languages as a warning to ardent lovers.

———————————♡———————————

Lack of love and kisses can stunt the growth. In January 1984, after a three-day hearing in a juvenile court and evidence from Dr. Richard Stanhope of the Middlesex Hospital, British magistrates found that a five-year-old girl had failed to grow because of emotional deprivation. She was a victim of psychosocial dwarfism, a medical syndrome first recognised in the 1980s. It produces children who, though strikingly small, do not look malnourished. They often have pot bellies and podgy cheeks, their legs are short and their expressions blank. Because their parents do not kiss and cuddle them enough, their growth hormone is arrested and their 'bone age' retarded. Removed from the hostile home environment and given a bit of love and affection their growth hormone level returns to normal within a few weeks, and they shoot up.

═══════════════♡═══════════════

DANGEROUS KISSES

On 13 March 1983 an unmarried Asian couple were gaoled for ten days for kissing on the cheeks while alone together in a room. The court in Abu Dhabi in the United Arab Emirates said the couple were guilty of 'committing an action that could be harmful to the general public'.

♡

A few years earlier the Criminal Court of Kuwait ruled that it was a criminal offence to kiss in public. Sentences vary according to the amount of indecency the court establishes has occurred.

♡

For the first time since the Cultural Revolution
tea dances are permitted once again in Peking.
Any couples caught waltzing cheek to cheek are
thrown out of the ballrooms.

♡

Most romantic, English-speaking visitors to France commit the worst French
faux-pas ever invented. It is a moonlit night and they are on the Left Bank of
the River Seine in Paris in the arms of a Frenchman or woman, when the
urge to say 'Kiss me' occurs. How many know that while *un baiser* means 'a
kiss', *baisez-moi* is a blunt invitation to active coition?

♡

Mr. Brian McCreath is a member of Wandsworth prison staff. He convinced
a Home Office solicitor that he could escape a tight bear-hug without moving
his hands or legs. How he did it was recorded in the journal of the Prison
Officers' Association: the sceptical solicitor was asked to apply a bear-hug to
McCreath, but as he tightened his grip on McCreath, the latter kissed him
full on the lips. The man from the Home Office dropped him as if he had
been stung.

♡

When the Democratic Party candidate, Walter Mondale, chose Mrs. Geral-
dine Ferraro as his vice-presidential candidate in the 1984 American elec-
tions, he was warned by his own party, by journalists and psychologists that
he must never kiss or embrace Mrs. Ferraro, who was also the first woman
ever to be on a vice-presidential ticket. Three reasons were given why Mr.
Mondale and Mrs. Ferraro should keep a careful distance between them:

1. Men, though not women, think that if there is a warm and close
   relationship between a man and a woman, something more has to
   be going on behind closed doors (the words of Dr. Joyce Brothers,
   the leading behavioural commentator).
2. Feminists would get outraged if he looked as if he were patronising
   her.
3. Looming ever present was the chilling possibility that either
   candidate might inadvertently let slip a *double-entendre* that would
   invite derision and divert attention from sober campaigning.

♡

Glandular fever is an infectious complaint, but
sufferers get more than sore throats, high fevers
and weight loss. Also known as the 'kissing
disease' and the 'love-bug', those inflicted with it
also get severely teased, as Prince Edward was
when he caught it in 1984.

♡

German scientists have found that a man's pulse rate increases from 72 to 110 when he kisses, and a woman's from 84 to 108. This proves that men get more excited than women.

Memory does not forget the promised kiss, but the remembrance of the kiss received is soon lost.
Finnish

A STIFF UPPER LIP

Henry VIII, bewitched by Anne Boleyn, wrote to her in 1528: 'Wishing myself (specially an evening) in my sweetheart's arms, whose pretty duckies I trust shortly to kiss; written with the hand of him that was, is, and shall be yours by his will, H.R.'

A fashionable lover during the time Erasmus visited the British Isles was expected to kiss his lady's hand, her fan, her nosegay, her petticoat, and 'to play with her little puppy'. The Dutch scholar, and other observers, suspected that this latest custom came from France or Italy. In 1499 he wrote to an Italian friend about English girls with angels' faces and added, 'wherever you come, you are received with a kiss by all; when you take your leave, you are dismissed with kisses; you return, kisses are repeated. They come to visit you, kisses again; they leave you, you kiss them all round. Should they meet you anywhere, kisses in abundance; in fine, wherever you come, there is nothing but kisses'.

A mournful Oxford bachelor, Robert Burton, thought that kisses could be dangerous, and warned against certain types in his *Anatomy of Melancholy*, written in the seventeenth century: 'There be honest kisses, I deny not, the respectful kiss, friendly kisses, modest kisses, vestal-virgin kisses, officious and ceremonial kisses, etc., kissing and embracements are proper gifts of Nature to a man: but there are too lascivious kisses . . . too continuate, and too violent; they cling like ivy, close as an oyster, bill as doves, meretricious kisses, biting of lips . . . with other obscenities that vain lovers use, which are abominable and pernicious.'
Was this a case of Eros denied?

The West Country city of Bath took the lead in manners and social behaviour in 1703 when a Master of Ceremonies introduced rules of deportment. Leading socialites in London were especially attracted to the new Bath way to bow, or 'make a leg' as it was called: with Gallic grace, Bath and London dandies offered each other snuff with a gallant flourish, kissed each other on the cheek, and swore pretty little oaths such as 'Why, blister me! Enfeeble me! Impair my vigour!' Some did.

This was the period of many tepid little phrases. 'Be kind,' a man would plead to one whom he wanted to bed. 'But my dear madam! Permit me, I beseech you!' was another much-heard request.

The writer, James Boswell, uttered many such pleas to Mrs. Louisa Lewis, a pretty young actress. She promised to make him 'happy' on Sunday at 3 p.m., and did.

♡

Kisses were snatched when a train entered a tunnel, in hansom cabs, on bus tops, and in the cabins of Ferris wheels in Edwardian England. And like H. G. Wells's character Mr. Lewisham, they loved 'thick fogs, beautiful, isolating grey-white veils, turning every yard of pavement into a private room'. They even had a secret code that could be invoked when kissing was not possible: a hand was squeezed in answer to 'Do you love me?', one or more times for 'How much?', and there was an extra big squeeze for intense passion.

♡

The BBC Radio 4 programme *Woman's Hour* took a look at British women of the mid-1980s. They found that the agony aunt of *Woman's Own* magazine gets letters asking how to kiss. One writer wanted to know if every woman felt as if she were blowing up a balloon every time she kissed. Another lady described her first kiss: 'Although it was stupid and fumbling I went back for seconds. I was only ten. His name was Eric Woodbine and he was in short trousers. He was over-enthusiastic like a St. Bernard.'

♡

The *Daily Star* asked its readers at the end of 1984 if they could remember their first love. Many wrote in about their two-timing Casanovas and some recalled their first kiss. Mrs. Eileen Graham of Woolton, Liverpool described her first love: 'We were both six, and he used to chase me after school. But he never seemed to know what to do when he caught me – so he hit me!'

♡

Ecuadorean beauty Lita Meneres kissed seventeen old boyfriends at her wedding reception in Quito in 1973. Pedro Basilio, the bridegroom, fled in tears and has not been seen since.

♡

BROTHERLY LOVE

If you are a boxer from Cuba, the United States, Wales or South Africa you will shake hands with your opponent before the encounter in honour of fair play in sport. Medieval knights kissed their opponents before a joust. British footballers kiss each other and hug and cuddle when a team-mate scores a goal. Kissing horrifies British referee Mr. Clive Thomas, who cannot bear to see a player submerged under the kisses and embraces of his fellow men. In fact, Mr. Thomas believes that kissing leads directly to the kind of violence that occurred when England football supporters rioted in Luxembourg. Mr. Thomas hopes that more will agree with him that a touchline love-in can be the forerunner of mayhem and violence, and that love-on-the-field will be banned.

♡

Prince Charles greeted his younger brother Prince Edward in public with a kiss on the cheek in May 1984. Some of their subjects were concerned about a French-style embrace bringing shame to the British monarchy. Most thought the correct way should have been for the princes to shake hands.

———————————————♡———————————————

The Poles spend more time kissing than anyone in the West, and their favourite time for making love is between eleven o'clock and noon. Professor Irenusz Kamelinski of the Polish Academy of Medicine discovered these facts after carrying out a survey among 100,000 Poles in 1978. The Professor, who is a specialist in social sexology, interviewed men and women between the ages of eighteen and sixty-five, and said that Poles were more tender as lovers than other races because they have not been corrupted by pornography. His survey showed that ninety-three per cent of the women and eighty-six per cent of the men rejected pornography on the grounds that it dehumanised sexual experience.

The Roman poet Ovid described a kiss that is intense and frenzied as a preliminary aphrodisiac to love. He gave other ways to best establish an erotic ambience: speaking with expressive eyebrows, gesturing, making conversation with the eyes, and expressing love with the lips.

One thousand, nine hundred years later, the Marriage Guidance Council of Britain issued a kiss-and-tell guide, warning that a quick peck on the cheek is a sign that a marriage is on the rocks: 'People find it easier to have sex with someone they no longer love than to kiss them.' And so those long, steamy kisses that Ovid preferred are still the best sign that love is in the ascendant.

———————♡———————   ———————♡———————

The Balinese like to change their love partners frequently, but kissing does not mean much to them. They much prefer to dance and display the beauty of their bodies as they move. The nearest thing to a kiss is a quivering movement of the head and shoulders as their faces nearly touch.

———————————————♡———————————————

TO KISS OR NOT TO KISS
Against Kissing

United Kingdom
Here the principal spoil-sport is the British Dental Association, who believe that fifty different species of micro-organisms exist in a kiss, but less if you wear dentures.

One reason given for the British love of bowing, curtsying and tipping of the hat in the seventeenth century was that it replaced kissing after the London plague broke out.

Books on English country folklore warn that a kiss on the nose is both unhygienic and unlucky, and will cause a couple to quarrel.

The Rest of France
In her best-selling book, *The Encyclopedia of the Kiss*, Dr. Martine Mourier describes how kissing can transfer bacteria from one kisser to another and can also put a strain on the heart. She quotes the findings of American doctors that each kiss shortens the kisser's life-span by three minutes because of increased heartbeats. As if all this is not enough, kissing can also cause sore throats, swollen glands, tiredness, and even epidemics.

Rome
Herpes is a great scare-word of the late twentieth century, but some 2,000 years ago the Emperor Tiberius tried to halt a herpes epidemic in Rome by banning kissing.

Sierra Leone
According to the Mendes of Sierra Leone, kissing leads to promiscuity, and you can always recognise promiscuous people by their bad complexion and physical weakness. In Sierra Leone promiscuous women are called 'the whole world's wife' or 'a man's mattress'.

Somalia
Kissing does not appeal to most people in Somalia because the idea of getting mixed up with another person's saliva revolts them. Others in Africa to feel like this are the Kikuyus, Rundis of Lake Victoria, Thongas, Mongo-Nkundos, and the Cewas, plus the Sirionós of Bolivia and the Lepchas who dwell in the Himalayas.

China
According to the *Worker's Daily* kissing helps transmit the hepatitis B virus, and so 'one can see' the dangers of kissing. The Chinese writer concluded: 'We must rid ourselves of this kissing habit.'

In Favour of Kissing

Virginia, USA
After studying the common cold, researchers at the University of Virginia have concluded that more germs are spread by shaking hands than by kissing.

Brittany, France
The inhabitants of the Pays de Mont in the Vendée part of Brittany have a style of kissing which includes the mutual exploration of each other's whole mouths with the tongue. These kisses can last for hours, and are specially named *un maraîchinage*.

The Gilyaks of Siberia
Though they seldom kiss in a way we would recognise, they eat each other's lice and see nothing wrong with washing each other's faces with saliva.

The Masais of Kenya and the Dinkas of Sudan
Saliva tastes so good to the Dinkas that they welcome visitors by showering them with saliva. Masais show how much they like people by spitting on their feet.

---♡---

The man who has stolen a kiss and does not
know how to steal the rest deserves to lose his
advantage.
Ovid in *Ars Amatoria*

---♡---

ORIENTAL STYLES

The Japanese do not have a word for 'kiss'. When Rodin's famous sculpture *The Kiss* was exhibited in Tokyo in the 1920s it was considered so decadent that it was kept behind a bamboo curtain so as not to offend sensitive Japanese eyes. Japanese women kiss their small children, but both they and their husbands prefer to kiss each other's J Spot (See page 3 for more about this).

The Chinese are shocked when they see their first Hollywood-style kiss, describing it as pure cannibalism. They also snigger if they come across two men showing affection publicly. Yet, there is nothing prim about the Chinese attitude to love: in Imperial China kisses were sometimes given to show the power of a woman over a man. When Empress Wu received government officials and visiting envoys she used to open her robes and they had to pay homage to her private parts.

---♡---

RUSSIAN KISSES

Two of the most famous Russians in the world were stripped of their Soviet citizenship in 1978. And that happened before Moscow knew about their love of kissing.

Galina Vishnevskaya, former star of the Bolshoi Opera and loved by Premier Nikolai Bulganin and other Soviet leaders, fainted after receiving her first kiss. The kisser in question was Pyotr Dolgolenko, a submarine lieutenant. In her autobiography, she described how 'when he kissed me for the first time, I actually fainted. We were on the street, and when I came to, I was sitting on a bench. Above me was his face, and around it the stars spinning'.

She later married the renowned cellist-conductor, Mstislav Rostropovich, who left his priceless 300-year-old Stradivarius cello on a train between Liverpool Street station and Ipswich. Alerted to the musician's plight, British Rail officials located the cello. Rostropovich was reunited with it two hours later when Kenneth Baird, general manager of the Aldeburgh Festival, handed the cello to him. How do Russians thank you for saving their lives or their treasured possessions? They give you a great big kiss and an even bigger hug.

———————————♡———————————

A curious kissing custom exists among the Ait Sadden Berbers of Morocco. If a woman is not happy with her husband she may flee to another man's house or tent. If she embraces and kisses the central pole which supports the roof, the owner of the tent is obliged to marry her and pay compensation money to the 'insulted' husband. If he cannot or will not, feuds will follow, and the 'injured' man will probably kidnap a woman from the village to which his wife has fled. An Ait Sadden Berber never knows what (or who) is around the next corner.

———————————♡———————————

An apple pie without cheese
Is like a kiss without a squeeze.

A lisping lass is good to kiss.

A woman kissed is half won.
English sayings

———————————♡———————————

In 1969 the police chief in the town of Inca on the Mediterranean island of Majorca staged a crackdown on kissing in public. A penalty of 500 pesetas a kiss was imposed *pronto*! Thirty couples rebelled. Their protest kiss-in cost them a fine of 45,000 pesetas.

Five hundred years earlier, a Roman prostitute called Veronica Franco asked for five crowns for a kiss and fifty for 'the complete transaction'. Her kiss cost as much as a domestic servant earned in six months.

Count Baldassare Castiglione, who lived in a hilltop palace in central Italy, was fascinated by women's legs, describing them as 'so secret a place'. On one occasion he recorded being intrigued at seeing 'her hose sitting clean to her leg'. Then he turned his attention to lips and mouths, and felt a need to warn lovers that 'anyone indulging in the sensual recreation of kissing would do well to remember that though the mouth be a parcel of the body yet it is an issue for the words that be the interpretation of the soul'.

In the Middle Ages, people unable to write used to sign a contract with an X and kiss it to show sincerity. That is how Xs at the end of a letter came to symbolise kisses.

When the *Daily Star* printed photographs of Boy George on holiday in Jamaica in 1984, the singer was so upset by comments about his appearance that he complained to the newspaper. The *Daily Star*'s editor published Boy George's letter and the newspaper's reply, signing off with:

Let's bury the hatchet, kiss, and make up.

Let's be friends again, George ...

The Editor

X X

A Kama Sutra position that requires practice.

Palm leaf drawing by Dharani Nayak of Orissa, India.

CHAPTER FOUR
LOVE LESSONS

GUIDES

The Japanese and Chinese call their love manuals 'pillow books', and most describe at least thirty love-making positions. The two leading Chinese guide books are the *Art of the Bedchamber* and the *Manual of Lady Mystery*. The top Japanese pillow book is the *Ishinpoo*.

Better known outside Asia are the two great 'K's from India – *Kama Sutra* and *Koka Shastra* – plus the *Anunga Runga* (which is fancied by Moslems of India and Pakistan, and Hindus alike). Each of these contains scores of pages devoted to love-making techniques and advice to lovers on how to top up their enjoyment.

The two great Arab books are *The Perfumed Garden* and the lesser known *Book of Exposition in the Science of Coition*, which begins with the promising greeting that goes straight to the point: 'ALHAMDOLILLAH – LAUD to the Lord who adorned the virginal bosom with breasts and who made the thighs of women anvils for the spear-handles of men!'

If you are interested in learning more about love techniques I recommend the *Kama Sutra* or *The Perfumed Garden* or any of the Chinese pillow books. Take them on holiday, or, if you are one of the lucky people who can take long-service leave or a sabbatical, take several pillow books.

It helps to be broad-minded *and* supple in mind and limb to manage some of the techniques advocated. It is very likely that you will discover muscles and dexterity you never knew you had. But there is a warning: if you practise some of the love positions in these books the chances are you may never walk normally again . . .

The chart that follows gives examples of the names given by the Chinese, Indians and Arabs to some of their most popular love positions. In some cases a particular position is unknown to one group, so there is obviously room for improvement and new ways of doing things.

LOVE POSITIONS

CHINESE (*Art of the Bedchamber* & other pillow books)	INDIAN (*Kama Sutra* & other love manuals)
The Rooster Perches on a Stick	—
The Dog Barks in the Autumn (Other races say this is impossible as it is done back-to-back; the Chinese advice is 'Try harder')	—
Shooting the Arrow while Running	Fixing a Nail
Old Man Pushing a Wheelbarrow	—
Cat & Mouse in the Same Hole	Lower Congress
The Hare Nibbles the Hair	—
—	Suspended Congress (Both stand & *he* leans against a wall)
The Cranes Entwine their Necks	—
The Monkey Shakes	Splitting the Bamboo
The Fish Eye	The Mare's Position
The White Tiger Leaps	Congress of an Ass
Swinging Monkey	—
Waters of the Fountain	—

ARAB
(*The Perfumed Garden*)

Fitting on the Sock

Reciprocal Sight of the
Posteriors
(This is the nearest anyone not
Chinese can get to the *Dog
Barks in the Autumn*, and even
this requires great suppleness
of the shoulders, neck & waist
for the woman & a rather long
reach for the male member of
the party.)

—

The Ostrich's Tail

—

The Screw of Archimedes

Driving the Peg Home
(Both stand & *she* leans
against a wall)

Pounding on the Spot

—

The One Who Stays at Home

The Ram

MARQUESANS practise this & call it
Stick the Bottom. *This position is also
known to the RUSSIANS, who call it the*
Crayfish Way.

The Toothpick in the Vulva

The Mutual Shock

Here are five famous suggestions for advanced students of love, who already know about the love positions listed in the preceding chart. The first three are Chinese, and it helps to be an acrobat by profession or inclination to manage them with ease.

Uplifted Woman
This love position requires four participants, though only two enjoy themselves. The woman is held high above their heads by two attendants; she curls up her legs and the man stands on a chair or stool, if necessary.

Flying Through the Air
The partners are unclothed. She sits on a swing with her thighs apart and he sits on another swing. They swing towards each other and try to connect.

The Balancing Act
This is much favoured by tea-lovers. The man and woman balance a bowl of tea on their heads and attempt union without spilling a drop. Indonesians also enjoy the Balancing Act.

As I have said, these are three Chinese techniques for advanced lovers. If you are disturbed by them you may be reassured by the current attitude to love as described in a Peking youth magazine: 'Making love is a mental illness that squanders time and energy.'

A popular love position, but not an easy one, is *El Kelouci* in *The Perfumed Garden*. It is called the Somersault in English:

> The woman must wear a pair of pantaloons, which she lets
> drop upon her heels; then she stoops, placing her head
> between her feet, so that her neck is in the opening of her
> pantaloons. At that moment, the man, seizing her legs,
> turns her upon her back, making her perform a
> somersault; then with his legs curved under him he brings
> his member right against her vulva, and, slipping it
> between her legs, inserts it.
> It is alleged that there are women who, while lying on
> their backs, can place their feet behind their heads without
> the help of pantaloons or hands.

For those who found this easier than blinking, here is another from *The Perfumed Garden*:

> Women of great experience who, lying with a man, elevate
> one of their feet vertically in the air, and upon that foot a
> lamp is set full of oil, and with the wick burning. While the
> man is ramming them, they keep the lamp steady and
> burning, and the oil is not spilled.

Not everything in the famous love guides is about love-making. For instance, *The Art of Love* is a famous Latin book that was widely read in ancient Rome, and it deals with many aspects of love. Written by the poet Ovid just two years before the birth of Christ, it still has many supporters today. It would appear that its principal appeal lies in its instructions on how to flirt, attract lovers, and consummate adultery.

Much of the detailed advice in *The Art of Love* is disconcertingly modern, and is to be found in etiquette books, sex-advice manuals, and in advertisers' announcements in the press, on the radio and on television. Here are some of Ovid's comments and instructions which I especially like:

- On the subject of a woman's having superfluous hair and body odour, he advises:
  > A hairy, stubbled leg your suitor will not charm,
  > And – dare I warn? – no goat below the arm.

  Furthermore a woman with a strong-smelling breath should not converse on an empty stomach [when, one assumes, the vapours must be at their worst], nor should she approach too near her lover. If her teeth are irregular or discoloured she should try to smile without baring too many of her poisonous-looking fangs.

- The man must flatter his loved-one, lose to her at gambling, and brush dust from her clothes. If she reminds him of his unsavoury past he ought to caress her and, in any event, he would do well to ply her with gifts.

- He will laugh with her and weep when she does, but if he cannot cry to order he will consider moistening his eye with his finger. He will always have it at the back of his mind that the best time to court a wife is when she has just discovered that her husband has been unfaithful, for then she will seek revenge.

- At the circus he must watch that those sitting behind her do not stick their knees into her back [still a frequent nuisance in theatres and aeroplanes].

- He must wear spotless, well-fitting clothes, keep his hair, nails, and nostrils well trimmed, and – like all women – avoid body odour and halitosis. Ovid also counsels a man to look pale at times, so that his loved-one will think she is the cause.

ADVICE FOR WOMEN

Many love guides contain special advice for women. The anonymous author of *La Clef d'Amour*, written 700 years ago in France, suggested: 'If you are short of stature, receive people sitting down or stretched out on your bed with a rug over your legs. Wear a lot of clothes if you are too thin and a tight band over your breasts if they are too large. If you have ugly teeth, do not laugh with your mouth open. The ideal laugh is short and sweet, with the mouth half-open, revealing two pretty little dimples. Never laugh loud and long. It is better not to laugh at all if you have a jarring laugh.'

No one knows for sure who Manu was, but those Hindus who have read his works say that his advice is as good today as it must have been all those centuries ago when he wrote them. How many women, though, could carry out this command:

> If he sing she must be in ecstasy; if he dance she must look
> at him with delight; if he speak of learned things she must
> listen to him with admiration.

The Greek philosopher Aristotle delivered valuable advice to any woman who feared that her love affair might not only be discovered by her husband, but that her baby might look like her lover:

> If in the act of copulation, the woman earnestly looks on
> the man, and fixes her mind on him, the child will
> resemble the father. Nay, if a woman, even in lawful
> copulation, fix her mind upon her husband, the child will
> resemble him though he did not beget it.

A BLUE-BLOODED GUIDE

In 1985 *Burke's Peerage*, that indispensable guide to 'who's got what', introduced a blood-and-gold list of Britain's top heirs and heiresses. The *Peerage*'s publisher, the untitled Mr. Harold Brooks-Baker, said: 'We are continually getting inquiries from Europe – mostly Italy, France and Germany – and from Canada and the United States. They want lists of the most eligible young people, wealthy heiresses and unmarried heirs to title. The inquiries are quite above board. They come from people in the "blood and gold" themselves, either of aristocratic descent, or in the millionaire class, or both.'

The operation was made possible by a socially conscious computer, which carries the whole of the *Peerage* in its tiny mind and has been adjusted to react, when told of a grandee's death, by promoting his heir and moving everyone up the correct number of stages. But the computer lacks a fail-safe device to prevent Texan oil barons or impoverished, deposed kings and potentates from turning up at a stately castle only to find that their quarry has halitosis and no teeth, or has willed her inheritance to the Royal Society for the Prevention of Cruelty to Animals.

The list merely gives the name of the goods on offer in terms of parenthood, future titles, and possible future wealth, leaving the hopeful suitor to do all the legwork.

ADVICE FOR MEN

The *Kama Sutra* gives a list of men who are generally successful with women. They include:

- Men well versed in the science of love
- Men who talk well
- Men who act as messengers
- Men who know their weak points
- Enterprising and brave men
- Men who surpass the women's husbands in learning and good looks, in good qualities, and in liberality

If male readers feel that life is too short for them to mend their ways and become absolute lady-killers, the *Kama Sutra* lists forty-one types of women who would be only too pleased to meet any man. The list includes:

- A woman who hates her husband
- The wife of an actor
- A woman whose husband is inferior to her in rank or abilities
- A woman whose husband is devoted to travelling
- A covetous woman
- A jealous woman
- A humpbacked woman
- An ill-smelling woman
- A lazy woman

WORLDLY ADVICE

A BIT ON THE SIDE 1

In Britain, Mrs. June Knowles claimed in the Marriage Guidance Council journal that adultery can sometimes save a couple from divorce: 'You can have a sexual relationship outside marriage without damage to the marriage. The marriage can be enriched by it . . . We are all capable of loving a lot of people.'

A BIT ON THE SIDE 2

Men with heart trouble should make love side by side with their partner, or let the partner take the initiative. Those who adopt other positions develop higher pulse and blood pressure rates. This advice from medical workers in

Illinois, USA, was published in the British *Sun* newspaper. A spokesman for Britain's Health Education Council commented: 'Sex puts a big strain on a man, whatever the position.'

THREE WOMEN'S ADVICE TO WOMEN

BARBARA CARTLAND, the world's most famous romantic novelist, advises: 'Greying, lank hair, wrinkles and lines on the face, a scraggy neck, drooping breasts are all the first results of a slimming treatment. What all men find attractive is *joie de vivre*, laughter, gaiety and a sparkle which comes from a happy disposition. No women can have that on a diet of lettuce leaves and grapefruit!'

Miss Cartland continues: 'A woman has to realise that at fifty she cannot keep her face and her figure. A thin woman will get wrinkles sooner than a fat one. So the choice is: "Shall I choose face or figure?" My advice has always been – have a lovely face and sit down.'

Hollywood actress ZSA ZSA GABOR: 'I never hated a man enough to give his diamonds back.'

LADY DOCKER was born Norah Turner, the daughter of a car salesman whose family home was above a butcher's shop in Derby. She revelled in the publicity her three marriages to three millionaires brought: she was banned from Monte Carlo, the Côte d'Azur, the Royal Enclosure at Ascot, and even from her local public house in Jersey. She explained her magnetism for rich men by the simple formula of always asking for the best:

'When other girls would be satisfied with fur I always demanded mink; when the other girls would be satisfied with zircon I would insist on a diamond. I always asked for champagne and it had to be pink because I loved the colour.'

Adam Petrie wrote *Rules of Good Deportment and of Good Breeding* in 1720. His advice to gentlemen was never to spit in the fire, never to break wind 'even among inferiors'. If women needed to go to the lavatory during a long journey Mr. Petrie recommended that suitable phrases should be employed so as not 'to put them to the blush'. One of his suggestions was: 'Let us allow the horses to breathe a little.'

♡

Descend a step in choosing thy wife: ascend a
step in choosing thy friend.
The Talmud

FEET

Ait Sadden Berbers of Morocco keep their slippers on in bed on their wedding night and for seven nights after, to stop evil spirits from entering their bodies through their feet.

The British SAS – Sock Advisory Service – says you can tell a lot about a man by the socks he wears. The SAS warns women against men who choose pink socks: 'You are unlikely to get this one into your bed, but your brother might.' No socks on is a sure sign that he is messy, slovenly and uncaring, and according to the SAS's director 'socks are the forgotten armament in the male weapon range for bird-pulling'.

A footnote: Frank Sinatra does it his way – never wearing the same pair twice. Multi-millionaire recluse Howard Hughes was so concerned about hygiene that he changed his paper socks at least four times daily.

Be careful if you talk about the weather to a Chinese person. This advice applies particularly to anyone who has business dealings with them or who likes to eat in Chinese restaurants. To the Chinese any mention of 'clouds and rain' refers to the act of sexual intercourse.

FOR & AGAINST SEX

Against

MAHATMA GANDHI, who said that the man who can achieve complete continence 'will be healthy and will easily live long. He will not even suffer from so much as a headache. Mental and physical work will not cause fatigue. He is ever bright, never slothful'

CONFUCIUS: 'In youth, when the physical powers are not yet settled, a man must guard against lust.'

WILLIAM ACTON, the nineteenth-century English physician: 'His mind had become enfeebled, and there was great pain in his back . . . I found that he had been in the habit of indulging in connection three times a week, without any idea that he was committing an excess, or that his present weakness could depend on this cause.'

For

The Chinese Yellow Emperor Huang-ti became immortal because he made love to several women every night. Some Chinese who doubt that the emperor is still alive believe that he lived to the age of 3,000.

The author of the Hindu love classic the *Ananga Ranga* believed in prolonging the pleasure of love-making. He advised men to avoid over-tensing their muscles, to smoke in the middle of coition or chew betel nut, and to preoccupy the brain.

The French also advocate pre-occupying the brain – by thinking of '*ma pauvre mère*'. This method is considered more effective for men than for women.

The humorist James Thurber thought that smokers smoke as an excuse to touch someone (when lighting up) and get attention. An article in *The Times* in December 1980 confirmed his view: 'It is a statistical fact, and statistical facts are acknowledged to knock the other sort into a cocked hat any day of the week, that cigarette smokers are more apt than others to be promiscuous or involved in criminal activity.'

TITILLATIONS

A popular item on five continents – maybe even six – is the Tibetan happy ring invented by Lamas 700 years ago. The original ones were made from goats' eyelids and were attached to a man's private parts. Today, they are made of nylon.

Burmese bells are another popular line, though the Japanese prefer to call them tinkling bells. Sometimes they were tied around the lover's private parts, but the really brave men had them inserted surgically. The aristocracy had silver ones, which tinkled prettily, but the poor could only afford lead ones, which rang but little. In Burma, China, Japan and Thailand a king or leader 'sometimes taketh his out and giveth them to his noblemen as a great gift' reported one English traveller called Ralph Fitch.

Emperor Yang-ti, the Chinese emperor with the 3,000 concubines whose exploits, techniques and advice are featured elsewhere in this book, had a special love-making chair on wheels. The lady's legs and arms were held by clamps in the best position to receive his favours. Such was his enjoyment that he commissioned craftsmen to invent more fascinating pieces of furniture. His favourite was a couch attached to four heavy silk ropes which, when pulled by four men, gave the lovers the sensation of being rocked in a boat at sea.

Jonathan Sale, a London-based journalist, once wrote off for catalogues offering special exotic equipment, the type sold with warnings such as 'if you feel they would cause offence we would strongly recommend that you dispose of it unopened', which has the immediate effect on many prospective customers to order six boxes right away.

Mr. Sale gave the names of some of the catalogue items available by post: Night Fingers, Dracula, Riffelfix, Alligator, Fakir-Lust, Pinky, Hell Fire, Micky, Handy, Jumbo and . . .

DRESS TO KILL

There is no shortage of advice from fashion designers and journalists about the type of clothes to wear if you want to seduce a man or appeal to a woman.

Pierre Cardin thinks cream linen trousers flatter a man's body (unless he is paunchy), and that jersey, cashmere or terrytowelling robes worn around the home are sensuously clinging.

Mary Quant, the darling of fashion-conscious Englishwomen in the 1960s, still has her followers twenty years on. In 1984 she announced her colour-code for women:

GREEN
Not immediately seductive,
but has the devil in it.

WHITE
Pristine linens longing to
be rumpled.

RED
Sexy, rampant – and it
always works

CREAM
Delicate seduction. Cream
blocking tops are amazing.

YELLOW
Smiles, sunshine & roses.

GREY
It has a conceited certainty.

ORANGE
Outrageous. A smack in
the eye colour.

BROWN
Warm, renewing and rich
with promise.

BLACK
Can be demure. So romantic
in lace, voluptuous
in velvet.

NUDE PINK
That pale, delicate, only-just
pink is very naughty –
especially with black.

BLUE
Royal blue & black are
aggressive, Parisienne chic.

FAWN
A delicious waiting quality.

You can tell a lot about a man who likes to 'say it with flowers' by the colour he chooses. American researchers interviewed florists and flower-givers, and found that:

Red = I love you
Blue = Reassuring; we belong together
Yellow = Cheer up! Life's not too bad
Pink = Our love is innocent and/or platonic
White = Sympathy and caring
Orange = A special friendship

Hardy Amies is dressmaker to Queen Elizabeth II and many famous women. He headed British Resistance operations in Belgium during World War II, he designed futuristic clothes for Stanley Kubrick's film *2001: A Space Odyssey*, and now he creates clothes for men. Though his advice is especially pertinent to British men it will be useful to any man who likes to please women: he hates men in bowler hats, and says sharply that men who wear frilly shirts with evening dress should confine themselves to hairdressing.

A few years ago *The Times* asked him what he disliked about his own sex. Never shy of a blunt answer, Amies held forth in style: 'I don't really dislike other men; I usually admire them. They often look more virile, richer and infinitely more intelligent than I do. Of course, I hate the way hair grows out of the ears and nostrils of intelligent ones, and the rich are usually too sleek or too portly. I love the rich working class: they are always so enthusiastic about life and anxious to learn. They give you a feeling that you can teach them something. It is the poor upper classes that I really cannot get on with. To bolster their sense of failure, they are always leaning on traditions of their schools, family and land, which is quite infuriating.

'Old men are tiresome with their string vests showing through their shirts and their terrible pipes. Most of them smell, because the English don't believe that a suit needs cleaning at least twice a year, not just when it shows the dirt. Young men are infuriating, too. They have far too much hair, which really looks marvellous.'

So much for men, but in these words lurks a lot of worldly advice.

———————♡———————

The English writer William Cobbett, known chiefly for his *Rural Rides*, penned this advice to young men: 'Get to see her at work upon a mutton-chop, or a bit of bread and cheese; and if she deal quickly with these, you have a pretty good security for that activity, that stirring industry, without which a wife is a burden instead of being a help. And, as to love, it cannot live for more than a month or two (in the breast of a man of spirit) towards a lazy woman.'

———————♡———————

STAYING YOUNG AT 100

Centenarians all over the world have their own methods of staying young, fit and desirable to lovers at 100. Here is the advice (practised by each, too) of five centenarians:

Joshua Whitehead of Huddersfield	never see a doctor.
Mrs. M. Cruttenden of Southend	become teetotal at 97 and resume drinking at 100.
Shirali Baba Muslimov of Azerbaydzhan, Soviet Union	never hurry and marry someone years younger. (When he was reputedly aged 167 his 'child' bride was 98.)

| Thomas Bridson of the Isle of Man | climb a 2,000 ft mountain every year on your birthday. |
| Javier Pereira of New York | eat rice three times a day, smoke cigars and drink rum. |

The mountain people of the Andes in Ecuador (the Vilcabambans), the Hunzas of the Karakoram mountains on the China–Pakistan border, and the Abkhasians of Georgia in the Soviet Union are the most famous and most numerous of the world's centenarians. Here are their 'recipes' for longevity and sexual strength:

Vilcabambans – smoke fifty cigarettes a day, but grow your own tobacco; hard work and lots of exercise.

Hunzas – drink huge amounts of mountain spring water; drink wine not older than 100 days.

Abkhasians – eat chicken, mutton or beef flavoured with lots of garlic and spices; drink unrefined rum.

Happy and sensuous centenarians have a sense of humour and enjoy a good joke. More women than men live to be a hundred. The best chance a man has of reaching his century is to be a eunuch (I take no responsibility for whatever male readers decide to do about this).

The Burmese have a system of laws called *Dhammathats*, which set out the types of beguiling women that men should be on their guard against: they include women who
– shake some concealed part of the body
– expose the thighs as if by accident, then pretend to cover them
– expose the breasts, the armpits or the navel
– raise the eyebrows
– bite their lips or stick out their tongue
– mimic a child's movements.

When can a Burmese man ever feel safe from a woman? The laws also warn him against five 'improprieties', the worse of which concern food. According to the laws, the three women he has to be most wary of are:
– the one who eats the best bits herself
– the one who eats immediately she gets up in the morning
– the one who has a bigger appetite than he does.

Another woman to treat with suspicion is one who 'is in the habit of looking at men when they are dressing or undressing, or when they are bathing'.

The *Daily Star* asked its readers, 'Are you looking for love?' Their advice was to start by looking in the right place, and gave department stores, do-it-yourself stores, on buses and the London tube, and fast-food restaurants as among the best places to meet a soul-mate. Another suggestion was to go jogging, but 'even if you dislike your exercise, remember to smile. Don't look in pain, even if you are'.

———————♡———————

To help understand women, the French writer Honoré de Balzac suggested that 'No man should marry before he has studied anatomy and dissected the body of a woman'.

An absence, the decline of a dinner invitation, an unintentional coldness, can accomplish more than all the cosmetics and beautiful dresses in the world.
Marcel Proust

———————♡———————

Two men with wildly different views each wrote a manual containing his advice to the love-lorn. On dating and petting Dr. W. E. Hulme wrote: 'Make your date a threesome with the Lord. Take Him along . . . He will show you a good time.' And in 1559 Giovanni della Casa addressed his worldly advice to courtiers bent on seducing a lady: he warned against yawning, sneezing or scratching in public, nor should a man ever be seen smelling someone else's meat (especially if it were on the loved-one's plate), and never, but never, should he make bad puns.

———————♡———————

A dating manual in China advises young men to carry a book and a badminton racquet on their first date to give an impression of intelligence and good health. The manual also warns women against 'the unscrupulous type who rounds corners at full speed on his bicycle'.

———————♡———————

CHAPTER FIVE
GO-BETWEENS

Cupid was a famous go-between. So was Puck. Other go betweens have been less high-flown. In ancient Rome maids were employed to carry love messages for patrician lovers. The messages were written in milk on their backs, and would remain invisible until the skin was rubbed with coal dust by the recipient. This secret service provided employment for dreary domestics whose features were decidedly plain: few mistresses would employ beautiful maids to act as their go-betweens.

Here I include a wide range of people whose role in life is to bring people together – either by introducing them or by improving a relationship that is deficient or turning sour. Such a role can be performed by machines (computers and video recorders for example), hired help (mistresses, companions, gigolos), love tutors, marriage bureaux, lonely hearts advertisements, agony aunts and psychologists. The love trade is large, lucrative, and important.

LOVE MACHINES

Just for your records I thought you might be
interested to know that on only my third run
your computer managed to match me to an
exceptional young man. He's handsome,
intelligent, kind. We have exactly the same taste
in music, politics, humour, hobbies . . .
everything. We could talk endlessly about
psychology, science, our backgrounds etc. He's
perfect! There's only one snag – he's my
brother!
From a letter to Dateline,
Britain's biggest computer dating agency

One man told a dating computer: 'I want a
companion who is small and attractive, loves
water sports, is fond of seafood, and enjoys
group activities.'
The computer replied: 'Marry a penguin.'
New Woman magazine, USA

♡

Your computer was right. Mitzi W. and I like all
the same things. We like the same food, we
both like the opera. Mitzi likes bike riding and
so do I. I like dogs, and so does Mitzi. Actually
there was only one thing we didn't like – each
other.
American matrimonial agency complaint
quoted in J. Godwin's *The Mating Trade*

♡

In a shed in the Forbidden City area of Peking is a Chinese-made computer
and 3,000 floppy discs containing the requests of lonely bachelors and
spinsters in search of someone to marry. Each applicant is asked to state the
political preferences, health, age and occupation of the desired partner. One
35-year-old girl said she wanted someone who was a Communist Party
member in excellent health, around forty, and had a good job in the
government . . .
The computer replied: 'No one is suitable for you. Be patient. Wait.'
Irene of California is much more sophisticated. She is a bag of chips
programmed to listen, and she will find you the ideal companion. 'What is
your lifestyle?' she asks, trying to find out which sex you prefer. She needs
fifteen minutes to run through her memory banks to locate your soul-mate.
A British equivalent to Irene is *The Dating Game* or *I Do* which asks
questions like:
'Your lover invites you to join him/her in the bath.
Do you:
1. Decline, saying there is not enough room.
2. Add some exotic-smelling oils and join in.
Or 3. Leap in, shouting 'Geronimo'?

♡

Video dating is a serious business in Japan and America. People record
themselves chatting, smiling, laughing, eating, cooking and doing anything
they think will show off their assets. Prospective partners hire tapes and
hunt for the man or woman of their dreams, but many are never successful,
turning up in the 'reruns' year after year. Somehow 'I'm a rerun' sounds
more poignant than being called a 'has-been'.
Mr. and Mrs. Gerald Burton use video in their marriage too but the couple
sued the Private Shop in Worthing, West Sussex, after hiring five allegedly

pornographic videos. They won their case and Mr. Burton, a plumber, claimed: 'I have proved my point. The films were insufficiently explicit. These shops cheat customers who are too embarrassed to complain.'

♡

Lee Kuan Yew, the Prime Minister of Singapore, enlisted computer programmes from Japanese match-making agencies to play Cupid on behalf of his country's women graduates. Mr. Lee complained that uneducated Singaporean women produced twice as many babies as their educated counterparts. Unless the trend were reversed, he suggested, the weakening of Singapore's gene pool would undermine the economy. A Government team was despatched to Japan to study computer dating, and Singapore University was urged to introduce a course in courting techniques for new students. As yet Mr. Lee's efforts have not had the desired effect – the uneducated have continued to procreate shamelessly.

A dating agency called Stifelsen Datastraffen in Stockholm is concerned that a lot of Swedes suffer from 'terrible loneliness in a meaningless world', so it undertakes 'systematic looking for partners' with what the publicity blurb describes as 'a speedy and cheap idiot which does as it's told' (the company computer).

♡

International spies are taught to beat lie detector machines by thinking about something sexy as they give their answers. The technique was advocated by British civil service union leaders when it was proposed to give lie detector tests to staff at the British Government's General Communications Headquarters (GCHQ) in Cheltenham in October 1983.

♡

A *shadkhan* is a professional Jewish matchmaker. When one young man caught a glimpse of his bride-to-be he took the *shadkhan* aside: 'You told me she had the appearance, the bearing, the grace of a queen. Look at her! She's pimply, cross-eyed and hook-nosed. She slobbers her food, she limps and she's hunchbacked.'
'No need to whisper,' replied the *shadkhan*. 'She's also deaf.'

♡

In Brooklyn's Borough Park area of New York matchmakers Mrs. Dov, Mrs. Weiner and Mrs. Levi ask their clients to fill in a card. Women are asked if they would marry someone with a beard – a euphemism for a devout Jew. Men are asked if they are a 'Cohen' or a descendant of the priestly tribe, which means they are forbidden to marry a divorced person. Such a careful approach to their work has earned the three ladies a good reputation.

AN IRISH–AMERICAN CONNECTION

In the small spa town of Lisdoonvarna in Co. Clare on the west coast of Ireland, where marriageable women are in scant supply, there is a Festival of the Bachelors every September. Jim White, a local hotelier and festival organiser, tries to revive the long and honourable tradition of Irish match-making.

For seventeen hours a day the village's twenty-six pubs play dance music to help the middle-aged, the elderly, the awkward and the shy get ac-quainted in a poor agricultural area where people traditionally marry late or not at all. In 1983 Mr. White's efforts were helped by an American travel agent anxious to promote package tours to 'Ireland in the mating season', who despatched forty-nine well-upholstered Chicago matrons intent on catching a husband if they could.

In Lisdoonvarna there was great excitement. Tony Garraghy groomed his donkey as well as himself for the arrival of the group from Chicago. Garraghy was sixty-seven, but compared to some of the bachelors he was quite a youngster. Tom Brennan was seventy, and when he waltzed divorcee Barbara O'Reilly Corbine across the floor the top of his underpants showed a good two inches above his trousers. Joe Nash, who used his shepherd's crook to hook the legs of the American visitors he fancied, was eighty-five.

Though one of the Americans had arrived with her Brooks Bros. wedding dress in her luggage, no marriages resulted. The American women learned that the Irish think there is more to life than women, and the men of Lisdoonvarna, some of whom have been on Mr. White's books for years, resigned themselves to waiting for another coachload of women to arrive – from anywhere.

VALENTINE

There are fifty-two St. Valentines and no one knows which gave his name to Valentine's Day on February 14. All the favoured candidates were martyred, but died with their knots of celibacy still securely tied. One Valentinus gave aid to persecuted Christians and while in prison for this formed a friendship with the blind daughter of his gaoler. When he was taken away to be executed he wrote her a farewell message which he signed: 'From your Valentine.'

In the medieval world St. Valentine's Day was associated with love because it was believed that birds began to mate on February 14. In the English countryside it is still believed that a girl can tell the occupation of her future husband by noting which bird she sees first on St. Valentine's Day:

blackbird = clergyman
robin = sailor
goldfinch = rich man
blue tit = happy man
dove = a good man
crossbill = argumentative man.

But if it is a woodpecker she will find no man at all.

In Victorian times so many lovers sent cards anonymously that in London the postmen claimed special allowances for meals to give them the strength to carry them. The three favourite types of cards were sentimental, silly and nasty, the latter type being directed to old maids, the pot-bellied, cross-eyed and one-legged cordially wishing them the three 'D's – disgrace, death and damnation.

The shop of A. S. Jordan at 2 Milk Street in Boston did a brisk trade in Valentine cards imported from England in 1847, when best-sellers included the following kinds: Hen-pecking, Suicidal, Raving-mad, Trifling, Serio-Comical, Heart-struck, Heart-rending, Heart-piercing, Heart-aching and Heart-killing.

In 1953 Wladziu Liberace – the pianist, owner of the 'most expensive fur piece ever designed for anyone including the Queen of England', whose master bedroom in America has a copy of the ceiling of the Sistine Chapel in Rome, owner of 26 dogs and 18 pianos (including Chopin's and Gershwin's) – received 27,000 Valentine cards.

❦

Love *can* be measured. For St. Valentine's Day 1985 lovesick lovers paid for advertisements to a loved-one in many of Britain's national newspapers. The vital dimensions were:

1. *The Times*   620 column inches
2. *Daily Mail*   484
3. *The Guardian*   375
4. *Daily Star*   191½
5. *Daily Mirror*   175
6. *Daily Express*   140
7. *Daily Telegraph*   51
8. *The Sun*   38
9. *Morning Star*   1

The problem is finding the message that might be for you. A lot of messages in *The Times* are addressed to Thunder Thighs.

The *Daily Mail's* lovers adore Victorian values, especially fidelity: 'Agatha, be my adorable wife forever.' *Guardian* lovers throw in frequent references to muesli, and one expressed himself in Welsh, while another showed feminine honesty: 'To Snouty: "It's true love because, when he's late for dinner and I know he might be either having an affair or lying dead in the middle of the street, I always hope he's dead."'

The messages have to be just secret enough to get a thrill out of exhibitionism without letting on for sure who the man or woman is behind the advertisement. Lovers see themselves or the desired-one as animals, with bears the firm favourite, but fleas, toads, rats and bugs are well represented. Food symbols occur often: sausages, prunes, cherry pies and thousands of items prefaced by 'yummy'.

Some lovers think the 'yuk' factor might appeal, so there are 'smelly feet', 'fatso', 'pot belly'. Others are more courageously sexual with stress on words like 'rampant', 'virile' or 'unquenchable'. Flowers with the most allure are the lily, rose and plain 'petal'. Probably most ingenious of all is the line of baby-talk that hundreds of otherwise sensible people indulge in once a year.

Having identified your love message the next step is to de-code it: then you might have an idea of who sent it and why.

♡

Last century it was common for a lover to attach a token of love to a Valentine card. A lock of hair was favoured by Englishwomen while men might send metal knives, forks or plates as 'a Trifle Towards Housekeeping'. A card that is popular in America has chewing gum attached to the message: 'We can be Valentines if you don't gum things up.'

♡

In Cuba February 14 is called Loving Day and couples queue to marry at the largest Cuban wedding palace, the Palacios de los Matrimonios.

♡

On St. Valentine's Day in 1975 the British Army arranged for 120 paratroopers returning from duty in Northern Ireland to make a St. Valentine's Day lovers' leap from an aeroplane into a field near Aldershot, Surrey. There was one casualty: a wife who dashed over to her husband twisted her knee.

On the last day of February 1288 (a leap year) the Scottish Parliament issued an ordinance whereby any man who refused to take a woman who proposed to him would be fined a pound unless he could prove he was betrothed to another. Similar laws were passed in France, Florence and Genoa. Some believe this to be the origin of the later custom for women to woo men in leap years.

♡   ♡

Have you decided what to give your special Valentine this year? Finger's has a lovely suggestion. Though flowers are nice and candy is filled with sugar and spice, a GE dishwasher is best for cleaning up your kitchen mess. It's a gift that will last. . . . Her dishes will sparkle, her eyes will gleam. Since her work is done there's more time to spend with her loved one. And through February 14 1984, Finger's will provide normal changeout installation in the Houston area at no extra charge. What a bargain! But then it's from Finger's . . . with love.

From an advertisement in *The Houston Post*, USA

♡

LOVE LETTERS

Henry VIII, Frédéric Chopin and Napoleon Bonaparte wrote love letters. So did Cimell, Mrs. Smith and A. K. Ghosh.

Cimell is a Murray Islander who proposed to a Mabuiag girl by letter on New Year's Day in 1899: 'You are a girl, I am a young man. Do you like me? Don't be afraid at all of a young man suitable for you. You suit me. God formerly made woman suitable for having a man, and man suitable for having a woman. I like you. What murrage for me? You know men, I am not like some men. I am a man of work. This is my message to you. The end.'

Mrs. Smith is just one of hundreds of British housewives who have written love letters to Ian McCaskill, an owl-like, plump and hyperactive BBC television weather man who became the most unlikely sex symbol of 1984. One pale primrose envelope was covered with kisses: 'Dear Ian. If you have been on holiday I hope you had a good time. What bliss you are back again, Ian dear.'

Another lady wrote: 'You always make me happy with your "cheeky lows".' Viewers who dislike him write direct to the Chairman of the BBC and complain that he waves his arms about like a windmill.

The Secret Art of Letter Write by A. K. Ghosh is sold on book stalls in College Street in Calcutta. Mr. Ghosh devotes a whole chapter to 'Letters Regarding Matrimony' in his guide to correct letter writing, giving samples for his readers to copy:

From a Young Gentleman to a Young Lady, with whom he was in love: urgent and passionate.

Dear Miss Kamala,

The moment you came into my life I loved you. The more I have seen of you the more I have liked. What little remains is where all my future happiness must lie. Dear Kamala, I love you more than anything else around. Will you be my wife? I eagerly await your answer. If it is 'yes' I shall be the happiest man. If it is 'no' is there no hope for me in any other position that you can think of?

Yours devotedly,

*From a Young Gentleman to a Young Lady, with
whom he was in love: courteous and formal.*

Madam,

I have three times attempted to give you oral
expression of the content of my fluttering
insides but my courage has so often failed. My
innermost parts crave expression now and I
must give it most sincere and urgent expulsion.
My happiness in these parts will depend upon
your answer. I am not precipitated, Madam, nor
would I want your hand if you should want to
cut it off with me. If this were so I would try to
bear it away like a man. My circumstances are
independent, my character hitherto
unblemished. Your mother knows my aunt. If
this proposal be to your satisfaction, the tip-top
concern of my future life would be to relieve
myself for ever in the company of her whom I
prefer than all others in the world.

Madam, your real admirer,

The Young Lady's Answer: favourable.

Dear Mr. Roy,

I will answer your letter quite frankly. I
believe it would be good for our mutual
happiness to marry at once. I want you to do the
needful. You better request your aunt to
propose to my parents. I do not step in the affair
without their approbation.

Yours devotedly,

The Young Lady's Answer: unfavourable and angry.

Sir,

I have read your letter with astonishment. I
consider it a gross impertinence. If you address
me in any way again, I shall not hesitate to
expose you in front of my parents.

Yours truly,

♡

♡

Unmarried Samoan boys are obliged by social custom to have a confidant and go-between called a *soa* through whom to pursue their clandestine love affairs. The *soa*'s task is to sing his friend's praises and to sweet-talk the right girl into making a rendezvous. Selecting a *soa* presents many difficulties. If the lover chooses a steady, reliable, younger relative he is likely to see the affair bungled through lack of experience and tact, but if he goes for an expert wooer the girl is as likely as not to go off with his *soa* instead of him.

The best *soas*, in fact, are girls – but they are difficult to find because a boy cannot choose among his female relatives, in front of whom it is taboo for him to mention anything concerning love or sex. Among young Samoans the most violent antagonisms arise not between ex-lovers, but between boys and the *soas* who have betrayed them.

♡

LONELY HEARTS

Lonely hearts can be fun to read, and it is often remarked how brave people need to be to place one. But those who really need courage, and a sense of adventure, are those who dare to reply. They are writing into the dark, and if they do not expose a lot of themselves they can never hope to hear from the advertiser. The advertiser can hide behind a box number, diverge far from the truth in self-description, demand photographs of applicants, and wait for the bait to be taken and the trap to be sprung.

Millions of newspapers and journals around the world carry notices from men and women in search of partners, and I include a mixed bag from some of my favourite places.

♡

Ranch owner, Henry Joneson of Alberta, saw an advertisement in August 1984 from a widow who 'wishes to start new life . . . will relocate'. He replied and was delighted to receive a warm letter from Ada Wittenmyer. Mrs. Wittenmyer was very willing to relocate from her home in a Tennessee gaol, where she was serving life for murdering her third and fourth husbands, and resuming her old way of life would allow her to go on poisoning men for their money.

Russian officialdom may be against lonely hearts advertisements, but when the magazine *Literaturnaia Gazeta* published two fake notices for marriage partners in 1976 they got more than 10,000 replies. Of these one per cent were from readers expressing horror at the idea.

TWENTY-YEAR-OLD jockey seeks active partner to keep weight down. No vices, also Labrador puppy for sale.

Tatler

DIRTY OLD LADIES. Quiet white male, 20, loves sex with single mature buxom woman 45–65 . . .

KEITH the rapist can make you fall in love by gently removing your panties. Anywhere . . .

both in *Freep*, USA

BEAUTIFULLY ASSEMBLED statuesque male 34, seeks friendship of female dancer, gymnast, artist for acrobatics and immortalisation.

UGLY, BORING male (31) seeks beautiful, witty, rich young lady to prove that opposites attract.

SINCERE SOPRANO (Gemini) would like to make music with brave bass/tenor/choir.

Private Eye

The townspeople were so outraged when Miss Helen Morison advertised for a husband in the *Manchester Weekly Journal* in 1727 that the Lord Mayor had her committed to an asylum for the insane for a month.

I award top marks to the Americans for down-to-earth descriptions of themselves and equally earthy accounts of what they hope to find. The following 'Strictly Personals' come from *New York* magazine:

GENTLEMAN, EARLY 50 – Athletic, virile, married, but starved for love and affection seeks equally hungry lady, sensuous, uninhibited for long term, mature, discreet daytime affair. Firm, well proportioned body important.

LADY WITH BEST OF MIND – And figure seeks man who can paint a ceiling, open a clam and tell a Rothko from a Cézanne. If you are over 6', over 45 and brave, write!

I AM REAL – Outstanding, financially independent, handsome, 50, warm, virile, youthful, intelligent, creative, witty, emotionally sound, genuine . . .

Time Out has a large and varied readership including many foreign visitors in London and the Home Counties. These lonely hearts notices were published in *Time Out*:

ENGLISH SPEAKING LESBIAN wanted by male Chinese gay 28, for permanent and rewarding relationship.

MAN, 37, looking for woman who can be honest and open in a physical relationship, and a close friend and companion, WITHOUT any emotional manipulation or implied ownership. Non-smoker only (who wants to kiss an ashtray?).

FORMER VENTRILOQUIST, speedway rider, academic, now senior, well-paid executive. Jewish, fortyish, wishes he had a simple involving relationship with a woman to cancel past, make a future.

WHO ARE those gorgeous, voluptuous girls that this attractive male, 28, runs past in the West End every lunch-time?

More money is spent by Indian parents than anyone else in the world to marry off their daughters and sons through newspaper advertisements. Every week hundreds of families insert descriptions of their offspring in *The Times of India*. These all appeared on the same day:

MAHARASHTRIAN LADY GYNAECOLOGIST AND OBSTETRICIAN M.D., D.G.O., D.F.P. from a respectable family, 30 years, 166 cm, intelligent, well featured, cultured, smart, good looking with wheatish complexion seeks matrimonial correspondence from smart, well natured Bombay based below 36 years, preferably with highly qualified post graduate medicos. PLEASE APPLY IN CONFIDENCE WITH HOROSCOPE.

[It is usual for Indians of all classes, educated and uneducated, to consult astrologers and compare horoscopes before a marriage can be contracted. Astrologers also choose the date when the wedding will take place.]

MATRIMONIAL INVITED FOR 26 years Punjabi girl, fair, 150 cm height, divorced within fortnight . . .

FOREIGN SETTLED BRIDE FOR TALL, handsome, smart, Agrawai, 32 advocate, businessman boy of millionaire – broad minded, reputed family. Willing to settle abroad. Absolutely no dowry. Girls in India may also write.

WANTED AN EDUCATED, BEAUTIFUL virgin for Hindu Jat M.D. doctor, 27 years, 172 cm, father senior officer. Brother engineer & advocate.

ALLIANCE INVITED BY PARENTS of a Brahmin girl aged 22, 155 cm, too beautiful, arts graduate, English medium. Candidate must be handsome industrialist or businessman, educated, wealth tax payer, yearly income above Rs:40,000 – and family socially wellknown. Advertisement is for very high choice.

HANDSOME GUJARATI DOCTOR M.B.B.S., D.A., 178 cm tall, 27 years, wants to settle in America. Green card holder girls reply.

But it was an Indian living abroad who had the courage to insert this advertisement in the March 1984 edition of *Select* magazine in Britain:

ABERDEEN-BASED
Indian engineer. Own flat and car, 25 and lonely. Well-versed in Kama-sutra. Tall, attractive and compassionate.

To the Ladies. Any young Lady between the Age of Eighteen and twenty three of a Midling Stature; brown Hair, regular Features and a Lively Brisk Eye; Of Good Morals & not Tinctured with anything that may Sully so Distinguishable a Form possessed of 3 or 400£ entirely her own Disposal and where there will be no necessity of going Through the tiresome Talk of addressing Parents or Guardians for their consent; Such a one by leaving a Line directed for A.W. at the British Coffee House in King Street appointing where an Interview may be had will meet with a Person who flatters himself he shall not be thought Disagreeable by any Lady answering the above description. N.B. Profound Secrecy will be observ'd. No Trifling Answers will be regarded.

Boston Evening Post, 23 February 1759

Polish men and women who advertise in the lonely hearts columns of newspapers try to describe all their best qualities in twelve words because the price goes up on the thirteenth. Many notices include the words 'foreigners not excluded', because many lonely hearts dream of migrating to other lands.

Marriage racketeers are exploiting this desire to get away from Poland. From lonely hearts columns and marriage bureaux they obtain names and addresses, smuggle their way into a woman's affections and make off with her savings.

Other sad lonely hearts stories come from China, which is the world's largest producer of coal. Miners top the list in China's lonely hearts advertisements, and newspapers are filled with pleas from men seeking compatible companions in some of the dreariest areas of the world.

♡

With the divorce rate spiralling – up by 600 per cent in Britain in the last twenty-five years – it is not surprising that magazines devoted almost exclusively to lonely hearts advertisements should flourish. In 1979 *Singles* featured a seasonal advertisement on the cover of its Christmas edition: 'Saintly single. Tired of hectic once yearly journey, would like to settle down . . . based in Greenland. Have reindeer, will travel.' Twelve people replied, including a woman worried that the reindeer might not get on with her dog.

111

LOVE CLASSES

Every year more than two and a half million people enrol in night classes in Britain. Some seriously want to learn everything about French and fretwork, while others spend their evenings on the look-out for a love partner.

In America there are classes available in:

How to meet people in museums

Wrinkles, wrinkles go away

How to identify, love and marry someone stable

How to kiss a rabbit correctly (title of a class in animal welfare, but for the curious the answer is 'between the ears')

In Houston, Texas, women can take crash courses in

Manhandling

Enticement

Marrying Money

More Manipulation

In Los Angeles married women can learn how to have affairs and get tips on ways to stop their husbands finding out. These include:

– Remember to cover a date with your lover by making an excuse your husband cannot check.

– Don't gaze longingly into your lover's eyes if you dine together in a restaurant.

– Choose your partner carefully: a married man, for instance, will probably want to be as discreet as you.

– Resist any temptation to confess: a white lie is better than the black truth.

Dr. Cynthia Silverman is responsible for these courses. She says: 'Deceiving a husband can help to keep a woman sane.' Of course, her advice would apply to men too.

♡

Dr. Leo Buscaglia has made a fortune in America with his hug-a-stranger-a-day philosophy based on the idea that the streets are full of people yearning to be loved. His answer is to throw his arms around anyone who gives him the slightest opportunity. Dr. Buscaglia teaches that cuddling extends natural life because it stimulates the hormones. He used to go jogging but now hugs so often that he finds he needs no other exercise. When he visited Britain preaching and demonstrating his philosophy in 1983, people were very surprised that he was able to leave the country without a black eye.

♡

Popular with Russian newlyweds are ten-day honeymoon cruises on the Black Sea where daily courses are given by Soviet 'experts' on sex and cookery. Radio Moscow reported that 'much fun was had in a competition for the best dish made by the young housewives'.

♡

In the Korean capital Seoul, there are fourteen government-approved establishments in which thousands of licensed *kisaeng* (trained hostesses) practise their skills on tourists. To qualify for her licence, a *kisaeng* must apply to the Association for International Tourism with proof of her academic qualifications. If she is accepted she is given a crash course in 'general culture', which includes sex education and anti-communist ideology. She must also pass an oral test, which covers hygiene and knowledge of the love positions most in demand with tourists.

---

4 HELP MATES

Dr. Barbara Hogan is a New York psychologist who specialises in human sexuality. She thinks sexual therapy is socially acceptable: 'It means at least there is nothing wrong with your head.'

El Indio wears a bone through his nose, a red feather through his ear and casts spells with garlic. A member of Colombia's Inga tribe, medicine man El Indio is planning to take his roots from the jungles of Colombia to New York where he will carry on his speciality treatments for impotence, lovesickness and obesity. His prescription for stopping a row between couples comes free: fill the mouth with water and breathe deeply till the anger subsides.

High Priest James Hillier of the American Church based in California claims to bring salvation to the 'sexually anxious and truth-seeking'. The Good Sisters of the church waft round dark corridors in black brassières, black suspender belts and possess black leather whips and, most probably, some

very nasty habits. Yet the High Priest says that the light they are shedding is not Red Light.

'Some of our clients have deep-seated problems,' says Mr. Hillier. 'We feel that by relieving these – we've got a stretch rack in the Inquisition Room – we are protecting them from harming themselves or society.'

Charges were brought by four women in Monterey, California on 8 October 1958 against a physician who, it was claimed, had taken liberties after injecting them

Mrs. Irwin testified that he had treated her for a minor internal ailment and gave her shots that made her lose all her inhibitions. Asked why she had gone back for treatment, she said: 'I craved for the shots.' When asked if she had tried to repulse the doctor's advances, she replied: 'No, I climbed all over him.'

Another patient, Mrs. Reynolds, testified that she became uncontrollably aroused even before the physician had removed the needle from her arm.

HIRED HELP

The beautiful Lais was desired so much by Demosthenes that he offered her 1,000 drachmas. She demanded ten times that amount but gave her attentions free to Diogenes, the unkempt philosopher who lived in a barrel.

♡

When you marry your mistress, you create a job vacancy.
Sir James Goldsmith

♡

A woman arrested as a prostitute claimed that she was too short-sighted to ply for trade. Mrs. Margaret Friend, aged 48, said she was blind in one eye, and vision in the other was blurred and short-sighted. She told Southend magistrates: 'I can only see if someone is right on top of me.'
Southend Evening Echo

♡

Fat Turks whose bellies are too large to allow love-making can engage lithe belly-dancers to straddle their thighs in a special attitude called *daq al-arz*.

♡

There is a rule in Grand Rapids, Michigan, which insists on strip-tease parlours providing ramps to their stages so that handicapped strippers can go on in wheelchairs.

♡

A woman who talked candidly about her sex life to a New York journalist in Peking was sent to a labour reform camp. The journalist wrote that the Chinese usually treat sex as if it does not exist.

♡

Beauty of the chaste is a virtue; that of a whore a quality.
Russian

Beauty and chastity have always a mortal quarrel between them.
Spanish

♡

A mistress should be like a little country retreat near the town; not to dwell in constantly, but only for a night and away!
William Wycherley in *The Country Wife*

♡

The inhabitants of Hong Kong lay out more money on one horse race than the British spend on a whole week's race meetings. When the tiny British colony reverts to Chinese rule in 1997 the inhabitants will be allowed to keep their gee-gees but not their G-strings, for pimps, prostitutes and strippers will be banned. China cannot abide what it calls 'this unwholesome aspect of bourgeois life'.

The ABC television network in America issued guidelines to its editors on how to handle the sexual contents of programmes. It says that love-making should always be accompanied by the sound of music not the sounds of love-making. Prostitutes should not be represented as 'happy, attractive, young ladies selling their wares like toffee'. Above all viewers are not to be aroused. ABC wants them to stay viewing.

♡

Ninon de l'Enclos was one of the most beautiful French courtesans of the seventeenth century. Men of rank, intellect and wit gathered at her *salon* to exchange ideas and literary thoughts. She would inform an admirer when he could expect to begin his term as her lover, a reign which would last several weeks or, at the most, months. When the affair ended he remained a friend and a member of the *salon*. Each man was permitted to contribute to her upkeep, but none was allowed to show any sign of affection in public at any time before, during or after his reign.

♡

Giovanni Rovai claimed to be 'the last of the gigolos' in a BBC television programme called 'Gigolo'. He confessed to having had more than 3,000 women from whom his rewards generally came in kind – 'watches, cars, that sort of thing. But I am not averse to a cheque slipped in my pocket.' He owns seventy pairs of shoes.

He has spent his sixty odd years devoted to making love. Chinese women are his favourites, but he plies all ladies with the three basic delights that, according to him, they require: love, music and flowers.

Beds and aphrodisiacs are important items in a successful gigolo's armoury. Signor Rovai recommends lobster and celery, but never *pasta*. The bed 'is vitally important. I have needed to ask hotel managers to change mattresses. The bed should not be too soft; that is a mistake many make. It must be hard for making love'.

Who are his clients? Most are bored wives, whose husbands have 'lost the art of romance and don't pay attention that they should. They may be busy at their work. But this *is* my work, so I can concentrate on it. I have had no other career'.

Where can Signor Rovai be found? His regular haunt in the spring and summer is the Italian resort of Viareggio, but he sometimes goes on hunting trips to Vienna.

♡

At a bingo hall for 'men only' in Granada the players competed for the services of sixteen young women. The prizes varied according to whether the winners had vertical, horizontal or slanted lines on their bingo cards, but the fun came to an end in December 1984 when Spanish police discovered that many of the girls were minors.

♡

There has been no shortage of recruits to the army of the African republic of Gabon since President Bongo ordered the round-up of the nation's prostitutes and gave them to the army in 1985.

———————————♡———————————

> The Love Club flourished in eighteenth-century England. It was created by the beautiful people of the time for the purpose of swapping husbands and wives. Gentlemen paid £10,000 to join, ladies half that amount. The journal of one lady member has been preserved and lists nearly 5,000 amorous rendezvous over twenty years, including 72 princes and prelates, 93 rabbis, 439 monks, 288 commoners, 2 uncles, 119 musicians, 929 officers, 342 financiers, 420 society men, 117 valets, 12 cousins, 47 negroes, 1,614 foreigners.

═══════════════♡═══════════════

NIGHT TOKYO

The Women's Special Course Club in Osaka, Japan, offers 'brawny muscles, over-excitement and beautiful men with no pantie'. The country of geishas, trained in the arts of pleasing men, does not let women go completely unprovided for, as I discovered myself at Night Tokyo in the Asakusa area of the Japanese capital where liberated women of Tokyo disappear for brief encounters with men trained in the art of pleasing women. Of the 100 hosts available for hire, one could have one's pick for £100, or take pot-luck at half the price. Every half hour of his presence would cost another £5, and all drinks and food are the client's responsibility.

While night club hostesses dress in slit skirts and plunging necklines to excite their customers, at Night Tokyo every host wears uniform tails and bow-ties: trousers too. Some clients employ three hosts at a time, one to dance with, one to talk to, and one to light their cigarettes.

The management could only find Mr. Ikede for me: he was the only host who was tall enough to see over my shoulder on the dance floor. Night Tokyo closes at midnight, but I asked Mr. Ikede – in the interests of my readers of course – how much he would charge for the rest of the night. '£650 till dawn,' he replied languidly [which seems better value in winter than in summer when dawn breaks before 5 a.m.], 'but it all depends on whether *I* like the woman in question or not.'

———————————♡———————————

A Nehmo is a Tibetan go-between whose job is to secure a sleeping companion for travellers away from their homes. If a child results, the fertile hostess is valued and her chances of finding a husband are improved. The father of her child can marry her if he wishes, but in any case he is expected to give money for the baby.

In this Nehmo song the lover calls his hostess a little black yak:

In the middle of the extensive grassy plain,
My little black female yak has become angry at me;
'Be not angry, do you understand, my black female yak,
I do not think in my heart that I will get milk from you.'

♡

When a Javanese man visits the house of a girl his parents have arranged for him to marry, he watches the girl's gestures, facial expressions and notes her deportment and the tone of her voice. This first glimpse of her is called a *nontoni*. If she looks around too much he will take this as a sign of wilful disobedience and he will ask his parents to go back to the go between to find a more demure wife.

───────────────────── ♡ ─────────────────────

THE JAPANESE CONNECTION

A Japanese travel agency offers wedding packages to Japanese tourists to Sausalito near San Francisco. For $400 extra a couple gets a chauffeur-driven limousine, bouquet, minister, organist, best man, maid of honour (or bridesmaid), two witnesses, wedding cake, photographs, marriage certificate and a cassette tape of American marriage counselling translated into Japanese.

♡

In a long-running popular television show young Japanese couples seeking marriage partners sit on a stage in front of an audience but hidden from each other. Both are given descriptions of each other by two comperes, and then they are allowed one minute's televised conversation before being asked to press a Yes/No button to show whether they want to meet again. The result appears on a screen accompanied by flashing lights, cymbals and drums. The show has been copied in Australia and America.

♡

At Mitsubishi, the top trading company of Japan, unmarried employees are introduced to each other by courtesy of a dating computer – made in Japan, of course.

You may have heard about the Japanese love of work and how few take their holidays each year. The managing director of the Mitsubishi Family Club said: 'Our young people are so busy at work they don't have time to meet the oppo-

site sex or go on a date. Our computer is fed all
their personal details, then we introduce suitable
partners to one another.'

♡

In Japan six in ten marriages are arranged by the company, school teachers, a
family go-between or marriage bureaux.

Genkichi Ishizaka of Matsumoto was one of the nation's most successful
matchmakers or *nakados*. In a forty-one-year career this *nakado* claimed to
have paired off 2,882 couples, saying that the secret of marriage is 'to get the
right boy for the right girl so that their sex energies will go bang and keep on
going bang'.

A girl applying at a marriage agency must produce a full colour portrait, a
history of her family going back three generations, and certificates showing
her age and examination ratings at school, college or university. Male
applicants are occasionally asked for medical certificates attesting to their
likely potency.

♡

Mrs. Kurihara's name when she is working as a fortune teller is Shinjuku
Mother or SM. SM earns £9 a minute whenever one of her 50,000 clients
consults her about love problems, in addition to the huge fees from her
television shows and appearances at Isetan, one of Tokyo's smart department stores.

At the age of twenty-two Machiko is the youngest madam in Japan, and a
millionairess. A former dish-washer, she is now president of the first-ever
Mistress Bank. Her clients include famous people in the Land of the Rising
Sun, and there is a waiting list.

Postscript: Japanese businesses spend about $12 billion a year on enter-
tainment, the equivalent of the national defence budget. Foreign business-
men and envoys are among those who benefit from lavish Japanese hospit-
ality in mistress banks, clubs, massage parlours, and the uniquely named
Japanese No-Pantie bars.

♡

Geishas are not, as most foreigners believe, the
Japanese equivalents of prostitutes or hostesses
who can be bought for a night's entertainment of
'loving'.

They are highly skilled dancers and singers,
and most play the *samisen*, a three-stringed
guitar. Each has a *dannasan* who possesses sole
rights to her talents. Called a second or business
wife, she entertains gracefully, dances and
sings, and has the wit to respond tactfully to the
witticisms of a drunken, tired or emotional
guest.

♡

PASSION WAGONS

Every night Parisians make love in the Bois de Boulogne. Most are in cars and, depending on the weather, many are in the woods. As a result tens of thousands of corsets have turned up in lost property offices after being found in the bushes of the Bois.

Claude Anet disliked corsets, which he described as contraptions which sheathed women from their armpits to their knees. His advice to men in *Notes sur l'Amour*, published in 1908 was: 'Never undress a woman who refuses to appear before you in the nude . . . Alas, how many women can do without a corset? They are careful not to reveal themselves naked and upright. This is the supreme test and how few are capable of passing it! When a woman is naked, she is usually careful to remain lying down with her arms behind her head; this gesture has the advantage of uplifting her breasts which then point to the ceiling as they should.'

One can easily understand that a corset would add to the complications of making love in a car. On an unseasonally warm night on 10 December 1984 I drove through the Bois de Boulogne to a formal dinner at the Pré Catalan restaurant in the heart of the woods. Along one stretch about thirty cars cruised along on the look-out for a *partouse*, which is a peculiarly French way of making up a party for a love-in of total strangers. The occupants of the cars were mostly in pairs: man and woman, two men, two women, man and Alsatian (dog), woman and Labrador (dog), Arab and Black, plus singles, threesomes and the odd two couples. We were flagged down by a man who stepped out from the bushes and four cars behind us squealed to a halt. All the car occupants gathered around us, and a tall, dark and quite handsome man asked: 'Shall we go to your place or mine?' I suspect that he was a transvestite.

The best chance one has of attracting attention in the Bois de Boulogne is to drive an English car, for somehow the sight of a GB registration excites the French. The sexual drawer in a Range Rover, though the Mini Metro has its turn-on effect, too. The least erotic are Japanese cars and the baby Simca; you can drive around all night in one of those and no one will bid for you.

♡

BEWARE! Back-seat sex can ruin your love life. This warning was issued by the National Marriage Guidance Council early in 1984. That may come as news to anyone who necked and investigated love topics in a car. The consequences are, said the Council, serious: for the man it means premature ejaculation and for the woman it can leave her unable to have an orgasm.

♡

In some countries a car number plate tells the world what type of person you are. Some American states, for instance, permit you to say whatever you like providing you do it in not more than six letters. The vice-president of a bank in Richmond, Virginia, chose 'POOPED' for his six-letter word, while a Mr. Jack Good opted for 'I'M GOOD'.

The British cannot play with words, but huge sums of money change hands if someone fancies a number plate that belongs to another person. Some will buy the car as well. A former Member of Parliament, Sir Gerald Nabarro, owned 'NAB 1' and 'NAB's up to 7. In America he could have paid a few dollars and had a number plate saying 'GERALD'.

State number plates tell a lot about a state. In America the state of Idaho has 'Famous Potatoes' as the slogan on every plate, and Missouri bills itself as the 'Show-me-state'. New Hampshire plates proclaim 'Live Free or Die' while Oklahoma settles for 'Oklahoma O.K.' My favourite was the number plate fancied by the state of Western Australia before a boat from the state capital of Perth won the America's Cup in 1983. In those lovely, love-strewn days before 1983 the motto for all Western Australian number plates was 'State of Excitement'.

THE BUREAUX

The little office at 46 rue Neuve St-Eustache in Paris was always full of clients when Monsieur Vuillaume ran his matrimonial bureau there during the days of the First Empire. When he was short of women he ran his eye down the imperial war bulletins for the names of soldiers killed and made discreet inquiries as to whether the new widow was likely to require solace. If the results of his investigation showed that the couple had not been particularly close, he allowed the widow two or three weeks before introducing himself. If the couple were known to have been on indifferent or warlike terms, he would offer his professional services at the first opportunity.

♡

Fun-loving Florence of Surrey – 'with eyes of blue, likes a social drink and music' – sounded like the perfect match for 23-year-old Andrew Stauton. He had joined a dating bureau for £30, but Florence turned out to be a 74-year-old pensioner.

Mr. Stauton, a salesman of Weston-super-Mare, got his money back.

♡

Exquisitely elegant Joyce Manning has a mission in life. It is to find honest, good looking women of integrity to marry millionaires. Miss Manning is manager of Execumatch, a glossy marriage bureau in California which is literally a lonely hearts club for millionaires. Potential partners on Miss Manning's books have to answer a five-page questionnaire to prove their suitability.

The bureau's advertisements in the *Los Angeles Times* plead 'millionaires need love too' and Miss Manning described one of her clients as a 37-year-old billionaire still looking for a more mature and intelligent woman than the average scatter-brained beauty queen. 'All he asks,' she said, 'is that his mate should adore him and let him shower her with gifts. If he lived with you for 30 days and liked you the honeymoon would be a world cruise. You would get several homes, a fleet of cars and a yacht.' All Miss Manning's Execumatch clients pay £77,000 for the chance the agency offers of finding Miss Right.

♡

> Heather Jenner is Britain's best known match-maker. Her own family ties are strong: daughter of a brigadier and widow of Lord James, but 'I only use my title at the passport office and Italian restaurants'. In conversation she can claim 'a nuptial rate of about a marriage a day'.

♡

AGONY AUNTS

Around the world exist a band of men and women who spend their days and some of their nights reading letters from people with love problems. They are often mocked by people who suspect that 'Agitated of Croydon', or 'Faithful husband of Minneapolis', or 'Edna of Moonee Ponds' are the trumped-up names of the agony aunt (or uncle) herself, and that all those letters of woe and despair that appear in newspapers are made up.

Most agony aunts and uncles are nice, concerned people. The up-market *Washington Post*'s auntie is called Miss Manners, which is the pseudonym of Judith Martin. Tokyo's *Shukan Josei* – *Woman's Weekly* – has an agony aunt who asks for the date of birth of both the correspondent and the lover. 'Dear Dolly' is the unseen face at *Drum* in eastern and southern Africa, while at *Bona* in Johannesburg the go-between is Auntie Barbara Zulu. Israelis can turn to the aunt of the *Jerusalem Post*, but she only replies in English.

All agony aunts get letters asking how to get kisses, how to get even more kisses, and how to stop them. Miss Dorothy Dix's advice column was published in America and syndicated round the world to millions of readers. When asked once by a girl if she should confess that she had false teeth, Miss Dix replied: 'No, marry him and keep your mouth shut.'

♡

Emily Post agonised more than most aunts, specialising as she did in matters of etiquette. She believed that girls should not go out with young men, even fiancés, in sailing boats because of the 'questionable situation' that would arise if the vessel was becalmed and could not return before night.

♡

Dr. Ruth Westheimer is 4 ft 7 in tall. She was born in Germany, is a grandmother, a fellow of the New York Academy of Medicine, and she is known to thousands of men and women as Grandma Freud. Dr. Westheimer has a radio show in New York called *Sexually Speaking* and people call her about their love problems. One woman complained that her vagina was too big. Dr. Westheimer told her: 'One is lucky to have a vagina; it can be such a pleasure, and it gives such pleasure. And never gets caught in a zipper.'

♡

In a country where men are much preoccupied with furbishing their fertility, Nigerian agony aunts keep the pages of magazines filled with articles on how to keep a husband from straying, skin bleaching, and the best sexual positions for conceiving boys. Women with rebellion in mind find little opportunity there.

♡

Seven out of ten women told top American agony aunt Ann Landers that they would prefer a hug to making love. Miss Landers, whose column of advice to the perplexed and forlorn is syndicated to newspapers around the world with a combined circulation of seventy million readers, asked her women readers: 'Would you be content to be held close and treated tenderly, and forget about "The Act"?'

Nearly 100,000 women replied to this loaded question, prompting Miss Landers to say: 'I was surprised at such a tremendous response, and at how many women were so angry they felt compelled to write three and four page letters. This shows us a lot of pent-up rage out there.' She added that the letters showed men were using intercourse purely as a physical release. 'It has no more significance than a sneeze.'

♡

CHAPTER SIX

INITIATION TO LOVE

THE LONG WAIT

♡ Chinese mothers have one thing in common with Jewish, Greek, Moslem and Koryak mothers: they want their daughters to be virgins until they marry.

My Chinese mother used to lecture me once a week on the joys of maidenhood, and her favourite advice given during the prime of my virginity was: 'Never give IT away to just any man. If you do, neither he nor any other man will want to marry you. However, I don't want you to die wondering.'

Those fine words contained one of the world's biggest problems: how long should a virgin wait before it is too late and she finds herself on her death-bed, unmarried, and still wondering?

In ancient Babylon, Sumeria and Greece women, including virgins, had to go to a temple and 'lie with a man' and offer the money he paid to the temple gods. When their godly duties were over, the women were free to return home. The Greek historian Herodotus recorded that 'tall, handsome women soon manage to get home again, but the ugly ones stay a long time before they can fulfil the condition which the law demands, some of them, indeed, as much as three or four years'.

The English in more recent times experienced the same problem, as Jonathan Swift wrote in his *Journal to Stella*: 'An old gentlewoman died here two months ago and left in her will to have eight men and eight maid bearers who should have two guineas a piece, ten guineas to the parson for the sermon, and two guineas to the clerk. But bearers, parson and clerk must all be true virgins and not to be admitted till they took their oaths of virginity, so the poor woman lies still unburied and so must do till the general resurrection.'

Barbara Cartland is one Englishwoman who prides herself on being a latter-day gentlewoman. Author of about 395 books (the number increases monthly) in 20 languages with export sales topping 200 million, Miss Cartland says: 'What a pity so many girls do not wait for their Prince, but "make do" with the counterfeit.' True to her word, Miss Cartland's heroines in all her romantic novels wait for several chapters to elapse before their first kiss, and not much else happens in love-making terms until the last few pages, by which time they are usually married.

Despite the Pill, and free abortion in some countries of the world, in what the older generations call 'these promiscuous years of the late twentieth century', there are a lot more virgins around than many would think. In the early seventies *Playboy* magazine questioned many women in the United States and found that 44 per cent were virgins. Several years later a *Time* magazine poll revealed that 42 per cent of those questioned thought women should be virgins at marriage, and 34 per cent thought men should be. My own findings conducted at a residential seminar organised by the British National Association of Youth Clubs were 60 per cent in favour of virginity until they met 'Mr. Right'. All those participating in my survey were young women between the ages of sixteen and twenty-two.

A final word about the Long Wait: four famous virgins did *not* wait long. Helen was twelve when she was seduced by Paris and taken to Troy; Daphnis was fifteen and Chloe thirteen; and Juliet was a mere thirteen, too.

PARADISE

The Christian paradise is a blissful, beautiful place where the angels – who are sexless – sing forever.

The Moslem concept of paradise is a garden of countless virgin houris, whose maidenheads miraculously reappear as fast as the faithful require them. In the words of the *Koran*, the holy book of Islam:

'And there shall wait upon them [the righteous] young boys of their own as fair as virgin pearls . . . and by their side shall sit bashful, dark-eyed virgins, as chaste as the sheltered eggs of ostriches.'

The Burmese believe that all those who go to paradise will have up to 500 lovers on their right side in bed and another 500 on their left.

I have always thought that the best languages for word-play and saucy double-meanings were English and French, until I heard about the type of chat that goes on in northern Thailand. If a man asks a woman what she had for supper, and she replies: 'Pepper sauce', she is telling him two things: first, that she is hot-tempered like peppers, and second, that she wants him to leave her alone and go home. The clue to this banter is the Thai word *phik*. *Phik* can mean 'pepper' as well as 'home'.

St. Wilgefortis, daughter of the King of Portugal, was betrothed by her father to the King of Sicily. She was determined to remain a virgin forever, and prayed for help, whereupon a beard grew on her face. The King of Sicily withdrew his suit. Her indignant father had her crucified.

Who wants to be Miss America? Miss America has to be beautiful, poised, intelligent, and a virgin – or an acceptable imitation. She will be an American citizen, aged between seventeen and twenty-six, a high-school graduate, and will never have been married nor lived with a man. The newest qualification is that she may not have had an abortion.

The girl chosen to be Miss America parades her qualities before a panel of judges in Atlantic City. None of the contestants is allowed to smoke, drink or gamble (this is the fastest growing casino-city in America), nor can they dine with a man or invite a man – including fathers – to their bedrooms.

Each contestant hopes to shine when it is her turn in the 'talent' spot. In 1961 the girl chosen as Miss America excelled at sewing. Another year saw Miss Montana showing off her equestrian skills, but her horse jumped into the orchestra pit. Nowadays, most contestants sing. In 1984 Miss New Hampshire sang 'The Simple Joys of Maidenhood', but Miss Alaska chose 'I Am What I Am', which also happens to be the anthem of the Gay movement in America.

'You're a man now, my son' are sweet words to the ears of some young boys, but there is a sting in the tail and in the mouth for some Australian and African boys. In Africa the Nandi, Wagogo, Bageshu, Mussurongo of the Congo River, Ambriz of Angola, and the Ovaherero of Namibia and Batoka of Mozambique all knock out some of the teeth of 'virgin' boys in ceremonies to celebrate their reaching manhood. The Ovaherero prefer to remove the two middle incisors, while the Ambriz think the loss of any teeth among the four centre ones of the upper row is attractive and desirable. It is still the custom for some Australian Aborigines to knock out their sons' teeth in the belief that if you sacrifice one part of the body another gains strength. If a boy's tooth comes out with difficulty it is assumed that he has already lost his 'virginity'.

The price of a bride has been reduced in Saudi Arabia because many local men are shopping abroad for foreign brides at bargain rates. The Saudi newspaper *Al-Nadwa* quoted 30,000 riyals (about £5,000) as the going rate for a virgin, with a third off if the bride-to-be is less than pure.

Mahammad Aloo did not care how much he had to pay to find a virgin. In Kenya in February 1984 he married a 14-year-old girl soon after he turned 100. The best man was aged 86.

In Namibia there is a royal court ruled by the queen of the Lovedus. Anyone who wishes to curry favour with her will present to her one of their own daughters, though the queen will probably accept only those whose parents are royals themselves or district chiefs. Naturally, she will accept the daughters of foreign rulers. These girls are called 'brides' and must be virgins. Those who retain their chastity are given areas of the country to rule as assistant queens. Many get pregnant, and are sent home in disgrace, so their fathers have to send another daughter as a replacement. From time to time the queen of the Lovedus gives one of her assistant queens to a man she wishes to reward, but this man is then required to give one of his own daughters in return.

Uzbeks will recite the words of the famous poet Omar Khayam while they organise a perfect cup of tea for their guests. To be perfect the tea must be made by a young virgin Uzbek girl, and she must smile when she pours for you. Next, you walk with your tea bowl to an open window where you will raise the bowl to your lips, kiss the steam rising from within, then you throw the tea out of the window. Your host will be waiting to fill your bowl with vodka.

BOWLING A MAIDEN OVER

For the English, Australians, New Zealanders, Indians, Sri Lankans, West Indians and a few others scattered around the British Commonwealth bowling a maiden over is a bit of sport.

It does not mean that they delight in putting virgins in a compromising position but comes, of course, from the English game of cricket in which a series of six balls bowled to a batsman without his making any additional score is termed a 'maiden over'.

The interest of the English in virginity is reflected not only in their national sport. The American state of Virginia was named after Queen Elizabeth I, who developed a personality cult for herself as the Virgin Queen. When a Member of Parliament gets to his feet for the first time to speak at Westminster he makes his 'maiden speech'. To encourage him other Members of Parliament try not to fall asleep or jeer him during this most tender moment.

♡

Almost 200 years ago William Cobbett's *Advice to Young Men* was taken seriously by those looking for a wife. Cobbett, English journalist and agitator, listed in order of importance the top eight qualities of a woman:

1. Chastity
2. Sobriety
3. Industry
4. Frugality
5. Cleanliness
6. Knowledge of Domestic Affairs
7. Good Temper
8. Beauty

♡

Place names such as Virginia Water and Maidenhead can still be relied upon to raise a snigger for reasons that would have been known to Sleepy Davie, hero of an eighteenth-century English ballad:

> Then she went up to his bedside
> Saying, Davie, are ye sleeping?
> I'm wearied of my maidenhead
> I have so long a-keeping.

♡

The hunt for virgins, or 'fresh girls' as they were called in the trade, was a full-time job for the operators of Victorian brothels in London. In 1885 Wickham Steed, the editor of the *Pall Mall Gazette*, published a brothel keeper's confessions: 'a pander [procurer] who understands this business has his eyes open in every direction, continually looking out for suitable numbers of fresh girls in order to keep up the reputation of his house. The hunt for fresh girls takes a good deal of time . . .' Packs of procurers took up the virginal scent in Hyde Park, Regent's Park and Green Park, and many nursemaids, governesses and domestic servants were lured away and tricked into losing their chastity. Nonetheless, another brothel-keeper admitted to Steed: 'We deal in virginity, but not virgins.'

Sarah-Jane Newbury, a virgin and proud of it, got a signed letter from her doctor in 1984 when she was 26, certifying that he had examined her and that her hymen was intact. Miss Newbury, a convent-educated legal secretary from Trowbridge, Wiltshire, said she saw nothing amazing about having written proof of her virginity, but had to deny to incredulous newspapermen that she was either frigid or a lesbian. 'I've got a good figure and big brown eyes,' she said. 'I've never had any trouble getting boyfriends. I've had several loving relationships. None have ended because I am a virgin.' She did add, though, that she planned to catch up on all the action she had missed when she finally went on honeymoon with Mr. Right. 'I might chain him to the bedpost,' she threatened.

♡

♡

Before the 1984 Los Angeles Olympics the British javelin star Fatima Whitbread, then twenty-three, claimed that she was proud to have kept her virginity. 'I aim to stay that way at least until I get that gold medal,' she said. Alas, it was Britain's other javelin thrower, Tessa Sanderson, who got gold. Fatima finished with bronze and faced another four years' self-imposed chastity.

♡

In 1984 the South African authorities lifted an eight-year ban on Jillian Becker's novel *The Virgins*. One newspaper told its readers: 'Virgins Declared "Not Undesirable"'.

If a girl from the Pedi community in the Transvaal loses her virginity, her girlfriends go into mourning for her diminished virtue. Zulu women are more realistic; they shout abuse outside the seducer's house.

♡   ♡

Every year 40,000 Japanese women have operations to restore their virginity. The operations are called 'hymen rebirths', and are performed to please the majority of Japanese men who prefer to marry a virgin. Plastic surgeons use sheep gut for the job, which has to be done with an eye on the wedding date, because sheep gut dissolves within a month.

English girls last century could have their lost maidenheads restored by an operation called re-virginising. Some young ladies went in hundreds of times to be re-sewn.

═══════════════════════ ♡ ═══════════════════════

3 LITTLE GIRLS IN WHITE

Lagos, Nigeria: pregnant brides in the Roman Catholic diocese of Lagos were told they could no longer go to the altar wearing white gowns. Archbishop Olubunmi Okogie said white was a symbol of purity and it would be ridiculous for a pastor to proclaim a pregnant woman pure, when her position was obvious to the congregation.

Conway, Ireland: a teenage couple were at the altar when the bride had to be helped to a pew, where she gave birth to a baby boy. The bridegroom said: 'It was the first I had heard of it, but Dora is an assistant nurse, so she knew exactly what to do. When it was over we carried on with the wedding as if nothing had happened.'

Nakuru, Kenya: a church wedding had to be abandoned when the bride succumbed to labour pains as she was about to cut the cake, reported the *Kenya Times*. The bride was rushed to hospital, where she gave birth to a girl.

─────────────────────── ♡ ───────────────────────

MY DAUGHTER THE VIRGIN

In the United States, Orthodox Jewish wedding invitations often state: 'We invite you to the marriage of the virgin Deborah [or Ruth, or . . .].'

♡

A favourite book of Chinese mothers and prospective mothers-in-law was the *Manual of Lady Purity*, in which the author described how one could recognise a virgin: 'She never looks you straight in your face. When she smiles, her teeth are not shown. Her face does not look shiny. Her voice is as clear as a new flute. While sitting, she does not keep her knees apart. Her breasts are firm, their nipples pink and tiny. Her belly and hips are both flat and firm. The inside of her private parts is pink, the maidenhair soft like down. When she stands there in the nude, you cannot see through between her closed thighs.'

♡

In 1978 *The Times* reported the case of an Athens court awarding 350,000 drachmas to the parents of a sixteen-year-old girl who had been seduced by her foreign-language teacher. This sum represented the amount the parents would have to add to the dowry 'in order to compensate a man of her own economic and social standing for the loss of her virginity'.

It is customary for many Sudanese husbands living in the cities of Khartoum and Omdurman to give their wives a gift of gold or money after the consummation of the marriage to say 'thank you' for being a virgin.

———————♡———————

In every house there should be two women – a wife and a statue of the Virgin over the door.
Italian saying

———————♡———————

The husband of Ann Lee complained to the church authorities in Manchester at the end of the eighteenth century that his wife would not allow him to make love to her. She then left him and became a leader of the Shaking Quakers, a group with many followers in England and America. They were united in their belief that there was no need to use the reproductive organs just because they were there.

———————♡———————

Chieftains in the Pacific islands of Tonga and Samoa like their daughters to remain virgins, but want their sons to have sexual liaisons with lower-class women who would not be able to adulterate the blood of noble families by marrying into the top class. In Congo-Brazzaville chieftains will entrust their weapons to the care of their virgin daughters, but if they lose their virginity the weapons are destroyed and replaced with new ones.

ROOFTOP VIRGINS

Like a great long curtain, the Himalayas tower above the kingdom of Nepal, the rooftop of the world and the country closest to the gods.

There are some very special virgins in Nepal. Among the high-caste Brahman-Chetri the girls are expected to be so pure that they may be given away as religious presents to village men thought worthy of them. Brahman-Chetri girls must never speak to boys on the village path because this constitutes loose behaviour.

The most intriguing virgin of all is the Living Goddess, or *Kumari*. Chosen from the goldsmith caste at the age of four or five, she must have perfect teeth and a scar-free body. Selected for the bravery she shows when left alone in a darkened room with a human skeleton and the bloody heads of decapitated buffaloes, she spends her childhood with two guardians in a pagoda in Kathmandu, which she leaves only five times a year. Then she is borne in a palanquin through excited festival crowds to a shrine. Even the King of Nepal, considered a god himself, worships her.

At the first sign of puberty the goddess will make way for her successor, but no man will marry her because the husband of the first Living Goddess died on the day after their wedding. When I saw her in her temple I smiled at her. She was the only person in Nepal who did not return my greeting.

Give me chastity – but not yet.
St. Augustine's prayer

A day at the baths was a popular pastime early this century for mothers of unmarried sons in Turkey. They assembled at Turkish baths to look over the young girls who went there deliberately to show off their bodies. Irfan Orga described a bath scene: 'My grandmother looked at the naked young girls with the critical eye of a connoisseur . . . saying that So-and-so was too thin altogether, that her backside rattled and that she would never be able to find a husband until her figure improved.'

Men of the Ulad Tidrarin tribe in south Morocco still enjoy the sight of eligible girls competing for attention. At special meetings, the girls run races in the nude while the men lay claim to the one who pleases them best. Later, the young couples are united in a group wedding.

---♡---

Thousands of couples are still virgins after years of marriage. In Manchester in northern England many seek help from Dr. Raymond Goodman, who runs a sex and marriage advice clinic.

Dr. Goodman's patients include a couple who chose to sleep in bunk beds on their wedding night. The wife knocked herself out on the bunk above. Other couples told the doctor their wedding bed had collapsed under strain. In all cases the state of shock induced by initial disaster had prevented consummation of the marriage ever since.

The doctor names three types of virgin wives: the Sleeping Beauty, who waits for a special kiss from her prince to wake her up; Brunhilde, the warrior maiden who, like her namesake in Wagner's opera cycle *The Ring*, can only give herself to a man who totally overwhelms her. The third type of virgin is the Queen Bee, who would like to have children, but fears the sex act.

---♡---

A CLUTCH OF MALE VIRGINS

St. Jerome called on all priests 'to cut down with the axe of virginity the wood of marriage'. He had to put up with marriage, though, so that the supply of virgins could be replenished.

♡

Tertullian, the holy man of Carthage in the third century, insisted that no man should ever marry. His reasons were that women were 'temples built over a sewer' or, worse still, 'the devil's doorway'.

♡

It is generally thought that Sir Isaac Newton died a virgin. He also suffered from acute insomnia.

♡

When a monk asked the early saint Abba Zeno, 'Behold thou hast grown old, how is the matter of fornication?' the saint replied: 'It knocketh, but it passeth on.'

♡

An Irish holy man of the sixth century named Scuthin always slept in bed with two beautiful virgins. When St. Brendan the Navigator reprimanded him for taking such a risk, St. Scuthin challenged him to prove himself equally able to resist temptation. St. Brendan tried and managed to resist the temptations of the flesh, but cut the experiment short because he was unable to sleep.

Mahatma Gandhi also lay with women to increase his willpower to resist temptation. Many Hindu and Chinese men practise sexual abstinence – some call it self-control. Formerly it was the Hindu belief that the body converts food to blood, then to semen, which is stored in the head. By practising sexual abstinence a man therefore conserved his spiritual and physical strength.

♡

Hundreds of tribes in Africa and South America resist all their cravings for sex before they set out on a hunting expedition or to fight a battle. So did the ancient Babylonians, Persians, and many American Indians, in the belief that their physical strength would increase. Not many modern soldiers in uniform follow ancient or tribal customs: 'Here today, gone tomorrow' is a more attractive philosophy.

———————————————♡———————————————

Mexicans living near Lake Pátzcuaro believe a virgin can stand in the middle of a swarm of bees at any time, and stay unharmed.

It is easier to keep a swarm of fleas in a basket than to keep the virtue of a woman under lock and key.
Hungarian

♡   ♡

Husbands kept the key to their wives' chastity belts safely hidden, but desperate lovers could sometimes buy duplicate keys from a friendly locksmith. Names given to chastity belts included the girdle of Venus, a Florentine (they used to be popular in Florence), padlocks of chastity, and drawers of iron. Yakut girls of northern Siberia wear leather trousers with many straps tied round their waists, and are supposed to keep them on till their wedding day.

Santa Rosa, the patron saint of Lima, Peru, became a nun in 1606. Worshipped for her chastity, she threw the key of her chastity belt into a well, which is now a place of pilgrimage.

♡

The virgins' bus was the name given to the last bus leaving Piccadilly Circus for west London at the turn of the century. Its late-night passengers were mostly prostitutes.

♡

A maid's virtue is unlimited; a wife's resentment without end.
Chinese proverb

———————————————♡———————————————

In the Swat Valley beneath the Himalayas and among the Bakhtiari of Iran, husbands are allowed to kill those who seduce their wives. But among the Kochi tribes in Afghanistan it is the wife who is killed if her husband finds on the wedding night that she is not a virgin.

At the beginning of the fourth century students and artists flocked from faraway lands to enrol for classes given in Alexandria by the beautiful teacher of philosophy Hypatia. Many fell in love with her, but she steadfastly remained a virgin. One student professed his passionate love for her whereupon she raised her skirt to the waist and said: 'This, young man, is what you are in love with, and not anything beautiful.' Hypatia, chaste to the last, ended up being murdered by Christian monks.

A maiden found herself stranded in a swamp. The mosquitoes were ferocious. An elderly gentleman invited her to share his mosquito net, but the maiden chose to spend the night outdoors among the reeds and rushes, where she was slowly stung to death by the mosquitoes. So vicious were they that by morning nothing was left but her skeleton.

At the next full moon the sister of the dead maiden found herself lost by the same swamp. She accepted the gentleman's offer, shared his bed for the night, and survived.

Virtue is its own reward, but who needs it when you are dead?

Taiwanese folk tale

RED LETTER DAY

I once spent a month in an industrial town called Gallarate, which is near the centre of the Italian footwear manufacturing base. At weekends men – single, married, widowed, betrothed – drove out from Milan to sample the charms of Gallarate's women and girls. Nevertheless, many of these women were 'virgins' on their own wedding nights, a feat achieved after first crossing the Swiss border to buy tiny capsules of red liquid, which could be relied upon to do the trick and produce living, vivid 'proof' that the *signora* (as she would be by the wedding night) was indeed pure, as well as beautiful.

Defloration of virgins can be a cause for celebration in some parts of the world. Among the Luo of Kenya, for instance, the marriage is consummated in the presence of witnesses. While the husband deflowers his bride he must make every effort to hide his enjoyment, for if he fails and the witnesses detect any sign of his glee, those who are members of his wife's family will shout: 'You have killed our sister!' If a Luo girl dies a virgin her ghost has to be pacified, so a stranger is called in to deflower her corpse.

Public defloration used to be performed by a stranger among the Todas of India and tribes in the Philippines, Peru and central Africa. In Cambodia till recently certain priests were each permitted to deflower one young woman a year. After the ceremony, they were carried away in their sedan chairs to another twelve months of celibacy, and the husband of the recently deflowered woman would join his bride. Defloration of a virgin is sometimes performed in front of others in Cyrenaica in Libya.

At Serb weddings in parts of northern Yugoslavia the guests eavesdrop outside the door to the room where the couple retire to share a toast with the father of the groom. Before he leaves them, the father shatters the empty glasses against the wall, whereupon the guests respond with another toast before proceeding to attempt to break an egg at the bottom of a sack. The egg denotes fertility to the Serbs.

Some old men in Ceram in Indonesia have a fine time at weddings. They join the queue of men hoping to be chosen by the bride as one of her lovers on the day she loses her virginity. Her husband is last in the queue, but usually gets his turn. The general consensus of opinion is that the more lovers who join the queue, the more esteemed is the bride, though she may have to stay in bed for a few days to recover.

A Totonác girl of Mexico is deflowered twenty-eight days after her birth by a priest inserting his finger, and her mother repeats it six years later. Fathers exercise the right to deflower their daughters in many Pacific Ocean communities, including the Sakais, Battas and Alfoers. It is common among gypsy groups in Spain for a bride to be examined by four women on the eve of her wedding – two from her own family and two from her fiancé's.

The plight of girls in Upper Egypt has been described by Nawal El Saadawi, the eminent Egyptian militant feminist writer, doctor and former Director of Public Health in Egypt. To some Egyptians, and indeed to many Moslems in general, it is worse for a girl to lose her virginity before marriage than it is to lose an eye or limb. According to an Arab saying, 'the shame can only be wiped out in blood,' and sometimes the family will kill the girl. In any case, young virgins will have a grim time in Upper Egypt if an old crone, called a *daya*, is engaged by parents to deflower their daughters to show to prospective suitors that they are virgins.

Some Berbers of Morocco are more enlightened. If an Ait Sadden family knows that a daughter is not chaste they will smear the blood of a rooster on the gown she will wear on her wedding night, and her husband will be none the wiser. His family will be shown the 'proof' of their daughter-in-law's purity, the husband will fire the family's gun to announce to the world that his wife was a virgin, then everyone celebrates.

VIRGINS NEED NOT APPLY

The elegant Baron Philippe de Rothschild, head of the great wine family, has two rules about love affairs: the first is never to make love to a virgin, and the other is 'never to persist if the lady doesn't want me'.

♡

To the Indians of Quito, capital of Ecuador, marrying a virgin is a total waste of time. They have a saying to describe this: 'She who has not been known to others can have nothing pleasing about her.'

♡

On Easter Island in the East Pacific, virginity is so despised that older women instruct growing girls in the art of love-making, then hand them over to an older male relative for the real thing.

♡

There is no word for 'virgin' among the Ilas of south east Africa, the Tukanos of the Amazon River, the Pukapukans of the Cook Islands, and the Trukese of the Pacific islands. The reason is simple: they consider virginity abnormal. All around the world there are races and tribes who cannot understand all the fuss made about virginity. Included among these are the Dards of Kashmir, the Zandes of central Africa, Tongans, the Kágabas of Colombia and the Seri of Mexico. In all these communities the chieftain has first pick of the virgins – a twentieth-century equivalent of the medieval practice of *droit du seigneur*.

♡

A Masai man in east Africa can send back a bride to her parents if he finds she is a virgin, or he can ask for compensation if he has to set about the troublesome task of deflowering her.

♡

Chastity before marriage is a total bore to the Kadars of Nigeria. Girls are betrothed before they are six years old, but they do not go to live with their husbands till ten years later, by which time many are pregnant by another man or some are already mothers. To Kadar men pregnancy is proof of fertility, and therefore welcomed.

♡

Cewa children of Malawi play a real game of 'doctors and nurses'. In this they are given full encouragement by anxious parents, prompted by the ancient belief that if a girl is still a virgin at puberty she will die young.

♡

Unmarried boys and girls are allowed by their Hausa parents in Nigeria to have casual sexual relationships. A girl's chance of marriage is slight if she is childless after having had two or three lovers.

♡

In the Stone Age it was generally believed that a baby was conceived by ancestral spirits who entered a woman's body through any of the orifices, including the nostrils and ears. Virginity was therefore not highly prized.

♡

'To be, or not to be' is more of a dilemma for Russians than for Hamlet, especially for those Russians who read magazines. An article in *Health* magazine warned: 'The girl who loses her virginity before marriage at the same time loses her charm, becomes less pretty and in particular loses all faith in deep and noble feelings, as well as in herself.'

Anyone who saw this and then read a 1977 edition of the *Literary Gazette* would be mystified: 'Women who look like cowboys enjoy great success. They are the ones who start families, and whose husbands do not leave them; whereas frail, defenceless young girls swell the ranks of the unmarried.'

What's the point of a halo? It's only
one more thing to clean.
Christopher Fry

CHAPTER SEVEN
IN-LAWS

♡ Mr. Glynn 'Scotty' Wolfe of Blythe, California, holds the *Guinness Book of Records* accolade as the world's most married man. The former Baptist minister has had 26 wives and suffered 24 mothers-in-law.

This is a modest performance compared to the achievements of some. King Solomon had 700 wives and hundreds of mistresses. A seventeenth-century Sultan of Turkey grew tired of his harem, ordered the drowning of all his women, and then created a new one. The Chinese emperor, Yang-ti, had at any one time about 4,000 women near at hand, and Tzu-hsi, the Dragon Empress who described herself as 'the cleverest woman who ever lived', was surrounded by more than 4,000 men and eunuchs. All these courts – like Imperial Rome – were hot-beds of intrigue, with in-laws of all types at the centre of many plots.

Jokes about in-laws are an international phenomenon, with the mother-in-law coming out on top – or worst – depending on which way you look at it.

═══════════════════════ ♡ ═══════════════════════

Among the Ait Warains of Morocco, the bride kisses her father-in-law's head and hands immediately after the wedding ceremony, but her husband must avoid seeing his father (her father-in-law) for forty days and forty nights. At first she addresses her in-laws as 'my lord' and 'my lady', but when they are really chums she may call them 'my sheik' and 'my mistress'.

Among the Hiaina Arabs near Fez, the bride refers to her father-in-law as 'sheik', but to her mother-in-law as 'the old woman'.

──────────────────── ♡ ────────────────────

Tears trickled down the cheeks of the tragic family as Roberto Rodriguez's coffin was lowered into his grave. Suddenly the lid burst open, and heart-attack victim Roberto rose up shouting that he was alive. The Venezuelan lived for several more years, but the shock of his resurrection killed his mother-in-law. She was buried in his grave.

———————————♡———————————

In the Narikot area of Nepal a daughter-in-law washes her mother-in-law's feet before each meal, then – as a daughter-in-law's mark of respect – she sips the water in which the feet were bathed. At night she rubs oil into her mother-in-law's feet. If her father-in-law has more than one wife, each will consider her to be their daughter-in-law, too.

———————————♡———————————

Kaingáng men of Brazil and men in Tsang province in Tibet share their wives with their fathers.

Women of the Lele community in Zaire and of the Chiriguano tribe in Bolivia share their husbands with their mothers.

♡

Everything has its drawbacks, as the man said when his mother-in-law died, and they came down on him for the funeral expenses.
Jerome K. Jerome

♡

Some husbands in Western countries like to be present at the birth of their children. In the Nanumba region of Ghana, the mother-in-law watches the baby being born.

♡

A Fulani mother-in-law in Nigeria is the first to be told whether or not her son's wife is a virgin. She is shown a blood-stained piece of the bride's underclothing, if the news is good.

♡

WANTED! Wife for the future Emperor of Japan. She must – the *Daily Mirror* was told while Prince Hiro of Japan was studying medieval water transport at Oxford University – be 'younger than him and shorter when she stands in high heels. She must never have worked in an office where she had a "boss", and her father must never have had extra-marital relations'.

No one could explain how Prince Hiro was supposed to make sure about his father-in-law.

———————————♡———————————

MOTHER-IN-LAW RULES – O.K.?

The status of a man who marries the youngest daughter of a Khasi family in the hills of Assam is rock bottom. He works in the fields under the constant supervision of his wife's brothers and maternal uncles. He is rarely introduced to visitors so, while his wife and mother-in-law play host to them he is expected to leave the room or, at best, stay silent in one corner. His treatment is similar to that meted out by the Cewa and Yao mothers-in-law in east Africa, in which communities he is known as 'the detachable husband'.

On the Pacific island of Dobu a man must serve an apprenticeship of a year as the servant of his future mother- and father-in-law. She is in charge of his work and issues the orders. He is not allowed to share meals with the family, and has to continue to work while they eat. His ambition is to have his own plot of land, marry, and find an apprentice who wants to marry *his* daughter.

♡

Women hold up half the skies, and the heavier
half contains the mother-in-law.
Chinese

A mother-in-law and a daughter-in-law in one
house are like two cats in a bag.
Yiddish

♡

A Banyai man who lives along the banks of the Zambesi River has to provide firewood for his mother-in-law for life. So as not to insult her by pointing his feet at her he always delivers the wood on his knees.

A Wataveta girl living in Mozambique is not allowed to leave home for a month after the wedding. But there is a nice surprise waiting for her; her mother-in-law and mother will have cut the wood for her new house.

♡

The only place in the world where a daughter-in-law and her mother-in-law are supposed to share a bath regularly is the village of Kurotsuchi on Kyushu, the most southerly island of Japan. It is the custom that they scrub each other's backs.

When a new bride enters the house of her husband's family in some villages in the hills of West Bengal, her new family may ask her to step in a pile of fresh cow dung for good luck. The cow is sacred and like it the new wife is expected to be serene, composed and at peace with everything.

♡

A man loves his sweetheart the most, his wife
the best, but his mother the longest.
Irish

All women become like their mothers. That is
their tragedy. No man does. That's his.
Oscar Wilde

The best way to a man's heart is through his
mother.
Turkish

Trust a woman so long as your mother's eyes
are on her.
Japanese

♡

If you visit New Guinea and make friends with a Bánaro tribesman whose
son is getting married, you ought to know that it is the tribesman's duty to
deflower his future daughter-in-law, but he usually hands over the job to a
friend. After the marriage the father-in-law retains the right to have sexual
relations with his daughter-in-law on feast days.

♡

With the Tallensis in west Africa the problem is not where you put your feet, but where you put your bottom. If a father-in-law sits on his daughter-in-law's mat it is the equivalent of making love to her.

If he wishes to improve his skills as a warrior an Aborigine of central Australia will wear a girdle of hair around his waist. The trouble is that the best and luckiest hair comes from his mother-in-law's head.

———♡——— ———♡———

What takes Satan a year to do is done by the old
hag of a mother-in-law within the hour.
Moroccan

Letting a daughter-in-law live with her
mother-in-law is the same as inviting the devil
into the house.
Laotian

The husband who lives with his wife's parents
is no better than the lazy dog who sleeps his day
away under a table.
Vietnamese

———♡———

A man who lives in the Hiaina region of Morocco is forbidden to speak to his mother-in-law and father-in-law if his own parents are alive.

In the days when the Assyrians were fighting fit and ruled huge areas of land, the best chance a man would have of winning the hand of a woman was to present to her father the private parts of an enemy.

No matter how keen a couple is, the Cebus of the Philippines are against any signs of undignified haste to consummate a marriage. In the old days a couple waited forty days and nights before sleeping together. Now it is three days, during which time the wife stays with her in-laws and the husband with his.

A mother-in-law, like a prickly yucca, is better buried.
Cuban

The French for mother-in-law is *belle-mère*. When a Frenchman tells a woman that her slip is showing he says: *'Tu cherches une belle-mère,'* or, 'You are looking for a mother-in-law.'

In French slang a mother-in-law is *un mélange de stout et de bitter*. In Britain last century, mothers-in-law were sometimes referred to as being 'a mixture of old and bitter beers'.

An unmarried girl looks good. A wife has many faults. The easiest woman to get on with is the one who is not yet a mother-in-law.
Malagasy (Madagascar)

She is well married, who has neither mother-in-law nor sister-in-law by her husband.
Albanian

The mother-in-law remembers not that she was a daughter-in-law.
Korean

FAMILY INTRIGUES

Because of curious laws concerning incest and marriage, a Barondo husband in central Africa must avoid the following people at all costs:

his mother-in-law
his wife's mother's sister
his wife's grandmother and sister
his wife's brother's wife
his sister's daughter
his son's wife
his niece's son's wife

– which leaves him very few relatives to choose from.

It is much easier on the other side of Africa for the Anyanja and Yao wives of Malawi and Mozambique. The only people they have to avoid are their mother-in-law's uncles.

A NEW PUZZLE

Among the Nuers, who live in savannah country near the Upper Nile, sometimes a sister's son will marry his mother's brother's daughter. If you have trouble working out that, try this puzzle. (It helps to be a Nuer.)

A Nuer man may not take his wife's sister or any near kinswoman of his wife as a second wife. He may be on familiar terms with his wife's sister, but any sexual relations with her are incestuous and it is only permissible for him to marry her if his wife has died without children. The Nuer regard a man and his wife's sister as related through the child of the wife. Her sister is a kind of kinswoman, seeing that she is also the mother of their child. Your wife's sister, being your child's maternal aunt, is your sister or, as we would say, sister-in-law. Now, when your wife's sister's daughter marries, your wife will receive a cow and the Nuer think there is something wrong about this cow coming to her if her sister is also her co-wife. In certain circumstances a woman may claim cattle on her sister's marriage, and in this case the man who gives the cattle would also be the receiver of them were a man to marry his wife's sister. And so, a man may not marry his wife's sister either on account of her (the wife's) children or on account of the cattle, which are different ways of saying that he cannot marry his child's maternal aunt.

Confused? Perhaps you have to be a Nuer to understand a Nuer.

Because the Prophet Mohammed married off his daughter, Fatima, to her paternal uncle's son, Ali, marriage between cousins is considered highly desirable by Moslems.

In the United Arab Emirates first preference *by a father* is for his son to marry his (father's) brother's daughter. Second preference is his (father's) sister's daughter. Third choice is the mother's brother's daughter. But there is a very big 'but'; you cannot marry any of your cousins if they have been suckled by the bridegroom's mother!

Why should anyone want to marry a cousin? Moslems have four good reasons:

1. To keep wealth within the family.
2. To strengthen clan bonds.
3. You can look inside the stable door, so there are no surprises.
4. You can deal with a wayward wife or half-hearted husband by getting the families to intervene.

> He is a fool who marries a stranger when his
> cousin awaits him.
> *Tunisian*

> I'll never forgive my mother,
> Who painted me for this wedding.
> I will never forgive my father,
> Who makes me marry this man.
> He is old, he is ugly,
> His belly is like the bottom of a grain sack.
> I wish I could marry my cousin,
> Whose face shines like the sun.
>
> *Berber bride's song*

And finally . . .

East Bantu	mother-in-law	must hide behind a bush if her son-in-law approaches.
East Bantu	son-in-law and mother-in-law	can only speak by shouting something important over a high fence.
Zulu	husband	must not look at his mother-in-law's breasts.
Zulu	wife	must not mention the names of her male in-laws.
Fraser's Islander	mother-in-law	will cause her son-in-law to go mad if their eyes meet.

Banyai (Zambesi River)	son-in-law	has to sit with bent knees if his mother-in-law is present.
Bondei (Tanzania)	son-in-law and mother-in-law	are not allowed to share a meal.
Anavils of Gujarat, India	daughter-in-law	cannot address her father-in-law or her husband's elder brothers; cannot mention her father-in-law's name nor serve him food; is ignored by her husband in the presence of his parents; must stand quietly in the doorway while her mother-in-law shows the babies to visitors.

The British brought out all their reserves – and a little bit more – for the Falklands War.
The girl on the right waving farewell to the troops is performing a sexual ritual familiar among
prehistoric tribes around the world where warriors are sent on their way with promised
rewards of sexual gratification if they come home victorious. Other enticements are described
in the chapters on *Love Nests* and *The Food of Love*.

You cannot give a Mursi girl too much lip. To improve on nature these Mursi tribeswomen from Ethiopia cut their lower lips and stretch them with increasingly large and heavy clay discs. When they have achieved a sufficiently loopy effect, the discs are removed. Then men try to win the loose-mouthed maidens by duelling with their *dongas* (long wooden poles). It is as honourable for the duellists to sustain injuries as to inflict them.

'Hearts will never be practical until they can be made unbreakable,' said the Wizard of Oz to the Tin Man, who lamented his lack of a heart. There is more about hearts in Chapter Two.

In central Africa a Mangbetu woman is beautified with decorative scars on her face and a body painted with soot and clay mixed with oil. Even as a baby the beauty treatment begins when her head is pressed between boards or stones to elongate the shape (Mayans in Mexico used a similar technique to foreshorten the head). The length of the head is further exaggerated by raising the Bo Derek plaits over a frame. Her husband is entitled to many wives, but even if she is the most beautiful she has no more claim to his time than any of the others. For more marital time-sharing see 'I Pronounce You Man and Wives' on page 200.

This vicious Valentine card, hand-coloured and with moving parts, dates from 1870 and was accompanied by the following verse:

> Lady, as I gaze I am smitten
>   At thy graceful form & features,
> By thy beauty I am bitten,
>   Most fair & lovely creature:
> This is what I ought to say
>   But from such a guy, I run away.

More off-beat love messages are included in pages 104 to 111.

A Dinka dandy having a wash and brush up: the cow's urine bleaches and de-greases the hair ready to be teased into an even shape. Cattle are the centre of life for the Dinkas of Sudan. When this man goes dancing with his girlfriend he tries to move like his favourite bull. See 'Wives for Cattle' on page 198.

The American actress Jean Harlow knew the appeal of protruberant nipples. To be sure hers would be sufficiently prominent she rubbed them with ice before making an entrance at press conferences and photo calls. For other tips refer to *Love Lessons* in Chapter Four.

This is a Solomon Islander's idea of *machismo:* a great leap into manhood. In a society with 87 vernacular languages, the way to say 'I'm ready for love' is to prove one's virility by jumping into the lake. In the Pacific islands of Vanuatu young men do it over land with ropes attached to their ankles, sometimes braining themselves in the process. Other ways in which men and women signal that they are 'ready for love' are included in the chapter on *Initiation to Love*.

CHAPTER EIGHT
THE FOOD OF LOVE

♡ Nothing that creeps, flutters, slithers, swims or crawls on land, sea and air is safe from mankind's search for that secret additive which will put human sexual passion into overdrive. For hundreds and thousands of years the peoples of Asia, the Pacific Ocean islands, South and Central America, Africa and – more recently – the Middle East have consumed foods, drunk potions or rubbed on ointments and unguents because they find in them pleasing amatory powers.

Europeans might be expected to be more sceptical, but the most popular aphrodisiacs in the West are products sold with such winning names as Seducing Powder or Fire Drops. In 1984 a number of products sold over the counter in Britain's sex shops were analysed by trading standards officers whose verdict on the best-selling lines was that 'the only physical effect likely to occur from these potions is a case of vomiting'.

An aphrodisiac is more likely to succeed if you believe in it; but then that is true of any medicine or treatment. Believing is half the battle. There are three types of love-inducing substances: the first type excite the senses and increase physical desire and capacity. Another group clouds the wits and banishes self-control, and these include dangerous drugs such as opium, heroin, cocaine and LSD. The third type are the potions and charms that are secretly administered to break down a person's resistance.

Whether or not you think you could benefit from love potions or love foods you will find in this chapter a whole range of items which have given, and will continue to give, billions of people additional pleasure in their love lives.

THE ROOT OF PASSION

Ginseng has a world-wide reputation as an aphrodisiac. It is a root which grows in China, Korea, Siberia and North America; the red root is more prized than the yellow. The name 'ginseng' is Chinese, meaning 'man root', and a perfectly shaped root is one which resembles the naked body of a well-formed man. A perfect sample costs tens of thousands of pounds – just enough for one person for a week. The best roots are bought by the Chinese of Hong Kong, Taiwan and Singapore, the Japanese and, more recently, by Arabs.

Men have killed each other in their quest for ginseng, so valued is it as a cure for impotence and frigidity. In Imperial China emperors, noblemen and rich merchants found that ginseng so increased their sexual drive that they could make love and take part in business discussions at the same time.

In 1982 I was invited by *Woman's Journal* in Britain to put ginseng to the test on six people. I summarise the results of three of them.

Prafulla Mohanti, who was born in Orissa, India, is the author of *My Village, My Life* and *Through Brown Eyes*.*** He sliced his Korean root and simmered it for four hours. 'The thought and smell of it while it cooked made me feel sensuous. My muscles tingled, especially in the thighs, and then followed such a sensational, firm reaction that I missed both my wife and my mistress, who were both in India. I couldn't sleep because of the fantastic physical power which would not go away, so I had to resort to Valium before I could go to sleep.'

Michael Sumner was not so lucky. The former Head of Talks and Features of the BBC World Service kept a diary of his *Ginseng Saga*. 'Ruined a knife trying to cut the root, which refused to yield. To bed early, instantly asleep. Next morning my wife cautiously enquires about my well-being, says she has to be at work early, dresses hurriedly, and departs.' In fact, his wife left for work early every morning during the *Ginseng Saga*. Michael Sumner's verdict: 'Four large scotches and ginger ale are the best thing for stimulating and losing inhibitions.'

Kenneth Lo is seventy-two and looks at least ten years younger. Born in China, he is a former member of China's Davis Cup tennis team and the reigning veteran doubles champion of the United Kingdom. He is also the author of more books on Chinese cookery than anyone in the world. He took his ginseng by infusion, drinking a cup of warmed liquid on awakening and another at night.

How important is sex normally to Kenneth Lo? 'Very, but not half as important as eating. Ideally it's good to have a wife, two steady girlfriends, and two unsteady girlfriends. When I drank ginseng I could feel a warmth in my palms, strength of grip in my hands and fingers, and firmness in my gums which created a desire to bite. Is this not aphrodisiac, the desire to bite? I played a lot of tennis and felt distinctly chirpy afterwards.'

Postscript: Kenneth Lo believes that for full aphrodisiac effect ginseng is best taken for three weeks with concentrated vitamin E (found in cold-pressed vegetable oils, especially wheatgerm, sunflower seed, safflower and corn oils). Recent research shows that if citrus juice is drunk within three

*** published by Oxford University Press in 1985

hours of taking ginseng, any beneficial effect from ginseng will probably be destroyed. My own researches reveal that the best results are achieved by chewing the dried root. There is, however, a high risk of breaking your teeth, but some people think it is worth a few chipped incisors if ginseng can work its wonders elsewhere.

———————————————————♡———————————————————

Every day hundreds, sometimes thousands, of men hurry along city streets and village paths in Sierra Leone, driven by the urgent need to make love. For these are men who have recently taken Efodi, a medicinal love potion guaranteed to work like a charm. A man who rushes away after work is accused by his colleagues of being an Efodi foodie. A wise man is one who is careful not to eat at the home of a girl whose mother has designs on him as a son-in-law: how can he tell whether she has slipped Efodi into his dinner?

———————————————————♡———————————————————

The perfect way to end the day for many Indians is to have a good *bang*.

While some like to smoke their *bang*, most prefer to chew it to savour the full flavour of the hemp seeds and leaves and to prolong the sense of euphoria and stimulus to love that a well-made *bang* can produce.

A chemical called phenylethylamine is produced by the human brain when lovers are in a state of excitement. It is also found in chocolate, which might explain why many people eat chocolates after a love affair ends.

♡   ♡

Popular Aphrodisiacs From Around the World

Crocodile kidneys	Popular in ancient Rome; Egypt; Madagascar; areas along the Amazon River. Australians are still trying to decide if the kidneys could possibly increase their sex drive; there are plenty of crocodiles in northern Australia. In Java the crocodile's testicles are preferred.
Alligator tails	China, where the best aphrodisiac results have been experienced by those who chose an alligator less than 3 ft long. (The one with the two big, sharp teeth sticking up from the lower jaw and outside the upper lip is the crocodile.)
Rattlesnake	America: for example on the menu at the Warwick Hotel in Houston, Texas.

Cobra, krait, common black snake	Snake restaurants in Jervois Street & Hillier Street area of Hong Kong; south China.
Python	Singapore
Rat snake	Thailand
Snakeburgers	Japan: e.g. at Takayanagi spa's municipal restaurant only small portions are served 'to avoid a too powerful effect on the diner', the local authorities said in 1978.
Fat palm grub	Philippines
Groo-groo grub	West Indies: tastes like roast chestnuts.
Sphinx caterpillar	Along the Amazon River.
Sea slug	South-east China; West Indies; Pacific islands.
Large bullfrog	South America; West Indies (where it is served to tourists as 'mountain chicken').
Small lizard e.g. skink	North Africa: the skink is mixed with cloves, ginger, olive oil and honey.
Figs	France; Greece; Saudi Arabia and the Gulf States.
Pumpkin seeds	China; United Kingdom (a source of zinc used to treat impotence).
Spinach, carrots, melons, apricots	Aphrodisiacs recommended by the Fresh Fruit and Vegetable Information Bureau of the United Kingdom.
Prunes	Served free of charge in brothels of Elizabethan England to revive flagging customers.
Dates	North Africa; in Shakespeare's *Romeo and Juliet* dates were planned for Juliet's wedding dinner.

Peyote cactus	Mexico
Rhinoceros horn	China, Hong Kong, Taiwan, Japan, Arab countries: the horn is powdered and believed to boost male potency.
Gold leaf	India: used to adorn sweets and believed to contribute to the sex drive.
Marsala	Sicily, where it is the honeymoon drink.
Amaretto	Italy; currently a top-selling liqueur in America: tastes of almond (thought by many to be an important and historically proven aphrodisiac).
Octopus	Japan – raw; China – with black beans; Italy – fried in batter; Spain – boiled and served in its own purple-black ink; Guadalcanal in the south Pacific – the raw eyes are the prime delicacy.
Whale	Eskimos enjoy its raw kidneys and heart; also the blubber.
Fugu (fish)	Japan, where it is considered such a delicacy and aphrodisiac that gourmets ignore the risk of death from certain toxic particles; special chefs are licensed to cook it, but people die every year.
Nŭoc-man	Vietnam: an extract of rotten fish mixed with garlic and pimento.
Pickled tea	Burma, where it is sometimes served at the name-giving ceremony of a boy.
Passion flower	Spain; but it is never taken with aged or mature cheese because of a risk of causing high blood pressure.
Pomegranates	Indians and Miss Barbara Cartland.
Celery	Norway
Caviar	Soviet Union; Iran; Rasputin the monk; Sweden.

EGGING THEM ON

The Western world is full of men who claim the only thing they can do in the kitchen is boil an egg. Perhaps they have read *The Perfumed Garden*. 'A man who wishes to copulate during a whole night, and whose desire, having come on suddenly . . . may have recourse to the following recipe. He must get a great number of eggs, so that he may eat to surfeit, and fry them with fresh fat and butter; when done he immerses them in honey, working the whole mass well together. He must then eat of them as much as possible with a little bread, and he may be certain that for the whole night his member will not give him any rest.'

Tibetans break a hard-boiled egg on their forehead and consume it with tea made from rancid buffalo-butter and salt as a pick-me-up after a hard day's night.

In parts of the West Indies, and Central and South America, iguana eggs are eaten as a source of amatory fervour, while in Hungary a liqueur made from quails' eggs was hailed as a love potion in the summer of 1984. Some Filipinos believe that a girl will not be able to resist a man who has put the egg of a black hen into a bowl of water then chanted her name before eating it. As a girl can only resist the spell by putting a similar egg into water, the moral is: always have an egg ready.

Dr. William J. Robinson was a leading medical consultant at the Bronx Hospital in New York in the 1930s. His advice to anyone wanting to boost vital energies was to drink an egg after making a hole in the top of the shell and adding a pinch of salt.

The *Sun* newspaper asked psychiatrist Jack Leedy whether it is possible to tell something about an egg lover's personality by the way he or she likes eggs to be cooked:

SOFT-BOILED	A little picky and fussy. Tends to be a perfectionist.
HARD-BOILED	Impulsive; a no-nonsense achiever.
POACHED	Nothing can hurry you. You appreciate the finer things in life.
FRIED BOTH SIDES	Easy-going, steady, reliable, kind and generous.
FRIED ONE SIDE	Willing to take a chance. You're assertive and know what you want in life.
SCRAMBLED	Harmonious, and you make good decisions.
RAW	Devil-may-care. You go your own way.

POWER

is the great aphrodisiac

Henry Kissinger, quoted in the *New York Times*

GREEDY PIGS

The French, Italians and pigs love to truffle. Truffles are among the most exotic and expensive of gourmet delights, whether served in a salad or poached in champagne. Their principal attraction is their aroma and reputation for awakening 'erotic and gastronomic ideas both in the sex wearing petticoats and in the bearded portion of humanity', the French gastronomic writer Brillat-Savarin observed.

Pigs are used to detect these fungi, and a good truffle-pig can sniff them out as much as three feet underground. The sow is especially gifted at finding truffles, probably because she recognises the scent of a substance called androstenol. Not only is androstenol contained in truffles, but it is also produced by boars in their testes, so when a boar is sexually aroused the substance is transported to his salivary glands, and it takes just one whiff of this smell to make the sow adopt the mating position.

What is good enough for a pig is good enough for humans: to test the effect of androstenol Dr. Michael Kirk-Smith (now of the University of Birmingham) showed a group of men and women a series of pictures and asked them to rate them for beauty and sexiness. Unknown to them, some of the human guinea pigs were exposed to a trace of androstenol in the air. They gave the pictures higher ratings than those who were not.

VERY PRIVATE RECIPES

Pius V was a pope and saint. He also employed a cook whose culinary masterpiece was a pie of bulls' testicles. The dish became a favourite of the leading men of the Renaissance era some of whom inveigled the chef into divulging his aphrodisiac recipe: boil four bulls' testicles in water and salt, cut them into thin slices and sprinkle with pepper, salt, cinnamon, and nutmeg. Put layers of the testicles in a pie dish alternating them with a mince made of lambs' kidneys, ham, marjoram, thyme and cloves. Bake in an oven.

The French expert in matters of the stomach and love was Dr. Nicholas

Venette, who recommended mixing cocks' testicles with egg yolks in his famous book *Le Tableau de la Vie Conjugale*.

That was in 1696. In England in 1633 Thomas Heywood had written in his play *The Dumb Knight* that 'cock sparrows stewed, doves' brains or swans' pizzles are very provocative'. Charles I was king at the time and both he and his predecessor, James I, were reported to have found that lambs' testicles increased their lusty powers.

The Chinese support Dr. Venette's theory that roosters' testicles produce the desired effect. In Hong Kong they feature on menus in many restaurants: when I first tasted them I did not know what they were, and their appearance was curious, wobbling as they were in a sea of sauce. Those who swear by them are the local Chinese themselves and long-term residents in Hong Kong from Britain, Australia and America such as tour operators, airline employees and journalists.

The aphrodisiac habit of the inhabitants of Siwa oasis in Egypt is to mix the sperm of a man with their food, but it is generally felt that to benefit most one should devour one's own vital essence rather than anyone else's.

In Java crocodile testicles are eaten by elderly men after their marriage to a young girl, while in Morocco and Algeria the testicles of an ass are considered very erotic inducements to love-making. Members of the Arunta tribe in Australia feed their women the testicles of the opossum and the kangaroo.

The Spanish brought tomato seeds from South America in the sixteenth century, believing the vegetable to be an aphrodisiac. Fearful of the fun the tomato might provide, the Puritans spread the rumour in England that the bright red thing was poisonous. To prove the English wrong Robert Gibbon Johnson of Salem in America publicly ate a dozen tomatoes in front of a big crowd. Two physicians attended the demonstration, but their services were not required.

In the seventeenth century the English called it a love apple; Americans still sometimes do. The French speak about *pomme d'amour* and Germans refer to *Liebesapfel*. But it is the Chinese who have produced the most spectacular evidence that, like love, tomatoes spring eternal. The English language *China Daily* reported from Sichuan province in 1985 that some 2,000-year-old seeds had been recovered from an ancient Han dynasty tomb. When sown they germinated and grew into plants which bore bright red tomatoes.

Researchers at Stanford University in California have found that a drug with a 1,000-year-old reputation for being a powerful aphrodisiac is strong enough to kick a group of sexually inactive animals into high gear. The drug is yohimbine, which is extracted from the bark of the yohimbe tree in central Africa. Although the animals used in the experiment were rats, the university was inundated with humans wanting to join in. Dr. Julian Davidson, who is in charge of the sex-drug tests, pleaded: 'Please, please, no more volunteers.'

Many people believe in the aphrodisiac qualities of onions and garlic despite the effect on their breath. The Chinese and the French go so far as to claim that garlic-haters make lousy lovers.

Americans and the British are the least keen on garlic, but since the invention of round, clean, inoffensive, odourless garlic tablets more Americans are swallowing the bitter pill, encouraged no doubt by recent claims that garlic also improves memory and digestion.

In Hong Kong an erotic ointment available on market stalls contains pig fat mixed with crushed garlic. 'Never mind the sting, watch for the uplift,' urged one poster near the Peninsula hotel.

Les Findlay lives near Glasgow, and finds the effects of onions less than erotic though he eats a lot of them. He is an onion addict, devouring them by the thousand, raw. His eye-watering addiction began when he was put in a trance by a stage hypnotist who fed him an onion and told him it was a juicy apple. Mr. Findlay says that his addiction has ruined his social life: 'After all, it's hopeless trying to pull a bird if you're reeking like me.' He grows them in his garden, and on a bad day he will eat three raw Spanish onions.

And to think that onions and garlic are members of the lily family!

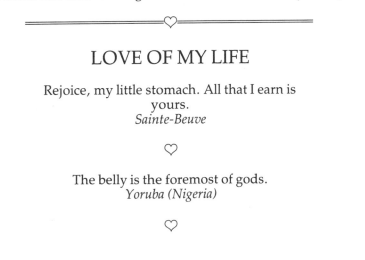

LOVE OF MY LIFE

Rejoice, my little stomach. All that I earn is
yours.
Sainte-Beuve

The belly is the foremost of gods.
Yoruba (Nigeria)

161

There is more honour in the belly bursting than in food going to waste.
Polish

♡

The food which their stomachs can scarcely retain is fetched from farthest ocean: they vomit that they may eat, they eat that they may vomit, and they do not deign even to digest feasts for which they ransack the whole world.
Seneca, writing about the Romans more than 1900 years ago

♡

To Americans a girl can be a dish, chick or honey. There are cold fish and those who like a bit of cheesecake or beefcake. Others are on the look-out for a tart or a sugardaddy. To the British a winkle is best eaten freshly pickled outside a shellfish stall on Fridays; it is also slang for penis, a point acknowledged in *Chambers Dictionary*.

───────────────♡───────────────

In the past the English have eaten cyclamens and orchids, sometimes putting their roots and stems in love philtres. Some psychologists say that if a man offers his loved-one an orchid he is thinking of his private parts: because of their shape, orchids are named after the Greek word *orchis*, meaning 'testicles'.

───────────────♡───────────────

Like the ginseng root (see page 154) mandrake has its 'disciples'. In fact, there are references to this erotic plant in the Bible: in *Genesis* (Reuben, Leah, Rachel and Jacob were familiar with it) and in the *Song of Solomon*.

Again like ginseng, mandrake often grows in human shape. Shakespeare refers to the plant in *Othello*, and the playwright's Cleopatra asks for it while 'My Antony is away', though she thought it would sedate, not excite her.

Arabs call it the man-plant, and Italians speak about the power of mandrake to make women fruitful. At the end of last century some orthodox Jews in America imported the root in the hope of curing their barren wives.

But nearly all who have tried it warn against taking it in excess; too much mandrake can poison the body.

───────────────♡───────────────

From the large number of vehicles stationary on the hard shoulder verges of the autoroutes and smaller roads in France, it would appear that more cars break down there than anywhere else in Europe. Do not be fooled; many of their drivers and passengers are looking for juicy, fat snails hiding in the deep grass. After the fine, tasty specimens from the Burgundy region, next favourite are the roadside species, which have the additional charm of being food for free.

The French add plenty of garlic and parsley to snails and the result is a pleasant amatory sauce (not to say source). An Imperial Roman recipe suggested cooking snails slowly to extract the full benefits of their aphrodisiac power: boil the snails with onions and parsley, then fry them in olive oil. Next, simmer them in a robust red wine for an hour.

Dopamine is the substance found in oysters and broad beans which, when absorbed in the bloodstream, quickly gives a lift to amorous desire. The effect is thought to last up to eight hours, by which time lovers should sleep off the effects of their activities, or swallow another plate of beans or let another few dozen oysters slither down the throat.

Beans may be cheaper than oysters, but their side-effects can be unusual as observed in the *Alphabet of Sex*, by Herr Scheuer: 'In some parts of Germany the men eat flatulent foods like beans, peas, lentils, and radishes in order that they may attain powerful erections by way of the accumulated gas.'

The Greek philosopher Pythagoras banned his ascetically inclined followers from eating beans.

After meeting D. H. Lawrence, the writer Norman Douglas used the pseudonym of Pilaff Bey for his book *Venus in the Kitchen*. His exotic love-recipes included skink with eggs and one which mixed sparrows' brains with goat's milk, turnips and carrots.

Simpler to do is his marmalade of carnations: crush the tops of red carnations then boil them in sugar and water. He especially recommended this for anyone with a chilly temperament.

THE CHINESE–ENGLISH CONNECTION

On a British Airways flight to Hong Kong an old lady once told me about a Chinese New Year recipe: slice a portion of begonia root and add a generous amount of cobweb; any spider's web will do. Allow the mixture to stand for ten days in a dark place. Twist the sediment that has formed into tiny pills, and drop one into your beloved's favourite drink. The old lady spoke in Cantonese dialect with a lisp, but I think she said the pills are effective against impotence and frigidity, but that too many can turn a reticent person into a sex maniac.

It was also the custom in medieval England to put certain ingredients in a dark place while they wove their love spells. One recipe required its maker to dry a large number of black ants, pour vegetable oil over them, and marinade them for about a week. Another recipe suggested taking 200 ants, 200 millipedes and 250 bees, and soaking them in water for a month. The liquid was thought to possess valuable aphrodisiac stimuli.

So convinced was Alan Hull Walton that certain foods could provoke sexual excitement that he thought it unwise to let ordinary men and women get their thrills in this way. His book *Love Recipes Old and New* was therefore published in a limited edition of 1,375 copies in 1956, with the provision: 'The sale of this book is restricted to members of the Medical and Legal Professions, Scientists, Psychologists, Sociologists, Ethnologists and Anthropologists.'

The recipes included Chinese egg soup with noodles and Marmite; bananas and beef (1 lb of meat to four bananas); fried cuttle fish; spaghetti casserole made from a tin of Heinz spaghetti; Marmite sandwiches; savoury jelly sandwiches made from Bovril, Lemco or Marmite (his favourite ingredient); and All-Bran.

The French gastronome and lawyer Brillat-Savarin created a recipe which successfully saved the lost sex drive of his friend, Monsieur Rabat:

Mince 6 onions, 3 carrots, and a handful of parsley, and heat them in a pan. Add a lump of butter. Stir in 6 oz sugar candy, 20 grains of powdered ambergris, a crust of bread (toasted), 3 bottles of water. While this boils kill and clean an old cock then mince it (flesh and bones) with 2 lb beef. Fry the meat with butter in a second pan. Pour liquid from first pan into the second, and simmer for three-quarters of an hour. Dosage: take a cup every two hours.

Cleopatra did not waste time talking about pearls of wisdom. She crushed pearls and dissolved them in wine, and created a perfect love potion.

A thousand years ago the ancient Persians made tablets out of pearls, rubies, gold and powdered ambergris (from the sperm-whale) which – when allowed to dissolve on the tongue – increased their sex drive.

In the United Arab Emirates today pearls are gathered from the Persian Gulf and powdered to make a tonic and aphrodisiac drink. A number of ingredients are added to the pearls: root ginger, senna leaves, caraway seeds, cinnamon, lavender flowers, red coral, aniseed, mace, mountain willow, and burnt tartar (taken from fermented wine).

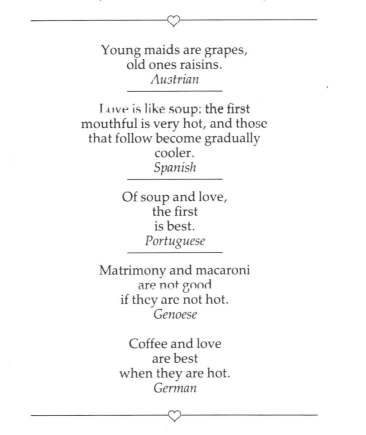

Young maids are grapes,
old ones raisins.
Austrian

Love is like soup: the first
mouthful is very hot, and those
that follow become gradually
cooler.
Spanish

Of soup and love,
the first
is best.
Portuguese

Matrimony and macaroni
are not good
if they are not hot.
Genoese

Coffee and love
are best
when they are hot.
German

The best chef in China is Liu Jingxian. He won the national chefs' competition with a menu that began with chicken and sea slugs served in boiling broth, followed by stewed bears' paws and fish stomach, and then chicken legs with abalone. Of these ingredients only chicken is thought by the Chinese to be low in aphrodisiac value. But bald-chicken potion is different. The recipe for this is jealously guarded by the few who know it, but the ingredients include a number of mountain herbs and specially fattened chickens. Its popularity is ages-old, and like most Chinese culinary treasures has its beginnings in folklore.

There was a civil servant who every day drank a potion made from chicken and herbs. Not only did he sire three sons after the age of seventy, but such was the frequency of his love-making demands that his wife was quite unable to sit or lie down. Thinking that the potion was the cause of his virility he threw it into a farmyard, where a rooster sipped it. The bird's lust increased a hundred times, and during its sessions of love-making it pecked at the hen's head till she was completely bald. If, say the Chinese, a man can find a genuine recipe for bald-chicken potion and sip it every day, he will easily be able to satisfy forty women most days of his life.

THE MILKY WAY

In May 1984 Dr. Harry Morrow Brown from Derby described a case in *World Medicine* magazine of a woman who suffered arthritic pains after making love. Tests carried out revealed that she was allergic to milk, and that protein in her husband's semen from milk he drank was causing her pain. To verify their claims, the doctors wanted her to make love with another man before and after he drank milk. She refused.

The famous French sexologist Jean Liebault found that rice that had been cooked in sheep's milk acted as an erotic stimulant to anyone who ate it before retiring to bed or for a siesta. Three hundred years earlier in the thirteenth century the Arab physician Avicenna recommended a drink composed of honey and chameleon's milk to several of his more libidinous patients. The Roman encyclopædist Pliny the Elder recorded that root vegetables cooked in goat's milk could excite most men and women, but that the same roots eaten without milk had the opposite effect.

Nero's wife Poppaea kept 500 asses to supply her bath. Today in the emirates of the Persian Gulf bathing in asses' milk is popular as an amatory stimulant; essences of myrtle and lavender, rose water, honey water and almond paste are added for extra power, though champagne baths are the current favourite. In 1984 Xavier Marchandise, the great-nephew of Jean Patou, whose firm in France makes Joy, the world's costliest fragrance, reported that a client from Jeddah had ordered a consignment of Joy to fill her swimming pool. Bulk-bought, Joy works out at £1,600 a pint.

Hungarian gourmet and publisher of food and hotel guides Egon Ronay says an ideal meal for lovers is fresh *foie gras*, followed by roast partridge and a light mousse, and 'a good champagne, but not too much of it'.

Actress Diana Dors thought that in romance 'food is the last thing on your mind. I have never known a man who had eyes for me to show much interest in what was for dinner. It is only when the romance is all over that a man starts thinking about his stomach'.

166

Anton Mosimann's culinary skills at the Dorchester in London are known on every continent. One year he created a love-inducing meal for St. Valentine's Day; the menu included warm artichoke hearts with Stilton cheese and quail; veal in a Madeira, cream and mushroom sauce; grilled breast of duck with passion fruit and honey-glazed figs; and coconut kisses, which were coconut biscuits sandwiched together with a light chocolate sauce.

Byron believed that lobster and champagne together did the trick. When Casanova entertained beautiful women they had oysters, truffles, hard-boiled eggs, anchovies, fish, game and wine.

HOT-BLOODED

Surprisingly, love owes more to blood and sweat than tears. In the Caribbean a drop of perspiration sucked from a philtrum – which is the groove running from the base of the nose to the centre of the upper lip – in a passionate kiss is regarded as the most powerful stimulant to love-making.

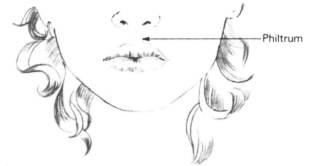

Philtrum

The power of sweat is known in Scotland, where it is thought that a man has power over a woman if she eats two sweets stuck together with his perspiration. In Norfolk and in Scotland if a man pricked an orange all over with a needle then slept with it under his arm, any girl who ate it would fall a victim to his charms. This Scottish ballad explains his chances:

> Frae below his arm he's pulled a charm,
> An' stuck it in her sleeve;
> And he has made her gang wi' him
> Without her parents' leave.

In Oklahoma there is a prairie custom that a woman gets her way with a man if she sprinkles his coat with alcohol into which has been pressed a piece of beef worn under her armpit for two days. Cubans also believe in the love power of sweat; a popular recipe in Cuban emigrant communities in New York and Miami is: add salt, pepper and drops of your own sweat to a hamburger. Cook and serve to the person you desire.

The good news for the bloody-minded is that blood has aphrodisiac qualities. Especially effective are steak tartare, rare (underdone) beef, black pudding from the north of England, and other blood sausages such as *boudins noirs* from France, *Blutwurst* from Germany, and Spanish *morcillas*.

In the Pacific a Lossu woman sprinkles a few drops of blood taken from a cut she makes in her breast on to a baked *taro* in the belief that the man who eats it will be attracted to her. The Dinkas and Masai in Africa are loth to kill their cattle (which represent wealth), but they tap the veins in the neck and mix the blood with sesame oil or sour milk to produce an energy-giving drink. Last century the Chinese emperor Hsien Feng drank deers' blood before a long session of love-making, while in America some doctors advised their patients to drink a small glass of warm blood before breakfast – but whose? I think we should be told.

South Italian wives send to their husbands working abroad a special powder containing their dried menstrual blood in the hope that this *filtro d'amore* will force an errant husband to return.

ANIMAL MAGIC

My Chinese father, like most Chinese from the southern province of Guangdong, found that cat, snake, dog and monkey – separately or together – made an excellent tonic and love-inducing food. The best cat for aphrodisiac purposes is a fat tomcat, and the most popular dog is the chow. Bones are also effective, especially tiger bones and dogs' bones – from the dog himself, not those he has dug up in the garden.

In ancient Rome and in France today, frogs' legs are enjoyed for their flavour and reputation for arousing passion; no one eats the front legs. The Japanese prefer dried beef because they believe it gives extra staying power to lovers. This view is shared by Peruvians and Argentinians, who get an extra thrill from eating *echarqui*, as the beef is called. They grab a large piece between the teeth and cut it with a sharp knife as close to the lips as possible.

A much-loved aphrodisiac ointment popular with Arabs in north Africa is made from jackals' gall, asses' milk and melted camel hump.

In the Seychelles islands the best known aphrodisiac is fruit bat curried or stewed in wine, while in Nigeria dried bat is believed to increase one's sex drive. The Hausas of Nigeria say:

> Throw out your bat ideas;
> The best charm for getting your woman
> is money.

Eskimos in Greenland think that the beaks of the king eider duck add fiery passion to those who eat them, and similar feelings are reported by Wagogos in Tanzania after eating lions' hearts and by the Bushmen of South Africa, though they prefer leopards' hearts.

Certain animals' feet are thought to give a sexual stimulus, if not to the beast itself then to the man or woman who devours them. The French eat a lot of pigs' feet and so do the Chinese. The Watavetas in Mozambique are a

168

hunting race, and enjoy elephant feet. The writer A. Hyatt Verrill found an elephant's foot tough: 'I boiled it from Monday morning until Friday night, and then I chewed it from Friday night until Monday morning.'

Ants are eaten as an aphrodisiac in many countries. The heads of the common black and the red ant are the sweetest part, but better value according to the Tariana Indians of the Upper Amazon are the larger species, which they catch in baskets and then cook over glowing coals.

Many African tribes enjoy termites, favouring the queen ant because she is fattest and longest. In part of east Africa, Haiti and the West Indies candied termite, made from honey and banana flour, is a great aphrodisiac and culinary delicacy. Mexicans sometimes serve honey ants, which when topped and tailed look like bright berries, at wedding parties.

Even rats have their followers. João Amaral, public nutritionist for Ceara State in Brazil, said in December 1983 that 'people should eat more rats. Eating rats not only gives a good supply of protein. It can also stimulate the libido in cases of sexual disfunction'.

Bear meat is praised by Germans, Swedes, Chinese, Russians and the Yakuts of Siberia, who feel its rich, energy-giving effects shortly after consuming it. The Chinese swear that the front paws contain a spicy elixir; the Germans are partial to bear cubs; Russians still follow a recipe of Monsieur Urbain Dubois, once the chef at the Prussian court, in which bear paws are stewed with bacon, ham, and vegetables before being rolled in breadcrumbs and grilled.

Alexandre Dumas, creator of *The Three Musketeers*, wrote about bears in his huge, rambling *Gastronomic Dictionary*:

'When the Yakuts, a Siberian people, meet a bear, they doff their caps, greet him, call him master, old man or grandfather, and promise not to attack him or even to speak ill of him. But if he looks as though he may pounce on them, they shoot at him and, if they kill him, they cut him in pieces and roast him and regale themselves, repeating all the while: "It is the Russians who are eating you, not us."'

CHAPTER NINE
LOVE NESTS

♡ A third of our lives is spent in bed. Some beds creak, others groan or sway. Some are made of solid bricks over a warm stove, others of padded cloth spread across a wooden floor. At its most basic a bed can be a layer of leaves in a forest glade. Useful as it is for resting, and inessential though it may be for ardent lovers, the bed remains the plinth on which most people choose to offer up their homage to love. Here, too, is the unpredictably shaky frame upon which marriages are built or founder.

———————————————♡———————————————

Describing their policy towards bedroom scenes a spokesman for the NBC television network in America announced in 1984: 'Within the past year we began to allow a man to lie on top of a woman. We are reaching the point of physical motion under the covers of a bed.'

———————————————♡———————————————

I am happy now that Charles calls on my
bedchamber less frequently than of old. As it is I
now endure but two calls a week, and when I
hear his steps outside my door I lie down on my
bed, open my legs and think of England.
Lady Alice Hillingdon

Wait in bed for luck.
Japanese saying

Unfortunately this world is full of people who
are ready to think the worst when they see a
man sneaking out of the wrong bedroom in the
middle of the night.
Will Cuppy

———————————————♡———————————————

Among the Mende of Sierra Leone a man who sits on his mother's or his sister's bed is deemed to have committed incest.

=========◇=========

TURKISH DELIGHT

The Turks and Chinese of old knew more about creating the right ambience for love-making in their bedchambers than any other race. With plenty of money and unlimited power, Turkish sultans and Chinese emperors and their favourite male supporters could obtain practically any woman they craved.

In the Turkish seraglio a strict hierarchy existed: top dog (or bitch) was the sultan's mother, then came the *kadins* (wives who had borne children to the sultan), next the *ikbals* (favourites who shared the royal bed), and next *odalisques* who had caught the royal eye but were still waiting to be summoned to the sultan's bedchamber.

Despite the lusty activities in the sultan's bedchamber, a code of behaviour had to be observed. For example, a *kadin* was expected to approach the foot of the sultan's bed, lift up the covers, and creep humbly in at the foot of the bed. Then she would gradually work her way up till she was on level-pegging with him. This 'creeping up the bed' was also fancied by some of the Chinese emperors. Curiously, if the sultan 'gave' one of his women (or a sister or daughter) in marriage to a loyal friend or favoured official, that man was expected to reverse the role so that *he* would 'creep up the bed' to his special wife.

The English writer Lady Mary Wortley Montagu visited the royal harem in the eighteenth century, and observed that Turks liked heavily built, big breasted women, who spent their days sitting cross-legged and devouring fattening foods: 'So many fine women naked in different postures . . . the lady that seemed the most considerable among them entreated me to sit by her and would fain have undressed me . . . I was at last forced to open my shirt and show them my stays, which satisfied them very well, for I saw they believed I was so locked up in that machine that it was not in my own power to open it, which contrivance they attributed to my husband.'

'Let her disappear!' need only be uttered by the sultan, and the concubine who displeased him would be taken away. If he decided to make a clean sweep of the whole harem and start afresh with a new supply of women he would command: 'Let them disappear!'

The idea of the harem has excited Europeans through the ages, and many paid large sums of money for information about 'life inside' to retired eunuchs, who were amazed to be rewarded for repeating such idle gossip which was everyday knowledge in every Turkish coffee house and bazaar.

Organising the Chinese emperor's love life was far more onerous than meeting the needs of a Turkish sultan. A group of trusted court officials had to ensure that the emperor received in his bedchamber the right wife, consort or concubine on the right day and in the correct order. Such skilful planning was needed so that the empress herself was received when the emperor's *yang* life force had been built to a maximum head of steam by reaction to the *yin* charms deployed in love-making by the lower ranking wives and concubines. With hundreds, and sometimes thousands, of ladies waiting for the royal summons, the officials in charge of the emperor's bedchamber programme were in a constant state of harassment and frequent panic. Not only were they responsible for getting the right girl to the emperor on time, they also had to make records of her menstrual periods, signs of pregnancy, and the time, date and duration of her visit to the royal bedchamber. On some occasions, ladies who had recently slept with the emperor had their bodies rubber-stamped to avoid substitution or getting another turn ahead of schedule. The rubber-stamp 'ink' was indelible for several weeks.

The love life of Chinese men in those polygamous times could be so demanding that many men fled to the green bowers (elegant houses staffed by hostesses) not for sexual attachments, but to escape from them.

---♡---

When Saudi Arabia's King Fahd goes on vacation he crams two jumbo jets and five smaller Boeings with friends, sons, princesses, bodyguards, and six or more bullet-proof motor cars. His own aircraft has marble bathrooms attached to the bedrooms, and near the master bedroom is an intensive-care unit which is linked at all times by satellite to leading medical specialists around the world.

If he prefers to rock the boat instead of taking flight the king has his 7,000 ton, £30 million yacht called Abdul Aziz (named after himself). Here the master bedroom is horseshoe-shaped with walls draped in fabric woven from gold thread. Mirrors cover the ceiling above the king-size bed.

But when Paul Kendrick arrived in Saudi Arabia from Wiltshire to sell beds to the king's subjects, brochures showing his products were seized by Saudi customs officers, who objected to the photographs of a well proportioned model clad in a nightdress and holding a teddy bear, because her face was not hidden by a veil.

===♡===

PASSING THE BUCK

In the first chapter I described how Pulaya women of southern India return to working in the fields shortly after the birth of their baby, while the husband goes to bed to recover, and that Andaman husbands may stay there for up to six months. This custom of paternal convalescence is called *couvade*, which is an old French word for 'brooding' or 'hatching'.

Couvade exists in many forms, but in most cases the husband takes to his bed. Some are given specially attractive and easily digestible food, others sit up in bed to receive the congratulations of relatives and friends. Some who really 'suffer' will groan and simulate labour pains. Cases have been reported from Asia, Africa, North and South America, and in island communities in the Pacific and Indian Oceans.

The Arapesh live in the steep mountains of New Guinea. Morning sickness is unknown to them, but after a baby is born, the father lies down beside his wife and everyone says he is 'in bed having a baby'. He stays beside his wife for five days, during which he must use a stick but never his fingers if he wishes to scratch himself. The infant is given a name immediately it laughs up into its father's face.

A Nayadi father in Cochin, India, gives up heavy work several weeks before his wife gives birth, then spends the next few days shampooing the hairs on his abdomen.

In 1984 a book called *Fatherhood* was published in Britain, but sadly the author Brian Jackson did not live to see the impact it made on expectant fathers. While he was researching the book Mr. Jackson found that little research had been done on fatherhood, and libraries and book indexes merely advised 'for fathers, see mothers'. According to Mr. Jackson one expectant British father in two suffers from the male *couvade* in the form of sympathetic birth pangs.

In some Catalonian clinics in Spain a husband is given a bed in his wife's room, and can rest there when the anguish of childbirth overcomes him. In East Anglia *couvade* pains often attacked the expectant father's teeth, a point documented in one edition of *Encyclopædia Britannica*, while an article in *Folk Lore* published in 1918 described how Winifred B.'s husband received a 'transfer' for life of his pregnant wife's haemorrhoids. She was never again afflicted.

At the end of last century readers wrote in to *Notes and Queries* with details of fathers (human) suckling their young, till the editor had to announce that 'further discussion is not invited'. At the same time it was believed in parts of Scotland that whoever rose first from the bridal bed would suffer the pains of childbirth when the babies arrived.

On October 2 1977 an article in the *Sunday Times* referred to some British men who take the Pill (for birth control) at the same time as their wives or girlfriends do 'just to be on the safe side'.

As late as 1726 the leading obstetricians in England were sympathising with a lady in Godalming, Surrey, who had, apparently, given birth to rabbits. The Court Anatomist, Mr. Nathaniel St. André, was sent by King George I and Queen Caroline to investigate. He arrived in time to find Mary Toft in labour, and had the alarming experience of delivering the fifteenth and sixteenth rabbit-babies himself. Though this is not a perfect case of *couvade*, Mr. St. André nevertheless felt a great sense of sympathetic responsibility for his patient, and suffered considerable discomfiture and embarrassment as a result. After examining the two conies he was convinced that Mrs. Toft had undergone a miraculous conception.

A baffled king then despatched Sir Richard Manningham, Kt., Fellow of the Royal Society and of the College of Physicians, to accompany Mr. St. André on another visit to Mrs. Toft. They brought her up to London though 'she was still big with a Rabbit', but under stern questioning she confessed that she had bought the rabbits: how they managed to be 'born' and how poor Mr. St. André was hoodwinked disappeared under a mass of technical language, but Sir Richard's account of the whole case became a best-seller in its day.

─────────────────── ♡ ───────────────────

THE FRENCH IN BED

As one might expect, the French have novel ways of using beds. It used to be customary to receive important guests in bed: Madame de Montespan, for one, accepted congratulations for her niece's nuptials from her own bed, though Madame de Maintenon went one better by inviting her niece to join her in bed where they both received congratulations on the niece's marriage. The Tsar of Russia was judged uncouth not because he entered Madame de Maintenon's bedroom without knocking, but because he opened the bed-clothes before opening the conversation.

On another occasion when Madame de Maintenon received the French king in her bedchamber she used to beckon him to go to a private corner, where a stool was in readiness and sometimes 'honoured by his contact'.

Mirrors above the bed were very popular at the time, but many were replaced by drapes decorated with naughty paintings after a Monsieur de Calonne – who was rarely to be found in his own bed – narrowly escaped vivisection when a large mirror dropped on to a bed he happened to be sharing.

When Cardinal Richelieu arranged the marriage between Charles I and Henrietta of France, such were the complexities concerning the protocol of which ambassador should walk where and beside whom that the cardinal took to his bed, and received them there.

The *lit de parade* was at its most glorious when the king got out of bed each morning. At *le petit lever* only intimate guests and friends were invited to watch, but at *le grand lever* (which involved a lot of getting in and out of bed) the guests were assembled for a more formal event.

People genuflected towards the royal bed even when it was empty. Many royal beds were surrounded by balustrades to keep dogs at bay, though it was a popular practice in Imperial France to have puppies trained as foot warmers.

In 1677 the extraordinary French law known as the *congrès* was repealed. *Congrès* was 'the practice of coitus ordered by decree of an ecclesiastical judge, performed in the presence of surgeons and matrons, to discover whether or not a man is potent, with a view to dissolving a marriage'. Couples were required to perform on a bed while the panel of 'judges' waited nearby on the other side of the curtains for the performance to begin. Even the most ardent lover in the world ran the risk of dying of shame.

On the eve of the Feast of Holy Innocents on 28 December Frenchmen had the right to slap female members of the household on the buttocks. In rural France there are still instances in which women choose to sit up all night rather than run the risk of being touched by their husbands.

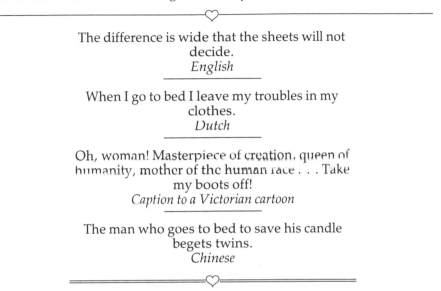

The difference is wide that the sheets will not decide.
English

When I go to bed I leave my troubles in my clothes.
Dutch

Oh, woman! Masterpiece of creation, queen of humanity, mother of the human race . . . Take my boots off!
Caption to a Victorian cartoon

The man who goes to bed to save his candle begets twins.
Chinese

RECORDS

The largest functional bed is 12 ft 6 in wide and 19 ft long, built for Philip Duke of Burgundy and Princess Isabella of Portugal in 1430.

Fakirs have lain on beds of nails for long periods, many of them unrecorded. The *Guinness Book of Records* gives 111 days as the longest, a record set in Brazil in 1969. Though the man responsible for this is not Mr. Vernon E. Craig of Wooster in Ohio, Mr. Craig nevertheless achieved something equally breathtaking: he once supported two men weighing a total of 58 stone on his chest while he lay on a bed of nails.

For anyone in a desperate hurry to make the bed before leaping between the sheets, the bed-making record to beat is 28.2 seconds, the time taken by Australian Wendy Hall in 1978. The leap cannot take place till an undersheet, two sheets, one blanket, an uncased pillow and a counterpane are in place. The average housewife in America walks four miles and spends 25 hours every year making and remaking *one* bed, revealed the United States Department of Agriculture in 1949. This would mean that in a family of four a mother would wear out a pair of shoes each year purely in the course of carrying out this chore.

SNORERS

Presidents Roosevelt, Lincoln and Washington, Beau Brummell, the biographer Plutarch, World War II Italian chief Mussolini, George II, my father, my husband and my father-in-law are, or were, all snorers. To date none can equal the world record for the loudest snore emitted in 1984 when Melvyn Switzer knocked up 87.5 decibels at Hever Castle in Kent. Switzer's snoring is louder than some pneumatic drills, and his wife is deaf in one ear.

With one person in eight in the world snoring (most are men), the consequences of this anti-social behaviour are widespread and far-flung. In Australia, for instance, doctors have announced that habitual snorers are more likely to suffer heart disease and high blood pressure. In Sydney Professor Nicholas Saunders has shown that snoring can adversely affect sexual performance, especially among men in their forties. The Dutch company Philips, though, attribute indifferent sex lives to bad lighting, but then they would: Philips manufacture light bulbs.

People all over the world have cures for snoring. The French doctor Louis Guyon wrote about gargling with hot vinegar fifteen minutes before retiring, while some Indians tell their children to sleep with their mouths shut to stop snoring now and in the after-life.

A letter to *The Times* from a clergyman called Prichard described the benefits of dropping pellets of soap into the offending mouth, mentioning that not only was this 'most reliable at Sherborne forty-five years ago', but 'further treatment was seldom needed'.

At the turn of this century all efforts were directed towards preventing the snorer from turning on to his back. A popular practice was to attach a ball to the back of the sleeper's pyjamas. If compressed the ball was guaranteed to emit a squeak louder than a snore. Another gadget was a leather thong, which would be attached at one end to the man's upper arm while the other was tied to a bed post, thereby preventing him from turning over on to his back.

Modern remedies are different, though who can say if they are more efficient except the snorer or the listener? The man shot in Dallas, Texas by the wife he was keeping awake might have preferred the old-fashioned methods, but Dr. David Fairbanks of Washington DC says that snoring not only breaks up marriages, but that it can also be fatal. In the words of Dr. Fairbanks: 'The most exaggerated form of snoring is obstructive sleep apnea, when loud snoring is interrupted by frequent episodes of totally obstructed breathing,' by which he means some snorers stop breathing! Some apnea sufferers 'experience 30 to 300 obstructed events a night and many spend as much as half of their sleep with blood oxygen levels below normal. This is serious if these episodes last more than ten seconds each . . . and can lead to elevated blood pressure and heart enlargement'. Dr. Fairbanks believes he can cure snoring by an operation, and many of his patients think this is the greatest thing that has happened to them since sliced bread, Band-aids or Aspros.

On the other side of the Atlantic Mr. Leslie Gamble of Tow Law in County Durham often wanders across the moors in the dead of night while everyone else sleeps. Since an accident in 1970 he has been unable to sleep, and his wife Ruth says that 'sometimes he has been so tired he has snored while we were walking along the street'. Perhaps a new British cure will help him: a gas mask is being developed to aid snorers, and there is hope that a bad sufferer will make twenty-three snorts a night instead of his usual 1,000.

Peter Rudd is one man who thinks snoring ought to be encouraged. He is the manager of the Hotel Nelson in Norwich, where he organised a Snore-away weekend with prizes for the loudest snorers: any guest who could be heard from the hotel car park got his bill cut in half while the top snorer received a golden clothes-peg. All snoring guests were given a prize: free trips to the nearby villages of Great Snoring and Little Snoring.

---♡---

SINGLE OR DOUBLE

The French novelist Honoré de Balzac agreed with Napoleon that 'twin beds are a menace to conjugal happiness and that they should only be resorted to by couples who have been married for at least twenty years, and who suffer from catarrh'. Balzac was also highly suspicious of sofas and divans, which he saw as temptations to adultery.

♡

One sleeps better than two
For two together all night
Means suffering, freezing and fright.
One coughs, one talks.
One's cold, one's hot,
One wanting to sleep, and the other one not.
Oh, one sleeps better than two!
Old French song

♡

Shared bed – severed hearts.
German saying

♡

There is not 'anything in nature which is more immediately calculated totally to subvert health, strength, love, esteem, and indeed every thing that is desirable in the married state, than that odious, most indelicate, and most hurtful custom of man and wife continually pigging together, in one and the same bed . . . to sleep, and snore, and steam, and do everything else that's indelicate together, three hundred and sixty-five times – every year'.

Dr. James Graham, inventor of the Grand Celestial State Bed (See page 183)

♡

In July 1948 Ilka Chase wrote in *Esquire* magazine in America that single beds were like 'self-imposed exile . . . a folly for which there can be no praise'. Single beds should only be found in hospitals, prisons and lunatic asylums, and fifty per cent of their inhabitants, the article argued, would not be there if they had not used twin beds at home.

♡

In 1961 a director of the American Family Relations Institute said: 'This movement towards twin beds must stop. It was started by furniture dealers who make twice as much money selling two beds instead of one. The change from a double bed to twin beds is often the prelude to a divorce.'

♡

In February 1975 Lady Reading claimed against the suppliers of her four-poster bed for causing a squeak in the bed. The squeak had apparently not been there before the company cut the bed in half to get it upstairs in Cadogan Place in south-west London. Lady Reading said that £250 was the amount required to have the squeak eliminated. She lost the case.

Professor John Fremlin has a theory that togetherness in one bed means a longer life, but this does not work if a couple sleeps too close to each other. The professor, a nuclear scientist, said in March 1984 that everyone has 100 grammes of radioactive potassium in their bodies which can help reduce the risk of cancer. When couples sleep together the chemical starts its magic. But if they get too close in a single bed, for instance, the energy flow between their bodies gets blocked.

The answer is evidently togetherness in a double bed.

When asked what chubby Italian singer Renata would have to say about Fremlin's theories, his agent replied: 'Renata has to sleep in a double bed because there isn't a single bed that will take him.' Renata's singing partner, Renee, added: 'On cold nights I like to share a double bed with someone, and if I'm saving their life at the same time that makes me feel even better.'

♡

Ashurbanipal was the last king of Assyria. When he decided to take his life he ordered the simultaneous burning of all his beds and each was to be occupied by his wife and concubines. None of the beds was a single; all 150 were king-sized.

♡

IRRESISTIBLE BEDS

Colombian law prohibits people from being arrested while in bed in their own homes. Some citizens never move far from their beds and stay dressed in pyjamas ready to pop under the bed-clothes in an emergency.

♡

Mrs. Hallock of Elmira in New York received a message from a spirit commanding her to stay in bed for ten years. From her bed she continued to run a farm, and after the term expired she got up but received another message to return to bed, an order she obeyed. She stayed there for the rest of her life.

♡

A hunter's bed is vitally important in some communities. If a hunter in parts of east Africa learns that his wife has been unfaithful on their bed he will give up an elephant hunt, believing that her infidelity gives the advantage to the elephant. The Moxos Indians of Bolivia say that if a man is bitten by a snake or a jaguar his wife has found a lover.

♡

At English medieval marriage ceremonies it was sometimes the custom for the wife to swear: 'I take thee, X, to be my wedded husband, to have and to hold, from this day forward, for better, for worse, for richer, for poorer, in sickness and health, to be bonny and buxom in bed and at board, till death do us part.' Many wives also signed letters to absent husbands: 'Your servant and bedswoman.'

♡

With tiny houses packed with three generations of grandparents, parents and children, young Cuban married couples frequently escape the family hubbub by renting rooms by the hour in government hotels. The price includes tots of rum.

♡

The naughty weekend in Brighton has been a favourite joke of British comedians for generations, but the weekends got official promotion from the English Tourist Board in the winter of 1983. Put to the test and asked to provide accommodation for 'a very famous man and his fancy woman' the staid Imperial Hotel announced it could provide masks, moustaches and wigs to avoid the possibility of recognition.

♡

Sleeping on trains in comfort has presented countless problems to the British traveller. Couples who booked the Honeymoon Compartment of the London–Chatham–Dover train found that there was no bed. Passengers in the Great Northern's sleeping car a century ago would have had to be lucky to avoid the three out of four beds which were attached to a door, especially if it were the bed hinged to the lavatory door. The unlucky occupier of this had to vacate the bed each time someone wanted to use the lavatory.

At London's St. Pancras station tickets were issued with warnings printed on the back that passengers must not retire with their boots on. Most English travellers were afraid to travel lying down in any case, and American visitors reported back home that there was no difficulty getting a berth. One American traveller wrote: 'An Englishman has a horror of being pitched into eternity in his underclothes . . . and they don't know who this Pullman is.'

All this happened more than a hundred years ago. In March 1983 I took a sleeper to Glasgow from Euston and the alarm went off eighteen times before we even reached the Border; all were false, but you should have seen who popped out from under the sheets . . .

———————————————♡———————————————

A study of Manhattan families in New York showed that the average time taken by a wife to put out the light after going to bed was fourteen minutes. A husband took nineteen minutes. During these minutes most husbands and wives 'did nothing' or read. More wives than husbands prayed or listened to the radio, but more husbands ate in bed or got up to close the window.

═══════════════════════════════♡═══════════════════════════════

FREE BEDS

The Murias of central India put their love beds in *ghotuls* which are wooden huts specially built as places where young people can make love. *Ghotuls* are seen as an effective way to avoid incest in crowded family homes, and they also give parents freedom for *their* sex lives.

Easter Islanders retire to *hare nui*, which are houses for boys and girls wishing to make love with someone they fancy.

In Vanuato (the New Hebrides) a woman called an *iowhanan* visits the *imeium* where circumcised bachelors live. Her job is to initiate them in sexual relations.

Young Masai boys and girls may live in villages called *manyatta*, where most will have their first sexual experiences. A girl can marry the boy of her choice unless he is already betrothed (from childhood) to another. If she gets pregnant, she can renounce her fiancé and marry her lover from the *manyatta*.

A *bukumatula* is a house where unmarried Trobriand men and women retire to bed when they feel attracted to each other. Many prefer to make love in the forest before relaxing in the *bukumatula*, as told by this young Trobriand chieftain to the anthropologist Bronislaw Malinowski:

'When we go out on a love-making expedition, we light our fire: we take our lime gourd (and chew betel-nut), we take our tobacco (and smoke it). Food we do not take, we would be ashamed to do so. We walk, we arrive at a large tree, we sit down, we search other's heads and consume the lice, we tell the woman that we want to copulate. After it is over we return to the village. In the village we go to the bachelors' house, lie down, and chatter. When we are alone he takes off the pubic leaf, she takes off her fibre skirt: we go to sleep.'

WHAT IS A BED WORTH?

Those who valued their beds used to leave them in their wills. William Shakespeare was one: 'Item: I give unto my wife my second best bed, with furniture.' Louis XIV gave beds as gifts to his illegitimate offspring.

Sometimes the cost of a bed was considered more important than the weight of the baby born in it. In 1612 the family of the Countess of Salisbury announced that the countess was 'brought of a daughter' and that the bed and chamber hangings 'were valued at fourteen thousand pounds'.

Slumberland, a major bed-manufacturer, researched the sleeping habits of Britons in 1984 and found that the average person buys a new bed every seventeen years. Speaking for the British bed industry, Slumberland could not understand how the British could manage with such curious bed customs, and asked how many would let their car go unserviced for seventeen years or use the same toothbrush for so long?

The Times reported in May 1967 that holiday-makers who sat on bed edges cost the Yorkshire resort of Scarborough £100,000 a year. They blamed this partly on bed-manufacturers who made mattresses strongest in the middle 'where people sleep' and not on the edges 'where mattresses need greatest strength'. But, concluded the report, 'holiday-makers are not normal people'.

Those frowsy, creaky, prehistoric, wooden concerns always six or eight inches too short, whose mattresses have not been turned round since they were made. What happens? You clamber into such a receptacle and straightway roll downhill, down into its centre, into a kind of river-bed where you remain fast, while that monstrous feather-abomination called a pillow, yielding to pressure, rises up on either side of your head and engulfs eyes and nose and everything else into its folds. No escape! You are strangled, smothered; you might as well have gone to bed with an octopus. In this horrid contrivance you lie for eight long hours, clamped down like a corpse in its coffin. Every single bed in rural England ought to be burnt. Not one of them is fit for a Christian to sleep in.

Norman Douglas (novelist 1868–1952)

♡

A survey organised by *Woman* magazine in 1984 revealed that British teenagers successfully badgered their parents to buy settees to smooch on. The magazine also found that one person in a hundred in Britain prefers to make love on the stairs rather than in bed, while one in eight chose the car as the favourite love-making spot. The same survey showed that while she is making love one British woman in twenty-five imagines she is embracing a woman or a stranger.

———————————————♡———————————————

Although most Tibetans believe that the Dalai Lamas are incarnated as celibate monks, the sixth Dalai Lama certainly enjoyed an active life of amorous adventures. He had built a house with many bedrooms at the foot of the Potala in Lhasa and named it the Serpent. It was here that he made his rendezvous with the women of Lhasa whose bodies and charms he craved. He was also a mediocre poet, who celebrated his visits to the Serpent in words as well as deeds. Marion Duncan has translated one of his poems:

From the very tips of eastern mountain peaks,
There emerges the shining white brilliant moon;
The lovely face of the virginal maiden
Has revolved around and around in my mind.

═══██

BED ACCESSORIES

Enrico Caruso, the great Italian tenor, sometimes needed a bed with three mattresses and eighteen pillows.

♡

When Madame Chiang Kai-shek, wife of the Nationalist Chinese leader, was in Washington she wanted her sheets changed on her bed after each time she lay on it. Twelve times in one day was the record.

♡

Napoleon had to share Josephine's bed with her dog, which prompted this letter written to a friend: 'My rival! He was in possession of Madame's bed. I tried to put him out – vain attempt. I was told I had the choice of sleeping in another bed or sharing that one with Fortune . . . I resigned myself. The canine favourite was far less accommodating than I – of which my leg bears proof.'

♡

In the Chou dynasty more than 2,300 years ago Chinese aristocrats engaged musicians to play chamber music to get them in the mood for love. In later dynasties many emperors asked for bedchamber music to accompany their love-making. So noisy was Empress Wu Tse-tien when she made love that she ordered a band consisting of gongs, cymbals and drums to play ear-splitting sounds throughout.

So insatiable was Princess Shan-yin of the Sung dynasty that her bed needed 100 legs to support her and the thirty men who used to share her bed at the same time.

♡

The Maharajah of Baroda had a bed specially built to fit around the contours of his corpulent body.

♡

Clients of the Everleigh mansion, a brothel in Chicago at the turn of this century, could choose which perfume they wished to be enveloped in by the automatic sprayers mounted over each bed.

♡

Much has been written about the Grand Celestial State Bed, a creation of the Scottish Dr James Graham in 1778. The bed could be rented at the Adelphi in the Strand, London at £50 a night, and anyone paying this fee was assured of an unforgettable night of stimulating experiences to improve his sexual vigour. The apparatus installed in the Celestial Bed included magnets, electrical fires (in the bedhead), harmonica, flute and vocal effects alternating with organ peals, live turtle doves cooing above, silk sheets selected to match the complexion of the client's loved one, and all the air around was alive with the scent of fresh flowers. Even the angle of the bed could be adjusted and 'converted by the gentleman into such an inclined plane, as that he can follow his lady downhill, as it is called, which is certainly the most favourable posture for the great business of conception'. The organ could be relied upon to peal loudly in the event of 'violent motion in the bed'. The whole experience was presided over by Emma Lyon, who later became Lady Hamilton and the mistress of Lord Nelson.

♡

Early this century the Longford Wire Company of Warrington, Lancashire, advertised a bed:

'Guaranteed for 5 years. On exhibit at Liverpool, Manchester and other cities CARRYING ONE TON.'

In 1947 Elliott White Springs shocked Americans with an advertisement for their Springs sheets, which showed an Indian couple on a sheet and the caption:

'A buck well spent on a Springmaid sheet.'

The Roman poet Juvenal wrote about the problem of a wife in bed: 'The bed that holds a wife is never free from wrangling and mutual bickerings; no sleep is to be got there! It is there that she sets upon her husband, more savage than a tigress that has lost her cubs. Conscious of her own secret slips, she affects a grievance, abusing her slaves, or weeps over an imagined mistress.' The poet had a solution to the problem: 'How much better to take some boy-bedfellow, who would never wrangle with you, never ask presents of you when in bed, and never complain that you took your ease and were indifferent to his solicitations.'

BED PESTS

The English poet and preacher John Donne had words of praise for a flea whose 'jet walls' contained the blood of both himself and his mistress and was therefore a living pledge of amorous unity.

♡

Such is their love of all living things that truly devout Jains of India will lie on beds in special houses so that bed bugs may receive the blood of life.

♡

An Italian machine is claimed to keep mosquitoes away from the bedside by emitting the love call of the male mosquito. Only female mosquitoes bite and they prefer to suck blood uninterrupted by copulation, so when they hear an amorous male nearby, they seek another bed with an unsuspecting sleeper to attack.

♡

Some old wives' tales actually work. The 'old wife' responsible for writing the medieval book *The Goodman of Paris* (*Le Ménager de Paris*) appeared to have inside knowledge of Keeping Husbands Free of Fleas and Flies in the Bedroom. The author included these three methods:

1. Put milk and a hare's gall into a bowl; the flies like the taste, but will die.
2. Smear slices of bread with glue or turpentine and stand a lighted candle in each; the pests will stick to the bread.
3. Put the juice of braised onions beside his pillow.

The belief was that no husband would ever want to leave a woman who watched over his welfare so well.

———————◇———————

ALARMS

Though modern lovers may curse the sound of the alarm clock ringing in their ears, early alarms seem to have been specially arranged to make love, if not always the lover, fly out the window. Joseph Tich of Vienna devised a clock that sounded the alarm with a charge of gunpowder. It is believed that Casanova used one of these.

Clock fanciers tell of an early alarm clock in the form of a vessel perched over the sleeper's face, into which drops of water fell and would overflow at the appropriate hour. To combat the in English industrial towns in the eighteenth century knockers would bang on doors for a small fee. If neighbours objected the knockers could be persuaded to tug on a length of thread which dangled out of windows; at the other end of the thread would be someone's toe.

Mr. R. W. Savage produced his alarm in 1851. His contraption could be relied upon to pull off the bedclothes if the sleeper ignored a bell. If this failed, the mattress slowly tilted and would tip the sleeper on to the floor. A few years later a similar alarm appeared in Germany, which would also pull off a night-cap, then thrust a notice saying 'Time to get up' in the face of the sleeper.

American alarms were quite as unromantic. An advertisement in *Daily Wants* in 1858 showed an alarm, accompanied by a warning against waking a sleeper suddenly. Such action could cause serious injury to the brain and the nervous system and 'dangerous, if not fatal effects, have resulted from the mental terror' of a loud noise. The advertiser suggested that if people did not buy his alarm they should burn feathers under the nostrils of the sleeping-one, and never, never shout except in cases of coma or apoplexy.

So how long should people sleep? According to an old English poem lovers need more than anyone else:

Six for a man,
Seven for a woman,
Eight for a fool.
Nature requires five,
Custom takes seven,
Laziness nine,
And lust eleven.

When Emperor Ai Di of China found that the boy he loved had fallen asleep on his sleeve, rather than disturb him he ordered that his sleeve be cut off with a sword. The Chinese expression for 'cut sleeve' is synonymous with 'homosexuality'.

It is also believed that the prophet Mohammed offered his sleeve as a bed to a sleeping cat, and that he too had the sleeve cut away so that he could leave without awakening the pet.

In past ages it was sometimes customary to share one's bed with strangers. The diarist Samuel Pepys shared a bedroom with his wife and maid, but Lord Alexander objected to the idea while on a visit to the Russian Marshal Tolbukhin's headquarters in Hungary in 1945. When it was suggested that a female valet should sleep on a couch in his room, the good lord commented: 'I didn't think that was quite the thing, and she spent the night outside the door.' In some hotels in the Balkans beds, not rooms, are let for the night, so there is always the chance of having to share a room with strangers.

The favourite wife of a high-caste Brahmin-Chetri in Nepal sleeps on a mattress at the foot of her husband's bed, while older or unpopular wives are given their own rooms. The husband has no problems about the choice of a bed: he sleeps in the one that his newest wife has brought as part of her dowry.

Norwegian beds used to be shorter than most beds because it was thought that lying flat was a sure way of inviting death to join the occupant in bed. The idea persists in a few outlying secluded

forest areas of Norway, though it is unlikely that
anyone would spend the whole night sitting up
in bed, as their early Norse ancestors did.

———————————————♡———————————————

Marriage is the result of the longing for the
deep, deep peace of the double bed after the
hurly-burly of the chaise-longue.
Mrs. Patrick Campbell

There are so many ways on this very longue
chaise.
Elsa Lanchester

Asked to comment on modern petting, Dr. Billy
Graham said that London's public parks 'had
been turned into bedrooms, with people lying all
over the place'.

═══════════════════♡═══════════════════

BEDSIDE COMPANIONS

Alexander II, the Tsar who abolished serfdom in 1866, found love in the
Winter Palace with Princess Catherine Dolgoruky. When he died in a bomb
blast his finger was found and given to the princess, who kept it in a glass
case beside her bed. She took it to Nice, where she died. The finger is in the
Russian cathedral there.

St. Simeon Stylites gets mentioned in most books of records for the time he
spent sitting on top of a sixty foot pillar (thirty years). Less known is his
fanatical quest to acquire spiritual goodness by tying a rope so tightly round
his waist that a maggot-infested putrefaction developed. Worms fell into his
bed, and in a form of grace before eating them he said: 'Eat what God has
given you!'

When Peter I of Russia suspected that his wife Catherine had a lover he
had William Mons beheaded in front of her. Then he had the head pickled
and placed at her bedside, but she continued to deny that Mons had been
her lover.

Isabella, Duchess of Bracciano, was embraced by her lover Paolo in 1577.
Then he took a noosed cord that had been lowered by his attendant from the
room above through a little hole in the ceiling, and strangled her. The cord
was raised and removed, but the small hole is still visible in the castle of
Bracciano today.

♡

Venus looks so lovely asleep and is an example
to women who forget it is important to look
beautiful in bed. Curlers, face creams, chin

straps, and scowlies are nails in the coffin of
marriage and effective antidotes to love.
Barbara Cartland

I don't mind seeing a child's lost tooth in a glass
of water by the bed or under the pillow waiting
for the tooth fairy to come. But I can't stand the
sight of a grown-up's gnashers beside the bed
lamp.
Author's mother

———————————♡———————————

NOR' NOR' SOUTH

To some people sleep can only be good if their feet are pointing in a particular direction. There is a popular Moslem saying:

Lying upon the right side is
    proper to Kings,
Upon the left to Sages.
To sleep supine is the position
    of the Saints
But flat on the belly is the way
    to the Devil.

Dr. Marie Stopes, who advocated birth control and shocked the English in the years immediately after World War I, announced that sex could be fun if beds were facing north–south to be 'in tune with magnetic currents'. Hindus disagree, preferring an east–west position.

Some English physicians early this century thought that sleeping on one's belly aggravated digestion, and that unless the head was held high by pillows any meat left undigested in the stomach would, through eructations, ascend to the top of the stomach. Others, more concerned with the effects on love-making, declared that women who loved their husbands favoured their right side for sleeping on, and that lying on the back induced nightmares and, more dangerously, talking in one's sleep.

Charles Dickens, an insomniac, could only get a good night's rest if he lay with his head facing north, for which purpose he carried a pocket compass.

More up-to-date is the Foundations of Manhattan Survey, a study of families which revealed that of those questioned fourteen per cent slept with their heads at the foot of the bed, while thirty-one per cent said they did so sometimes.

——————————♡——————————

Mangaian men of Polynesia like
women with huge hips, which are
best for rotating in *hula* dancing.
They describe a woman with especially big hips as 'a bed with a good
mattress'.

——————————♡——————————

188

THE ART OF LYING IN BED

Many famous people have stayed in bed, preferring work to making love: Alexander the Great, the kings of France, writers Milton, Swift, Rousseau, Voltaire, Gray, Pope, Trollope, Proust, Edith Sitwell, and Wordsworth; Winston Churchill; composers Glinka and Rossini; artists Salvador Dali, Matisse and William Morris to name but some.

Mark Twain also wrote in bed, but warned against the danger of too much lying there since it is the place where most people die. G. K. Chesterton wrote about the 'great art of lying in bed: if you do lie in bed, be sure you do it without any reason or justification at all. I do not speak, of course, of the seriously sick. But if a healthy man lies in bed, let him do it without a rag of excuse; then he will get up a healthy man. If he does it for some secondary hygienic reason, if he has some scientific explanation, he may get up a hypochondriac.'

My Chinese father also had something to say about being in bed: 'Lying in bed is better than lying in the bath for thinking. The water does not get cold.'

BUNDLES OF FUN

Amorous but unmarried couples used to go to bed together and practise bundling, which meant that either the girl was clothed in garments which prevented her from making love, or the couple would be separated by a bolster or a wooden board over which neither was permitted to climb on to the other's side of the bed. In desperate cases where it was thought that self-control would not prevail, both measures were taken.

Bundling was quite widespread till the turn of this century in Europe, the eastern colonies of North America, and in Afghanistan. Often the girl's ankles, calves and thighs were tied together, or her lower regions were protected with tight-fitting garments or layers of impenetrable petticoats. In Ireland tying tight clothes with a special knot was referred to as 'the knot that cannot slide', while in Wales bundling stockings resembling single-legged pyjamas were worn by the girl from the waist down. In France it was common for the girl's parents to attach bells to the legs of the bed so that they would ring if the action above became too hectic.

The custom began in poor rural communities, where it was more economic for families to huddle together for warmth than buy firewood. Even this century many cases of bundling have been reported. Between the two World Wars there were instances in Lewis in the Outer Hebrides of girls' legs being inserted into large stockings which the mothers tied above the knees. In 1941 the *Daily Mail* reported that in the Orkneys girls' legs were tied by 'a special, traditional, and very complicated knot', and in 1910 the English writer Havelock Ellis (who studied the sexual behaviour of humans) noted that in Norway the girls who bundled wore extra skirts, hardly effective one would have thought for 'the prevention of liberties'.

Similar practices have been described in Spain where, for instance, the girls sent to watch over the cattle receive their suitors in mountain huts and 'protect' themselves by bundles of blankets or by wrapping their legs in cotton sheets.

The Kikuyu of Kenya also practise this form of love-play, calling it *ngweko*, or 'caressing'. Jomo Kenyatta, who became president of Kenya in 1964, provides the following account:

> 'Girls may visit the *Thingira* (hut) at any time, day or night. After eating, while engaged in conversation with the girls, one of the boys turns the talk dramatically to the subject of *ngweko*. If there are more boys than girls, the girls are asked to select whom they prefer as companion . . . After the partners have been arranged, one of the boys gets up, saying: "I am going to stretch myself." His girl-partner follows him to the bed. The boy removes all his clothing. The girl removes her upper garments and retains her skirt and her soft leather apron, which she pulls back between her legs and tucks in together with her leather skirt. The two V-shaped tails of her leather skirt are pulled forward between her legs from behind and fastened at the waist, thus keeping the soft leather apron in position and forming an effective protection of her private parts. In this position the lovers lie together, facing each other with their legs interwoven to prevent any movement of their hips. They then begin to fondle each other, rubbing their breasts together, whilst at the same time they engage in love-making conversation until they gradually fall asleep. Sometimes the partners experience sexual relief, but this is not an essential feature of the *ngweko*. The chief concern in this relationship is enjoyment of the warmth of the breast and not the full experience of sexual intercourse.'

---♡---

As you make your bed you must lie on it.
*English saying meaning 'everyone must bear the
consequences of his or her own acts'*

When you have made your bed everyone wants
to lie on it.
Russian

190

Early to bed, early to rise
Makes a man healthy, wealthy and wise.
English

Early to bed, early to rise
Ain't never so good if you don't advertise.
American

Early to bed, early to rise
Makes a man surly and gives him red eyes.
Qatar saying

Those who are early up and have no business,
have either an ill wife, an ill bed, or an ill
conscience.
Scottish

Love motels are popular in Brazil, with most bedrooms accessible by driving right up to the door. A serious treatise has been written about Brazil's love motels by Lauro Cavalcanti, who sees a similarity between a car penetrating the inner recesses of a motel and the sex act.

Japanese love motels are situated mostly near motorway exits near the cities. Some have extraordinary architecture: scenes from Disneyland, halls of mirrors, onion domes copied from the Kremlin, and one called the Queen Elizabeth, which is more like the ship than the British monarch.

Municipal authorities in Japan are trying to curb further expansion of the love motels by banning double beds, but some couples simply find small, single beds even more exciting than a king or queen sized model.

With typical candour and lack of prudery, Japanese motoring magazines describe, with drawings, the best love-making positions to adopt for the greatest satisfaction within the limited space in a car. And the reports are thorough, too; all the popular car makes and models are discussed in separate reports.

CHAPTER TEN
VOWS, OATHS AND CURSES

For better or for worse, for richer or for poorer, most people get married. But love and marriage do not always go together like a horse and carriage, despite the words of the song.

I include examples of marriage from around the world. You may decide that you are better off as you are – single, married, separated, widowed or divorced – after reading about people in other lands. On the other hand there may be a system of matrimony on the other side of the world which appeals to you. Like a bird you might choose to migrate.

Before they marry the Yapese of Yap, an island in the Pacific, make love in a manner called the *gichigich*, which is so frenzied that the women become weak and helpless, experiencing a multiple series of orgasms so hectic that they are unable to prevent themselves from urinating. The men feel that they are on fire. The climax comes when the woman puts her finger in the man's ear. All this stops after marriage, when the 'usual' missionary position is adopted, but while the couple practise the *gichigich*, the frequency of love-making is one of the lowest in the world – not more than once or twice a month – after which they need time to recover before the next energetic encounter.

'I DO'

For her wedding day, a Galla bride of Ethiopia stiffens her hair with butter and rubs her body with civet, causing it to smell like the cat house at the zoo. The wedding ceremony begins when the bridegroom climbs into the bride's lap and sits there while a mixture of butter and honey is poured over them.

As part of a Moslem marriage ceremony in Indonesia the couple throw betel leaves at each other. As she moves the bride will sometimes pray to Allah, asking him to turn her into a snake if her husband has had sexual relations with other women before his marriage.

♡

In the Arabian desert in Sharjah, a plump bride is greeted with 'God be praised, you have become very fat' by the admiring guests. At the feast which follows, everyone chants: 'Allah, Allah, you have made roast meat of my heart!'

♡

It is very rare to hear the word 'love' mentioned at a Chinese wedding, for much more precious to the Chinese are good luck, good health, having a lot of children (boys are much preferred), and wishing someone a long life.

According to the Chinese there are two ways of finding out who will outlive the other. The first is for the newly-married couple to light candles in the bridal chamber on their wedding night: the one who outlives the other is the one whose candle burns longer. Another way is to see who has a mole on a particular part of the face.

FEMALE

MALE

If a woman has a mole here she will live longer than her husband.

If a man has a mole here, he will live longer than his wife.

In the unlikely event that both have this mole they can expect to quit this life together.

♡

In Niger the Wodaabe men who dance well succeed best with women. They decorate their faces and roll their eyes and smile broadly to show off their dazzling white teeth. An especially good-looking man is greeted with shouts of 'Yeehoo!' by the women, then, like prima ballerinas, they dance on tip-toe, working themselves and the watching women into a frenzy.

Couples pair off for a night of love, then the beauty parade and dancing continue next day. Most of the liaisons are ephemeral with a new partner each day. The festival lasts a week, then the nomadic Wodaabes disperse until it is time for the next festival after the next rainy season.

♡

A Dinka man has to have style when bidding for a bride on the east bank of the White Nile. The most successful is the one whose charcoal-black skin shines in the sunlight, who is tall and slender, and whose head of hair is made paler by dyeing it with cows' urine. Before choosing a wife a Dinka man watches the eligible girls dance. They giggle and shuffle their feet, their bracelets jangling on wrists and ankles as they sway and jerk their thighs suggestively backwards and forwards in a simulation of love-making. When he likes the look of a girl, the Dinka man thrusts his loins forward, and joins her in the dance.

♡

The world's most frosty wedding was celebrated in the ice when Randall Chambers and Patricia Manuel said 'I do' in an outdoor ceremony at the South Pole on 11 February 1985. The couple, who met while working for the United States Operation Deep Freeze Antarctic programme, were married by an American Navy chaplain in a temperature of −45 Celsius (−49 Fahrenheit).

♡

The very moment a Kamchadal man of Siberia touches the naked private parts of a woman, they are considered man and wife. If a man fancies a particular woman who is not attracted to him he may try to touch her even while she is fully clothed, and he will feel he is engaged to her. In such cases, her women friends will surround and protect her, and there are some men who have been trying for a little touch for years: all they get are bruises.

♡

In China, marriage certificates are printed on red paper, the traditional colour for good fortune. In some provinces a message on the back of the certificate reads: 'Practise thrift, frugality and birth control.'

Not all Chinese brides want to marry in red garments, as their ancestors did. After leaving the marriage office many go straight to a photographer's studio, where the bride can change into a white, Western-style wedding dress and her husband can choose a Western-cut suit. Photographs in the studio's display case show that nine out of ten brides choose the same dress. Only the smile is different. (See page 68.)

Less than a fifth of China's population of one billion live in the cities, and a

194

country bride would certainly not choose to wear a white gown. To her, and most Chinese, white is the colour of mourning worn at funerals.

♡

At the marriage ceremony of the Santal tribe in Bihar in north-east India, a few drops of blood are taken from the bride and groom and mixed together. The husband puts a little on his wife's forehead, and the rest is added to milk and water, which the couple drink. With these acts the couple swear eternal union.

In the dense jungle along the banks of the Amazon, all the guests at an Urubu wedding are encouraged to get drunk on a potent drink made from manioc, but the bride and groom cannot join in the fun. Instead, they follow their chieftain's instructions to 'make a lot of children', and spend as many nights as possible making love constantly in the groom's hut. The record to aim for is ten nights – without sleep, of course.

♡

♡

Breaking objects and making a lot of noise are ways of keeping away evil spirits and bringing luck to a newly married couple.

Eggs are thrown and smashed underfoot to the accompaniment of much shouting in Morocco, Iran and Java, while in west Africa, women of the Ishi-speaking peoples often run around nude at weddings except for two hens' eggs fastened above their pudenda. Armenians chuck a plant on the ground and squash it by jumping on it and shouting their joy. To noisy encouragement from the wedding guests, Zulu brides in Africa throw spears while Yukaghir bridegrooms in Siberia take aim with their arrows in the direction of imaginary demons' eyes.

Gypsies in Turkey, Germany and the Basque regions of France and Spain delight in smashing dishes. Spanish gypsies hurl theirs in the direction of the sun; French gypsies

shatter a special clay vessel and believe that the broken fragments represent the number of years the couple will stay together. If, at the end of that period, the pair are still living with each other the chances are they will break another dish and start counting all over again. German gypsies and some rural families in Germany and Switzerland keep their crockery-hurling for the wedding eve party.

Americans hold charivaris (or shivarees, as they are sometimes spelt), when guests are expected to make a din with kettles, pans and bells late at night outside the home of the newly-weds.

The Moroccans can probably claim the record for the noisiest celebrations, for it is a custom to hire musicians who will make a lot of noise, but if this is too restrained, members of the groom's family will probably fire their guns.

♡

The highlight of the wedding night festivities for many families in Kuwait is for the members of the family to crowd together in a room next to the bridal chamber and listen to the sounds coming through the wall.

It takes longer in some countries than others to consummate a marriage. On the Loango coast in Congo-Brazzaville, for example, the couple have to confess their sins to each other during the marriage ceremony. Failure to do this means illnesses galore will follow.

THE FOURTH FINGER

Almost everyone who wears a wedding ring chooses to put it on the fourth finger. In some countries – Germany, Russia and Poland for instance – the right hand is preferred, but not many people today know why the fourth finger is number one favourite.

The ancient Chinese and Egyptians found a link from the fourth finger of each hand that went directly to the heart: the Egyptians thought it was a nerve, the Chinese called it a meridian (which is the name given to the power 'lines' in acupuncture). The ancient Romans also sometimes wore wedding rings on the fourth finger. In Spain in the sixth century St. Isidore of Seville spoke about a connection between the finger and the heart.

From the eleventh century till the Reformation, the diocese of Salisbury in England accepted what the *Manual of Sarum Use* ruled about the ring-finger: 'Then let the Bridegroom put the ring on the thumb of the Bride, saying – In the Name of the Father; (on the next finger) and of the Son; (on the next finger) and of the Holy Ghost; (on the next finger) Amen. And there let him leave it, because in that finger there is a certain vein which reaches to the heart.' In 1853 a correspondent of the English publication *Notes and Queries* wrote to ask if a lady who had lost her fourth finger in an accident could be married in the Church of England.

Whichever it is – fact or superstition – the fourth finger is here to stay.

FIRST CATCH YOUR WOMAN

Gonds do it,
Uapes do it,
Ipurina Indians of Brazil do it . . .
and many more races and tribes practise marriage by capture.

It was legal in England till the thirteenth century, and even today in Britain and many nations the bridegroom takes his best friends to the ceremony to help him 'capture' the bride (the best man and ushers) while the bride surrounds herself with 'protectors' (bridesmaids). Later, he carries the bride over the threshold of their new home, which again represents the custom of carrying away the bride by force.

One of the most dramatic forms of marriage by capture is carried out by the Banyankole tribe of Uganda. Here the groom holds down his bride while *her* family tie her up with ropes. As she weeps her family and his have a tug of war, which his side is allowed to win. Next she sits on a blanket, and as she is whisked away her people run after her shouting and doing their best to get her back. The more poignant the acting, the more successful the wedding has been.

Araucanian Indians of Chile seize their bride and carry her off on horseback, but an Ipurina Indian girl of Brazil must get her father's consent before she can run away. The moment her man catches her she is deemed married. When a Bushman husband carries off his bride in southern Africa, he is hit by her relatives with sticks, but he must grin and bear it. At the pre-wedding party of Uape Indians in the upper reaches of the Amazon, the future groom's party suddenly gets up and leaves after seizing the bride-to-be. They bundle her into a canoe and paddle away, but her family continues eating without blinking.

Among the Lisus on the China–Burma border when the bride-to-be is carried off screaming, kicking and biting her future husband and in-laws, her own family shrieks for help but stands comfortably flat-footed. As the groom's group approaches its village the captive is warmly welcomed, she then prepares for a wedding party.

In India a Gond bride is expected to weep as often as possible before her wedding day and an east Greenland Eskimo bride must appear reluctant; while the groom attempts to catch his Eskimo bride by the hair or arm in full view of the assembled village, she will fight back violently – a sure sign of her maidenly modesty.

The Balinese see the whole marriage business as one of fun: after running off with his bride the husband later visits her father and will probably pay a fine. But there is absolutely no fun for a Gond man, who is sometimes seriously injured by women determined to 'protect' the girl he wishes to marry. They attack him with sticks and stones and, being unaware of their strength and pelting power, lose control and inflict severe damage.

A similar instance of female power occurred in Ireland in the late seventeenth century, when the Lord of Howth lost an eye at a dart-throwing ceremony held simultaneously with the beginning of the 'dragging home the bride' event. Fortunately, this Irish custom has lost its popular appeal.

WIVES FOR CATTLE

Around Lake Rudolf in Kenya men can pay for their wives in instalments: a dozen cattle this year, another dozen next year until the asking price is reached. Then they set to work to buy another wife, preferring a strong and plain one to a beautiful one because the former will work hard (she draws water, builds huts, tills the land, produces children) while a beautiful woman will be sought after by other men.

♡

In December 1983 the government of Temotu province in the Solomon Islands ruled that $600 was the maximum price for a good wife. Anyone found guilty of paying more would be gaoled for three months or fined up to $90, or in some cases the Council of Chiefs might decide on both.

♡

Because Antandroy women of Madagascar find it difficult to conceive, the best price is paid for a woman with children; widows are welcome, especially those with a lot of children.

♡

In central Africa a teenage Nandi girl is worth six cows, while the Wataveta evaluate a woman to be worth one bull, one cow, seven goats and six jars of beer.

Further east a Masai man is prepared to add two sheep and some goatskins to the usual price of two cows and two bullocks if he especially fancies a woman. Furthermore, he is allowed as many wives as he can pay for, and no matter how unhappy a wife might be she is not allowed to return to her parents' home unless accompanied by her husband. Before marriage young girls spend their days dancing, singing, and having fun. After marriage they do all the work and become the over-burdened hewers of wood and drawers of water.

In South Africa a Zulu man values his cattle above everything: if a woman wishes to flatter a man she will tell him that he must have been belched up by a cow, meaning that his birth is a blessing to everyone.

♡

In many islands in Melanesia young girls are tattooed, and when they become eligible for marriage the bridegroom has to pay the girl's relatives for the cost of this 'beauty' treatment. Even if the girl's body is covered in tattoos, a very keen man will pay up the extra cost.

♡

It is the custom of the Cape Ngunis for a bride and her bridesmaids to assemble in the cattle-byres, where they undress and allow themselves to be inspected by the men. If the men are satisfied with what they have seen, the performance is repeated in a hut for the benefit of the female members of the man's family.

♡

Fourteen-stone Sam Lukhele went with the Swaziland Commonwealth Games team to Australia in 1982 as its press officer. So thrilled was he by the beauty of Australian women that he tried to buy one for the price of a few cows. When he learned that Australia's strict quarantine laws would have meant paying for six months' penning of the cows after their arrival from Africa, he changed his mind and offered £2,000 plus the warning that he planned to buy several other Mrs. Lukheles. When told by Australian reporters that this seemed rather greedy, he replied: 'In Swaziland monogamy is seen as a sign of laziness.'

♡

A British wife is worth £227 a week. The sum represents the amount a husband would have to pay to hire someone to run his home if his wife died. Although the insurance company executives who initiated the evaluation in 1983 told their computer that a 'typical mum' works a 94-hour week, they dared not give it details about her extra work at weekends, holidays, and the 24-hour-a-day emergency cover she provides.

———————————————♡———————————————

'Don't look a gift-horse in the mouth' is a popular saying in many languages including English, Italian, French, Spanish (where you are also asked not to examine the beast's teeth), and even Latin.

Two men who made sure that their loved-one would not look in their mouths were Mark Antony and Richard Burton. When he fell in love with Cleopatra, Mark Antony gave her Phoenicia, Cyprus, Coele-Syria, and parts of Arabia, Judaea and Cilicia. Though not quite as rich, Richard Burton nevertheless bought from Cartier's a 69.42 carat diamond for $1,050,000 to give to Elizabeth Taylor.

In some countries, so that she does not receive 100 milk jugs and 91 vases, the bride-to-be draws up a list or register of gifts in a department store or boutiques for her friends and relatives to consult. There can be no surprises about the value of the gift because the list shows exactly how much each item costs. As each plastic egg cup, tin pan or 22-carat gold trinket is purchased it is crossed off the list so that there can be no duplication.

Those who leave their visit to the store late run the risk of finding only the expensive items still outstanding, but one company in America coaxes everyone to remember Oneida stainless steel products at all times: 'Some things you decide with your heart. The things that matter. Like your stainless.'

———————————————◇———————————————

'I PRONOUNCE YOU MAN & WIVES'

Husbands are shared in numerous communities around the world. This includes the Todas and Nayars of India, many Tibetans, and also the Bhots, Lepchas of the Himalayas and many mountain tribes in Asia.

Chukchi hunters and herders of Siberia also seek safety in numbers, marrying in a group and sharing sexual rights to each other's women. The marriage ceremony is called *newtumgit*, which means 'partners in wives'.

Wives are also shared by Margis in west Africa and Kamberis and Katabs of Nigeria, while Pahaariis of north India will pool their resources with other members of the family – usually their brothers – to raise the bride-price to purchase a wife. They get another wife when they can afford it.

On July 1 1982 Sun Myung Moon officiated over the marriage of 2,075 couples in Madison Square Garden in New York. The largest mass wedding ceremony took place when he repeated his numbers game three months later in Seoul in South Korea. On that occasion 5,837 couples from eighty-three countries were married.

◇

The British get a thrill out of a good, hot-blooded political and sexual scandal, especially when one of the protagonists is a Cabinet minister. One that attracted considerable excitement was known as the Parkinson Affair, when Mr. Cecil Parkinson's liaison with Miss Sara Keays hit the headlines during the Tory Party Conference in Blackpool in 1983. Shaik Mubarak Ahmad, Imaam of the London Mosque, offered his (and Islam's) solution: polygamy. Referring to Mr. Parkinson and Miss Keays, the Imaam wrote: 'Some people today find themselves placed in the position of being adulterous, whereas, if the taking of a second wife were legal, this too could be avoided.' However, the Imaam did not think that the British were ready yet for total polygamy, so he suggested it could be introduced 'where there is a need and where financial means permit'. I wonder what Allah thought of this elitist suggestion considered by the Imaam to be 'a simple solution provided by God, the Wise, the All-knowing'?

An editorial in the *Indonesian Observer* reflected yet more Moslem concern for what it called the Perkinson Affair:

> 'The inference one can gain from the attitude of Mrs. Thatcher's on this Perkinson's sex scandal was that from now on she would not mind

that sex goes public in Britain in whatever form of manifestation as long as it does not affect her own interest.

'On that score it can happen that other ministers in her Cabinet and even her ambassadors stationed overseas are at liberty to have extra-marital sex life in public as long as they remain loyal and pledge allegiance. How long Mrs. Thatcher can stay on top to provide complete sex freedom to her aides is hard to tell, but while she is still on top there might be many who will not miss the chance of having a gay time in public without minding the baby who is born out of wedlock. Britain led by Mrs. Thatcher has indeed developed into a fast, happy-go-lucky and gay world.'

♡

In my country, and probably yours, we can have as many husbands or wives as we wish . . . so long as we have them one at a time.

══════════════ ♡ ══════════════

GAY VOWS

Male homosexual couples are made welcome by the Ila, Dahomey, Lango, Nama, Siwa, Thonga, Wolof, Zande, Fulani, Gisu and Margole communities in Africa. Lesbians can expect a warm greeting from the Nandi, Mbundu and, once again, the friendly Namas. They will also find themselves among gay friends if they call on the Woleaians in the Pacific Ocean, the Tupinambas of Brazil, the Chukchi in Siberia, the Mongos of central Africa, and many Kuwaitis.

♡

All gays should stay away from the following communities if they value their lives or limbs: in Africa the Kwomas, Nuers and Kikuyus; the

Pukapukans and the Trukese in the Pacific; Lepchas in the Himalayas; and in South America the Timbira, the Kaingáng and the Sirionó.

The Chinese and Saudis sometimes execute gays and adulterers, and both are toughest on female adulterers. Neither would have got on well with the ancient Greeks who thought that the ideal love affair was between a mature man and a youth. The relationship disintegrated, however, when the lad grew whiskers, but then it was his turn to look for a youth he could love.

♡

The famous Sacred Band of Thebes was a corps of shock troops, composed almost exclusively of gay couples because bravery was said to result from the love between two men. The great Athenian general Xenophon, who successfully marched the Ten Thousand (not all gays) home through enemy country, said that lover and youth would rather die than act in a cowardly way in each other's presence. Once, when he was at a banquet at which the guests had been struck dumb by the beauty of a youth, Xenophon commented: 'The people who do not choose handsome men for commanders of their troops are mad.'

♡

In November 1984, by a clear two-thirds majority the 36,000 residents of West Hollywood voted to become an independent city and gave the United States its first city council controlled by homosexuals.

———————————♡———————————

It is true that I never should have married, but I didn't want to live without a man. Brought up to respect the conventions, love had to end in marriage. I'm afraid it did.
Bette Davis, *The Lonely Life*

A woman, who at the moment of death enjoys the full approval of her husband, will find her place in Paradise.
Mohammed

———————————♡———————————

Not only does a Narikot daughter-in-law in Nepal wash her mother-in-law's feet before each meal as a sign of respect (as we saw in Chapter 7), but the same girl is also expected to wash her husband's feet *and* drink that water by splashing some of it into her mouth to show the extreme respect expected of a wife towards her husband. In some cases a Narikot husband watches while his wife eats the food he has left on his plate. Naturally, such a wife walks behind her husband and carries burdens for him, rushing to serve him in every possible way. Only on one occasion does she have the upper hand: after their marriage ceremony she is allowed to grab his big toe and hang on to it till he gives her some money. But then the initiative returns to him: the new bride massages her husband's legs with oil, beginning with his feet, then his calves, and next his thighs until he becomes aroused or falls asleep.

A wife, to a Kabyle mountain man of Algeria, is his property to use and dispose of as he wishes. Her only possession is the garment she is given to wear, and her husband has a right to 'persuade' her with his fist, sticks, stones or knives. He is, however, forbidden to kill her if he does not have a reasonably serious motive. If she is very beautiful her bride-price may have been more than one donkey, but most fathers need little persuasion to sell their daughters for a worn-out donkey.

Life is more tolerable for the women of the Cook Islands in the Pacific, where they can walk all over the men. When a girl marries, the young village men form a human path (each man lying face-down) while she walks over their bodies from her family's home to the house where she will live with her husband.

WOMEN ON TOP

It was announced at their British headquarters in Yorkshire that the Ancient Order of Hen-Pecked Husbands would be calling off their annual Easter get-together for 1984 because their wives would not let them go.

From Shanghai, China, comes this report about men's liberation: one day a group of hen-pecked husbands held a secret meeting to discuss a way to restrain their bossy wives and restore some of their rights. As their plot hatched, one husband said: 'If our wives hear about our plan they will ambush us and beat us up one by one.' Fearing the wrath of their wives, the men called the meeting off and rushed home before they were missed. Only one remained, and the others admired him for his courage. But he had already died of fright on the spot.

♡

The lost kingdom of the Minaros was 'discovered' in a mountain hideaway 16,000 ft up in the Himalayas by a French explorer in 1984. The Amazon-like women totally dominate their men, marrying several at a time and keeping them in line by brute force.

The explorer Michel Peissel said: 'I've seen the women striking their men in public. They are terribly argumentative, noisy and bossy – the men are petrified of them.'

In ancient Chinese texts this remote region in the Himalayas is referred to as the 'Kingdom of Women', so female power on the rooftop of the world has been going on for a long time.

♡

A Cabrai woman of Togo in west Africa lets a man know when she wants gratification by placing a leaf at a particular angle on a path he uses, or she approaches him with a leaf clenched between her teeth.

On the other side of the world a Tarahumari Indian girl of Mexico throws small pebbles at a young man. If he is interested he throws them back.

Kwoma men of New Guinea wait for their women to make the first move, because it is well known that if a man tries to touch a woman who is not in the mood for love she will scream 'Rape', and the men from her side of the family might be persuaded by her to kill him.

Much gentler with her 'message' is a girl from the Lesu tribe of New Guinea or the Kurtatchi tribe of the Solomon Islands: if she finds a man she desires she simply lies down in front of him and spreads her legs wide apart.

♡

The wife of a Marshall Island chief in the Pacific has considerable power over her husband's subjects, and had till recently the right to force any man she chose to make love to her. This was extremely dangerous for her lover because the chief could, if he so wished, kill any man who committed adultery with his wife. Some men even took drastic steps to disfigure themselves so as not to appeal to the chief's wife.

═══════════════════════ ♡ ═══════════════════════

MANLY WAYS

Unable to stand his friends' taunts about his bad breath any longer, Hiero – as reported by the Greek biographer Plutarch – went home in a rage and demanded to know why his wife had not told him about his breath. She replied naively: 'I thought all men smelled like that.'

That occurred nearly 2,000 years ago. In Nigeria today, merely to ask a married man if he has children is to accuse him of impotence; the number of children he has can be taken as a reflection of his virility.

Grant Bagraazian advised Russian husbands to remember that they are the 'stronger sex', and that washing up the dishes was unmanly. Comrade Bagraazian regaled his readers in *Pravda*, the Russian Communist Party newspaper, with the story of a wife who 'caught' her husband washing dishes with an apron on. She was quoted as saying: 'I saw my man had changed – even his voice wasn't what it used to be.' She demanded: 'Take off that apron! I don't want to see you bent over the kitchen sink again. Be a man!'

According to an EEC report, of the jobs Western European men thought were most reasonable to take over from their wives, shopping was considered the most manly chore, followed by washing up, then organising a meal and cleaning the house. Ironing was near the bottom of the list. Italian men showed least inclination to wash up. A final result of the study showed that women who commit murder do it in the kitchen, while murderous men prefer the bedroom.

AN EYE FOR AN EYE

An Islamic court in Iran gave Mrs. Maryam Zavarei permission to blind her husband after he had been found guilty of gouging out her eyes with a knife in the desert outside Teheran. The court ruled that she could choose how she wished to carry out the punishment. She chose scissors.

If incest is committed between mother and son, father and daughter, or brother and sister by a Kágaba Indian of Colombia, expiation of the crime requires that it be repeated so that all may be forgiven. The only difference is that second-time round the man's semen must be caught and the cloth offered by a priest for sacrifice.

Committing adultery gave the ancient Romans as much pleasure as modern men and women get from avoiding income tax. As Imperial Rome approved of all love unions except adultery, so making love to another person's spouse became the game that Romans everywhere longed to play.

In some countries today adulterers run a risk of horrible punishments. The Islamic punishment is stoning to death. In Saudi Arabia a woman found guilty of adultery is often buried up to her waist in a pit before the stones are hurled. Afghans prefer to tie up the couple in separate sacks before inviting the neighbours to join in. A stoning-to-death event took place in Pakistan in October 1983, after a married Afghan woman and a Pakistani Pathan were discovered having a sex relationship in an Afghan refugee camp.

In Uganda King M'tesa caused adulterers to be dismembered alive and each part was thrown to the vultures. In other parts of Africa, in Bornu for example, the guilty couple is bound hand and foot before their heads are smashed together. The Hottentots consider adultery a very grave outrage on their property, especially if a wife is caught with a lover; husbands have the right of life and death over members of the family, so a guilty wife has to hope for leniency.

According to the Twi tribe of Liberia, a husband or wife who dreams of making love with someone else is guilty of adultery.

There is no stigma in Jamaica, Trinidad, Martinique, the Seychelles and many other countries in being illegitimate. In fact, in many countries most people are illegitimate, and after the children have reached adulthood a party is held for members of the family to meet and compare life stories.

Yet in the early 1970s students at a secondary school in Estonia, when asked why they thought marriage was 'a good thing', replied that it was necessary 'to have intimate relations officially registered, and to do this one ought not to remain a bachelor or spinster'.

———————————♡———————————

After a lifetime of walking naked through the desert, a family of nine Pintubi Aborigines took their first steps into twentieth-century Australia in October 1984. None had seen white people before, but their decision to give up a nomadic life was necessary if they were to survive: the group were reduced to members of one family so that any sexual relationship necessary to produce children would have meant committing incest, which their tribal laws forbid.

The Pintubi tribe has lived in central Australia for more than 40,000 years using spears, clubs and boomerangs to hunt wild cats, emus, and kangaroos. The family who emerged from the desert were especially alarmed by the movement of the windscreen wipers on the jeep that took them out of the Stone Age. As night fell the nine – three women, two men, two boys and two girls – dug holes in the sand to sleep, as they and their ancestors have always done. Soon they will look for suitable husbands and wives for their children among other Pintubi groups so that their family will carry on into the twenty-first century.

══════════════♡══════════════

TEACHER'S PET

From America, Vietnam and India come three types of teachers' pets.

In December 1983 the University of California's academic senate voted to declare romantic or sexual relationships between faculty members and students a serious breach of professional ethics.

Buddhists in Vietnam forbid students to marry the widow of their former teachers.

According to the ancient Hindu law books and a code of conduct drawn up by the sage Manu, adultery is committed with another man's wife if a man is with her at the junction of streams, kisses her, winks at her, touches her in unseemly places, or sits on a bed with her. But far worse is 'intercourse with the teacher's wife', and for such a foul deed Manu decreed that the guilty man shall either sit on a red-hot iron plate or cut off 'his own offending member'. After this he is to 'go away with uplifted eyes'.

Arranged marriages are widespread in Egypt, where nineteen is considered the age of a very old, old maid. Families living in rural areas believe that a special feminine devilry begins after a girl reaches puberty, and that by twenty she is a possible murderess. If she is still unmarried at nineteen no effort will be spared to marry off the daughter whom they refer to among themselves as a 'lump of grief' or a 'domestic calamity'.

Although arranged marriages are customary in Japan, an increasing number of parents are encouraging their children to take package marriage tours to south-east Asia, where wedding ceremonies are cheaper.

In Tokyo £100,000 buys a few hours at a wedding hall, which includes the use of the shrine and reception rooms, food, drinks, flowers and the services of a video cameraman and a photographer. Every couple is photographed cutting the wedding cake. The same cake is shared by countless couples: it is made of plastic, and has a slot at the side into which the knife is plunged. Despite the huge expense though, a marriage takes place at each wedding hall every twenty minutes.

In parts of Asia it is an ancient Buddhist practice to arrange the marriage of the spirits of those who die too young to have had a chance to share their lives on earth with another person. When a Korean Airlines jumbo jet was shot down after straying into Soviet air space in September 1983, several Korean families found spiritual partners for the spirits of their children killed in the tragic incident. A steward and a stewardess both of whom 'had to die without knowing the full meaning of love in this world' were united in a marriage of their souls by their families in a sad ceremony near the spot where the airliner plunged into the sea.

To the Sarakatsani shepherds of Greece it is a disgrace to die a spinster or a bachelor, so unmarried men and women are buried in wedding clothes, thereby joining them in wedlock to Mother Earth.

In the eastern Indian state of Orissa, it is shameful to the family to have an unmarried daughter for any length of time. It is not such a disgrace for a man not to marry, but it is believed that if he dies unmarried a man becomes a ghost.

THE MERRY WIDOW

The merriest widow in the world is an Amba lady. As soon as her late husband is buried she is guest of honour at an all-night orgy given by her African friends in the Congo River basin to help her forget the past and begin a new sex life. A

Gisu widow in Sudan ceases to be one the moment her husband is under the ground, but life is tougher for a Zande widow of central Africa, who is not allowed to make love for a year. There are fewer restrictions on African widowed men, but one who must bide his time before being allowed sexual relations with his other wives is an Ashanti widower in Ghana, because it is feared that any child conceived within a few weeks of the death of any one of his wives will die at an early age.

———————————♡———————————

An archaeologist is the best husband a woman
can have; the older she gets, the more interested
he is in her.

*Attributed to Agatha Christie, but denied by her.
Also attributed to Dorothy Parker, Mrs. Cohen,
Woody Allen, Spike Milligan, the author's
father-in-law, and others*

———————————♡———————————

Old, rich Tiwi men of Australia and their Zande counterparts in central Africa have a greedy, lusty habit in common: both marry all the eligible women they can lay their hands on, so that young men are usually about forty years old before they can inherit a wife from an old man who has died or when some of these senior citizens decide that it is time to get rid of a wife, or two.

═══════════════♡═══════════════

LOVE'S LABOUR'S LOST

IRISH (Armagh)

If you wish to be reviled, marry.
If you wish to be praised, die.

POLISH

The woman cries before the wedding
and the man cries after.

There were two brothers who had brains,
and a third who was married.

Marry – and you will be all right for a week;
Kill a pig – and you will be all right for a
   month;
Become a priest – and you will be all right for life.

CZECH

A wedding lasts for a day or two, but the misery forever.

RUSSIAN

There is no such fiery love that it will not be cooled down by marriage.

SPANISH

Bachelor – a peacock;
Betrothed – a lion;
Wedded – an ass.

ITALIAN

He who has had a wife deserves a crown of patience,
but he who has had two deserves a strait-jacket.

♡

Marriage is for women the commonest mode of livelihood, and the total amount of undesired sex endured by women is probably greater in marriage than in prostitution.
Bertrand Russell

One was never married, and that's his hell; another is, and that's his plague.
Democritus

♡

Men marry because they are tired;
women because they are curious; both are disappointed.

One should always be in love; that is the reason one should never marry.

Oscar Wilde

♡

GOING-GOING-GONE

America has the highest divorce rate in the world. In 1984 doctors and social scientists produced statistics to show that the distress of an unmendable marriage and a divorce was likely to cause a greater emotional and physical toll than anything else – even the death of one's husband or wife. Higher rates of mental illness and disturbance were evident, as were pneumonia and high blood pressure. In fact, new studies revealed that in divorced men heart disease doubled, car crashes increased more than three times, suicide went up fivefold, cirrhosis of the liver fourfold, and lung cancer almost doubled.

Research into the effects of divorce on the British was carried out in the same year at the Central Middlesex Hospital, when it was shown that divorced people were five times more likely to commit suicide than married people, and this increased to twenty times among those *separated* from their mate. The divorce rate in England and Wales is the highest in Europe.

♡

Americans, who make more of marrying for
love than any people, also break up more of
their marriages. This is not so much a failure of
love as it is the determination of people not to
live without it.
Morton Hunt, *The Natural History of Love*

♡

While the United States was at war following Pearl Harbor in 1941, a clever lawyer in Georgia used a forgotten law to get his client a divorce from her husband. The law, passed during the Civil War when Georgia and the United States were on opposite sides, gave grounds for divorce if the husband was in 'the military service of the United States'.

American lawyers have lost none of their expertise nearly fifty years on. Their skilful tactics for securing enormous alimony awards bring them clients from all over the world. Mr. Marvin Mitchelson is the man everyone seeking alimony tries to engage; he obtained $81 million for a client in 1983, and every day hopeful clients pray that his magical powers will keep them in the luxurious style to which they have become accustomed.

♡

Filipino comings and goings depend on exactly which gods are worshipped. Moslems and tribals are allowed more than one wife per man, but Christians, most of whom are Catholics, are monogamous. Many Christian men have a mistress who is called a *querida*, and the favourite way for a wife to humiliate her is to pull her hair in public.

Grounds for divorce in the Philippines are as complicated as the marriage patterns. Though denied to Christians, divorce is permitted to Moslem men on the grounds of their wife's incompatibility, infidelity or desertion. A

Negrito man can be rid of his wife if she is lazy, unfaithful or cruel, while among the Bontoc highlanders and the Sulods of Panjay sterility on the part of either spouse is enough to be rid of one's husband or wife.

♡

Nawal El Saadawi, the Egyptian writer and former state health administrator, described the rules governing Moslem divorce in her book *The Hidden Face of Eve*. A man can divorce his wife if she does not allow him to satisfy his sexual desires even if she is ill, or if she refuses, or if she is prevented by her parents. Her husband must be able to fulfil himself sexually so that he can concentrate on worshipping Allah, seeking knowledge and serving society. Mrs. Saadawi points out that Moslem men keep their wives at home because of their fear that men cannot resist the temptations of women, and she quotes a popular Palestinian saying: 'My woman never left our home until the day she was carried out.'

♡

The Chinese sage Confucius thought of seven reasons for divorcing a wife; they were later incorporated into the legal code of the Manchu dynasty. These are the defects of the disposable wife:

1. Rebellious towards her mother-in-law and father-in-law
2. Failed to produce a son
3. Unfaithful
4. Jealous towards her husband's other women
5. Has a repulsive and incurable disease
6. Given to hurtful talk and tale-telling
7. Is a thief.

But no Chinese husband could get rid of his wife if:

1. She had mourned for her husband's parents for three years or more
2. She had no family to return to
3. She married her husband when he was poor, even though he may be rich now.

♡

Adulterers in the Middle Ages were sometimes made to ride naked through the streets on an ass, while in Babylon in earlier times guilty wives were drowned. In June 1984 Greece's Supreme Court ruled that searching a wife's or husband's wallet or pockets for evidence of adultery is ground for divorce. The Court added that such an act was evidence of irreconcilable breakdown of a marriage.

♡

Shortly after he divorced his wife, Terentia, the Roman orator and philosopher Cicero was asked if he would marry again. Certainly not, he replied, because he 'could not cope with philosophy and a wife at the same time'.

♡

A Burmese man can legally separate from his wife if she fails to conceive after eight years of married life. But not everything is in his favour: if he remarries and again no children are conceived, it is assumed that he is the barren one, and so any property that he kept from his first marriage is restored to his first wife.

♡

Wife-selling was a flourishing business in England, and public auctions took place until the end of last century. In 1832 Joseph Thomson, a farmer, put his wife Mary Anne up for sale in Carlisle to the highest bidder, and 'after waiting about an hour, Thomson knocked down the "lot" to one Henry Mears, for twenty shillings and a Newfoundland dog'. This represented a good price compared to a sale reported in *The Times* of 30 March 1796, when John Lees sold his wife for sixpence. By the late 1800s the best offer a man might get was a pint of beer.

♡

A letter introduced in a Minsk divorce case in the Soviet Union in 1955 is quoted by many observers of Soviet marriage trends as evidence that many unmarried pregnant women will try to find a husband at any cost: 'I need a father for my daughter, be it only documents . . . I am agreeable to the conclusion of a marriage with anyone regardless of age, position or appearance. I can provide a large reward and promise peace and quiet. That is, depending on his desire, I will immediately hide myself so that it will *never* be remembered that I exist.'

Three-quarters of divorce petitions in Russia and East European countries are filed by wives. Czechoslovakia's best known adviser on sex problems and author of books on marriage difficulties is Dr. Miroslav Plzak of Prague. The Czech psychiatrist upset a reporter from *Izvestia* when he told her that women ought to stop divorcing bad husbands because 'they are not going to find any better ones anywhere else'. Dr. Plzak believes three months is quite long enough for a wife to 'get over her wrongs and take her husband back if he is repentant'.

———————♡———————

A man is often too young to marry,
But a man is never too old to love.
Finnish

If a man is too old, it is his wife's fault.
Ukrainian

When an old man takes a young wife, the man
becomes young and the woman old.
Yiddish

An old wife at home and a hill in front of his
house weary a man.
Saying in Ethiopia

Mrs. Gillian Bartley, aged thirty-nine, of Great Bookham in Surrey, England, was granted a divorce from her husband because of his smelly feet. The judge referred to Keith Bartley's 'unreasonable behaviour', but it is probable that Mr. Bartley would have been spared the publicity concerning his feet if he had heard about Mr. David Usher. Mr. Usher is a disc jockey who lives in Sandy in Bedfordshire. So bad was his problem of smelly feet that Mr. Usher spent a considerable amount of money each year on fourteen pairs of size fourteen shoes but all were rotted by his perspiration. 'I used to take girls dancing. As the night warmed up, so did my feet – and the girl quickly cooled down,' confessed Mr. Usher. 'I used to have a dog. It was very courageous – it staggered in with my slippers at night. I could empty a room just by taking off my shoes.'

But Mr. Usher has been cured of his problems. Surgeons cut some of his spinal nerves to reach the sweat glands through his stomach. Although this sounds horrible, and Mr. Usher has two fourteen-inch scars on his abdomen, he is now sweet-smelling and no longer has to pickle his socks each day in vinegar.

FOR THE RECORD

If you would like to be in the record books for having the most wives or husbands the number to beat is 9,000. King Mongut of Siam (the king in *The King and I*) had a good time with his wives and concubines before dying of fatigue and exposure while watching an eclipse of the moon in 1868. Second place is shared by Emperor Yang-ti of China who had a queen, deputy queens, royal consorts and 3,000 palace maidens, and one of the Monomotapa kings in what is now Zimbabwe.

If you have left your run too late the answer is probably to tackle one of the modern record-holders such as Octavio Guillen and Adriana Martinez, whose engagement of 67 years is the longest to date. They finally took the plunge in Mexico City in 1969.

The most married man in the monogamous world has had 26 wives and 24 mothers-in-law (more details on page 137) and the most married woman has had her nose broken by five out of her 14 husbands. When asked why she had married so often, Mrs. Beverly Nina Avery of Los Angeles replied: 'It's because I'm so provocative.'

The record to beat for bigamous marriages is 104, and to be the oldest bride and groom the ages to topple are 95 (the bride) and 101 for the groom. The longest recorded marriage is 86 years and the most expensive wedding cost about £22 million, when Mohammed, son of Shaik Zayid ibn Sa'id al-Makhtum, married Princess Salama in Abu Dhabi in May 1981. The biggest wedding in history was the day Menachem Teitelbaum married Brucha Meisels in December 1984. More than 20,000 people crowded into the Nassau Coliseum, home of the New York Islanders ice-hockey team, for a pre-wedding reception. One hundred and fifty buses were hired to transport the guests there, but only 8,000 were invited back for the more intimate sit-down dinner.

I'm a practising heterosexual – but bi-sexuality immediately doubles your chances for a date on Saturday night.
Woody Allen

♡

HAIRY LADY. Otherwise unkinky professional man (35), tanned, goodlooking, affluent and sensitive, seeks slim woman with abundant unshaven body hair. Any age or nationality.
Lonely hearts column in *Time Out*

♡

To live happily together the husband must be deaf and the wife blind.
French

♡

The heart beats faster during a heated argument than it does when you make love.

♡

Love is that delightful interval between meeting a beautiful girl and discovering that she looks like a haddock.
John Barrymore

♡

Women are like elephants to me; I like to look at
them, but I wouldn't want to own one.
W. C. Fields

♡

After I have gone, there will be no greater
danger menacing my nation and more liable to
create anarchy and trouble than women.
Mohammed

♡

Love rarely dies a sudden death.
French

♡

When you fall out of love you don't actually cry.
You only cry when someone has fallen out of
love with you.
Carla Lane

♡

Those who come together in passion
Stay together in tears.
Japanese

♡

The best present a woman can give a man is a
sleepless night
Spanish

♡

Whoever marries for love without money, has
good nights and sorry days.
Italian

♡

I wasn't kissing her, I was whispering in her
mouth.
Chico Marx, caught by his wife kissing a chorus girl

♡

Say what you will, 'tis better to be left than
never to have been loved.
William Congreve

♡

To be loved, be lovable.

Seneca